BIRDS IN KANSAS

University of Kansas
Museum of Natural History

Public Education Series No. 11
Joseph T. Collins, Editor

BIRDS IN KANSAS

VOLUME ONE

Max C. Thompson

Department of Biology
Southwestern College
Winfield, Kansas

&

Charles Ely

Department of Biology and Allied Health
Fort Hays State University
Hays, Kansas

UNIVERSITY OF KANSAS
MUSEUM OF NATURAL HISTORY

The Public Education Series is intended to provide publications on natural history for the people of Kansas. This volume is the result of studies sponsored, in part, by the Museum of Natural History, Southwestern College, Fort Hays State University, the Kansas Biological Survey, the Kansas Department of Wildlife and Parks, and the Kansas Ornithological Society.

Distributed by the University Press of Kansas
Lawrence, Kansas 66049

Library of Congress Cataloging-in-Publication data

Thompson, Max C.
    Birds in Kansas / Max C. Thompson & Charles Ely.
        p.   cm. — (Public education series / University of Kansas,
    Museum of Natural History ; no. 11–)
    Bibliography: p.
    Includes index.
    ISBN 0-89338-028-8 (v.1) — ISBN 0-89338-027-X (pbk. : v. 1)
    1. Birds—Kansas—Identification.   I. Ely, Charles A. (Charles
Adelbert), 1933–   II. Title   III. Series: Public education
series : no. 11, etc.
QL684.K2T47   1989
598.29781—dc20   89-5017

This publication is funded in part by the *Chickadee Checkoff* of the Nongame Wildlife Improvement Program of the Kansas Department of Wildlife and Parks. All persons filing a Kansas income tax form have an opportunity to make a special contribution that is earmarked for conservation of nongame wildlife. Do something wild! Make your mark on the tax form for nongame wildlife.

Dedicated to our colleagues
who waited so patiently
and continued to provide us with new data

PREFACE

Kansas was one of the first states west of the Mississippi River to have a book devoted entirely to the birds located within its boundaries. This event came about when Colonel N. S. Goss wrote his first *Catalogue of the Birds of Kansas* in 1883, updating it in 1886 with a *Revised Catalogue of the Birds of Kansas*. The latter listed 335 species and races and predicted that the total could eventually reach 350. Little did Goss imagine that over a century later the total would reach 424 species plus additional races.

We began thinking about writing a book on the birds of Kansas when we worked together in Hawaii in the 1960s. Two decades later, this volume represents the fruits of our labor. Because of the large numbers of bird species recorded from Kansas, the book is being produced in two volumes. Volume One will deal with the 222 species of nonsongbirds, including all birds through the woodpeckers. Volume Two will include the 202 species of songbirds, beginning with the flycatchers. These volumes are not intended to be a thorough technical work, but rather are written for the enjoyment and use of both the amateur birdwatcher and the professional ornithologist.

We have included in the book all known information on the distribution of birds in Kansas. Many members of the Kansas Ornithological Society donated records to the data bank. During the accumulation of data, one of us (Ely) compiled and partially computerized all the literature records, while the other (Thompson) began computerizing data from all known bird specimens from Kansas in various collections. The latter information is now stored at the University of Kansas Museum of Natural History. We would like to acknowledge Marion Mengel, who was a tremendous help in computerizing this data, and the Ohio State University Computer Center, which kindly provided computer time and keypunching for some of the initial input.

For data, photographs, and assistance in the field, we would like to thank Sylvia Albright, Jerry Arnold, Ron Barkley, Byron Berger, the late Amelia Betts, Walter Boles, Bessie Boso, Jan Boyd, Roger Boyd, the late Ivan Boyd, Margaret Boyd, William Brecheisen, John Brockway, Martin Brockway, Tim Broschat, Steve Burr, Ted Cable, Thomas Cannon, Stephen Capel, Joan Challans, Wallace Champeney, Calvin Cink, Randy Clark, Lorena Combs, Jeffrey Cox, John Davis, Charles Edwards, Effie Edwards, Guy Ernsting, Elmer Finck, Thomas Flowers, Stephen Fretwell, Jo Garrett, Robert Glazier, Bob

Gress, Charles Hall, Steve Hansen, Erma Henley, Larry Herbert, Jane Hershberger, Ken Hollings, Lloyd Hulbert, Allen Jahn, J. C. Johnson, Jr., Nanette Johnson, Kenn Kaufman, Katharine Kelley, Steve Kingswood, Robert Kruger, Dan Larson, Robert LaShelle, John LaShelle, Dan LaShelle, Patricia Latas, Bill Layher, Eugene Lewis, Eulalia Lewis, Renne Lohoefener, Paul Long, Mick McHugh, Edmund Martinez, Jim Mayhew, Lloyd Moore, Mary Louise Myers, Jay Newton, Art Nonhof, John Palmquist, James Parker, James Piland, Jean Piland, William Piper, Galen Pittman, Dwight Platt, Barb Pratt, Martin Pressgrove, James Ptacek, Margaret Ptacek, Mrs. W. H. Qualls, the late Orville Rice, James Rising, Marvin Rolfs, Stan Roth, Jr., Richard Schmidt, Steve Schmidt, the late Ed Schulenberg, Jean Schulenberg, David Seibel, Scott Seltman, Dianne Seltman, Tom Shane, Frank Shipley, Theodore Sperry, Dennis Stadel, Donald Stout, Robert Sutherland, Marie Swisher, Allen Tubbs, Don Vannoy, Byron Walker, Barbara Watkins, Michael Watkins, Roger Wells, Gerald Wiens, Celia White, Kevin Wills, Robert Wood, Eugene Young, Dennis Zehr, and John Zimmerman.

We would like specially to thank Jane Church, who unselfishly gave of her time to criticize the initial manuscript. Sebastian Patti and Marvin Schwilling kindly read the manuscript and provided some additional information. A special thanks goes to Jan Ely for her understanding in all the hours her husband spent compiling data and for the delightful cuisine provided to us while we were working on the manuscript. We thank Philip S. Humphrey, who encouraged us to do the project and then gently pushed to get it finished. Lastly, we thank and dedicate this book to our colleagues, who waited patiently and constantly provided us with more data.

Max C. Thompson
Charles Ely
15 September 1988

CONTENTS

Rails

Gallinules

Cranes

Plovers

Stilts

Avocets

Sandpipers

Woodpeckers

INTRODUCTION

The number of bird species reliably reported for Kansas is 424. A species is admitted to the state list on the basis of a specimen, a photograph, or an observation that is verified by more than one competent observer. People who observe birds as a hobby are called birdwatchers. There are an estimated ten million birdwatchers in the United States. Professionals who study birds—ornithologists—are much fewer in number. Most of the larger universities in the United States employ at least one ornithologist in the biology department.

Kansas has been fortunate in having ornithologists at our universities since 1866. In the early days of the state, birds were collected and deposited at the University of Kansas. Later, the Museum of Natural History was established by the Kansas Legislature to house the vertebrate collections of the state at the university. It has since become one of the leading university museums in the nation. The University of Kansas Museum of Natural History bird collection now contains nearly 90,000 specimens. Other bird collections of note include those at Southwestern College in Winfield (9,000 specimens) and at Fort Hays State University in Hays (3,500 specimens). The curators of these collections are happy to answer questions on birds or to help you identify any birds that you may have seen.

All birds in Kansas have state and federal protection except the alien European Starling, Rock Dove (= Feral Pigeon), and House Sparrow. It is illegal to possess nongame birds, their nests, or their eggs for any reason without a permit from the Kansas Department of Wildlife and Parks and the U.S. Fish and Wildlife Service. Should you find injured birds, it is best to call your local game warden for advice.

Several field guides are available for the birdwatcher. Check with good bookstores or with museum gift shops to find the ones best suited to your needs. The Kansas Ornithological Society welcomes those who are interested in birds. You can obtain information on the Society and its benefits by writing to

Kansas Ornithological Society
Division of Ornithology
Museum of Natural History
The University of Kansas
Lawrence, Kansas 66045

A BRIEF HISTORY OF ORNITHOLOGY IN KANSAS

The history of Kansas ornithology begins with an expedition by Maj. Zebulon Pike (Pike 1810), which set out in 1805 to explore the sources of the Mississippi River. The journey began in Louisiana and headed northwest to find the head of several rivers, including the Arkansas River. Pike entered Kansas in 1806, but the only ornithological observations made were from hunters bringing in turkeys. Those turkeys were the first bird records for Kansas.

The Lewis and Clarke (1814) expedition set forth in 1804, one year before Pike departed. However, the results of the expedition, which entered Kansas in a small area along the Missouri River, were not published until 1814. The second (and only) bird added to the Kansas list was the Whip-poor-will.

Maj. Stephen H. Long led the next expedition entering Kansas, though he covered only the northeastern portion of what was to become the "Sunflower State." A member of the expedition, Thomas Say, took a detachment up the Kansas River to the Blue River and then northeastward to join the main group on the Missouri River. On the return trip of the main expedition, Say joined a party that traversed the entire Arkansas River through Kansas. Say (1823) had notes and descriptions of new birds attributed to Kansas but without specific localities. His list included eight new state records.

In 1832, Maximilian, Prince zu Wied, went up the Missouri River and made some observations in Kansas, adding 12 birds to the list (1839).

A trader by the name of Josiah Gregg published a book on commerce of the prairies in 1844. He added the Whooping Crane and the Sandhill Crane to the Kansas bird list, which then numbered 24 species.

John C. Fremont twice traversed northern Kansas on his way to the Rocky Mountains. He added only that he saw a colony of Bank Swallows on the Kansas River (1845).

The first notable accumulation of bird records was by J. W. Abert (Abert's Towhee was named in his honor). His expedition left Fort Leavenworth in 1846 and crossed Kansas on the Santa Fe Trail. His published findings (1848) listed 26 new species for the state.

The next large compilation of species reported from Kansas was by Spencer F. Baird, John Cassin, and George N. Lawrence, in a publication based on specimens collected while surveys were being made to lay a route for the railroad from the Mississippi River to the Pacific Ocean. Collections listed in this report (1858) were made by such noted naturalists as Kreuzfeldt, Hayden, Wood, and Cooper. Collections were also made by Lieutenant Couch and Dr. W. A. Hammond at Fort Leavenworth, and by John X. de Vesey at Fort Riley and on the Republican River. The 1858 report added 42 species, increasing the state list to 95 species of birds.

In 1854, P. R. Hoy, working under the auspices of the Smithsonian Institution, reported several species from eastern Kansas, including the first positive record for the Lark Bunting. Remarkably, this was an eastern distributional limit for the species.

Elliott Coues journeyed through Kansas in 1864 and published several new state records in 1865 and in 1871.

In 1866, the University of Kansas opened its doors to students. Francis Huntington Snow was employed that year as one of its first faculty members. Arriving at the university a few days early, he was told by the chancellor that nothing could be done until opening day, and was advised to "get a gun and go shooting" (Snow 1903). It was almost virgin territory, and over several years Snow added numerous birds to the state list. In 1872, he published his first list of Kansas birds in the *Kansas Educational Journal*. This catalogue contained 239 species and subspecies. Snow was criticized by J. A. Allen of Harvard University for omitting several birds that Allen had earlier added to the Kansas list, but it detracted little from the significance of Snow's discoveries. Several editions of Snow's catalogue were published, the last being the fourth edition. Altogether, Snow listed 305 species and 9 varieties of Kansas birds.

In 1878, Colonel N. S. Goss published his first paper on Kansas birds. He and Snow worked closely together, and Snow deferred any further publishing to Goss. Goss's first catalogue, appearing in 1883, contained 320 species and varieties. Goss updated his catalogue in 1886 and eventually published his *History of the Birds of Kansas* in 1891. In June 1899, D. E. Lantz published a review of Kansas ornithology in the *Transactions of the Kansas Academy of Science*. His first paper was a bibliography of Kansas birds, and his second was a historical list of Kansas birds. Lantz made some unkind remarks about Snow's work, to which Snow replied in 1903 in a point-by-point rebuttal. The rebuttal is too long to summarize here, but it is fascinating reading for anyone interested in the ornithological history of the state.

Various other ornithologists worked in the state after Lantz and Snow. W. S. Long published a lengthy article (1935) on western Kansas birds. He later wrote a checklist of Kansas birds, published in the *Transactions of the Kansas Academy of Science* (1940). In 1946, Arthur L. Goodrich published *Birds in Kansas*, which was mainly a review of previous works. In 1950, Richard and Jean Graber made a three-and-one-half-month trip to the southwestern part of the state and added many new species to the state list (1951).

Another major milestone in Kansas ornithology was the formation of the Kansas Ornithological Society in 1949. The first formal meeting was held at the University of Kansas, Lawrence, on 21 May 1949. The group was led by Charles G. Sibley. At the first meeting, Ivan L. Boyd was elected the first president of the society. Since those formative years, society members have played a key role in helping to better delineate bird distribution in the state. The Society has continued to grow since 1949, and it publishes the *Kansas Ornithological Society Bulletin,* for scientific articles, and the *Kansas Ornithological Society Newsletter,* for items of more general interest. C. G. Sibley was elected the first editor of the society, but moved to California before he could produce the first *Bulletin.* Arthur L. Goodrich then became the editor *pro tem.* Max C. Thompson, as assistant editor, produced the first *Newsletter* in 1963. The *Newsletter* was later given its own editorship, separate from that of the *Bulletin.*

It was not until 1956 that a new authoritative checklist of Kansas birds was published, when Harrison B. Tordoff, curator of birds at the University of Kansas Museum of Natural History, published his *Check-list of the Birds of Kansas.* Tordoff listed those species that had been verified by a specimen examined by a qualified biologist. Any unsubstantiated records were included as hypothetical. His list contained 375 species. Tordoff was an active field ornithologist, who added several birds to the state list and clarified the status of others.

In 1958, Richard F. Johnston became the curator of birds at the University of Kansas Museum of Natural History. He updated Tordoff's checklist in 1960 and again in 1965. He instituted a breeding-bird survey with the help of the Kansas Ornithological Society and used the resulting data to publish the *Breeding Birds of Kansas* in 1964. In addition, the Kansas Ornithological Society has published a field checklist to permit its membership to keep abreast of the current species list; the list is now in its sixth edition. Although called a field checklist, it actually is a list of birds whose occurrence in the state has been documented.

There are certainly other recent ornithologists who have contributed much to our knowledge of Kansas birds: Robert M. Mengel, James D. Rising, David Parmelee, Marvin Schwilling, Roger Boyd, and Calvin Cink, to mention a few. Amateur birdwatchers have been especially active in recent years, as noted in the preface.

But there is still so much to be learned about Kansas birds, and this book is by no means the definitive publication. New checklists will continue to be published in the future, and new books will be forthcoming. Such information is always welcome—a sign that the study of birds in Kansas in healthy and ongoing.

BIRD DISTRIBUTION AND VEGETATION

There have been 424 bird species recorded in Kansas. The great diversity of this avifauna is partly attributed to the early start of Kansas ornithology, which preceded the massive disturbance that resulted in the extinction of such species as the Passenger Pigeon and Carolina Parakeet, and the local loss of the Common Raven, Ruffed Grouse, and others. Of equal importance to the large species count of birds in Kansas is the state's central location, because it includes both eastern deciduous forest and the central grasslands and is on a major migratory flyway. Kansas is also a wintering area for far-northern birds, as well as a breeding area for typically southern species such as the Mississippi Kite and (formerly) the Black-capped Vireo. A group of species, including the Greater Roadrunner and Curve-billed Thrasher, enter the state from the arid southwest. Our major rivers also funnel in stragglers from the Rocky Mountains when those species experience their occasional irruptions.

All birders should become familiar with the physiography and vegetation of Kansas in order to appreciate the diverse ecology and wildlife found in the state. Excellent general references include Self (1978), Collins (1985), and the vegetation map by Kuchler (1974). In Kansas, birds are associated with one of three major types of vegetation—deciduous forest, grasslands, or wetlands.

To the casual visitor, especially one traveling on an interstate highway, Kansas seems a treeless expanse of plain and prairie. However, a short distance on either side of these main routes, one can find a great variety of habitats. These areas, usually small and widely scattered, are concentrated habitats that are often as productive or more so than larger blocks of the same habitat elsewhere.

The topography of Kansas is usually gently rolling rather than flat and slopes upward from the southeast to the northwest. From about 700 feet in elevation in southeastern Kansas near Coffeyville, Montgomery County, there is a gradual rise of about 10 feet per mile to 4,025 feet on Mount Sunflower, Wallace County, in the far-western reaches of the state. Climatic conditions in Kansas are varied, with annual rainfall increasing from about 18 inches in the far west to more than 40 inches in the southeast. The average growing

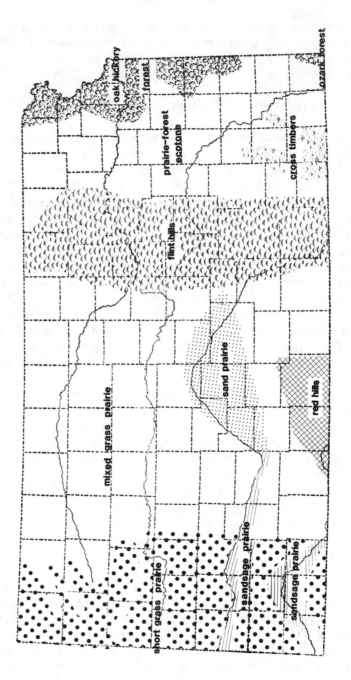

Approximate locations of major native vegetation types in Kansas.

season ranges from less than 150 days in the northwest to more than 200 days in the southeast. Vegetation is determined by temperature and precipitation, as well as the type of parent rock, soil development, and, more directly, human land use over the last two centuries.

Forest

At present, deciduous forest occurs in extreme southeastern Kansas as an extension of the Ozark Plateau, and in the northeastern part of the state as a westward extension of the eastern deciduous forest. Oaks and hickories dominate, and both areas are multilayered, with an understory of shrubs and herbaceous plants. Islands of bluestem prairie occur in the east-central and southeastern parts of Kansas. Westward to the Flint Hills, the proportion of trees decreases as prairie increases. Originally, this was a mosaic, or intermingling, of forest and prairie "forest islands in a sea of grass." In the southern portion, chiefly on sandstone and upland soils, open groves of blackjack and post oaks are interspersed within bluestem prairie; these are the Chautauqua Hills, or "cross timbers," which extend northward from Oklahoma. Thus, much of eastern Kansas has woodlands, to the delight of birds which like to inhabit thicker stands of trees.

Riparian woodlands extend westward along all major rivers and are particularly well developed along the Kansas River from Kansas City to Lawrence. In the east, riparian growth involves a variety of tree species, including cottonwood, sycamore, willows, elm, hackberry, ash, and various oaks, typically with a thick understory of saplings and woody shrubs. The number of tree species and the extent and density of vegetation decrease rapidly as one progresses westward. Nowadays on the Republican River, such eastern birds as the Wood Thrush occur in the understory west to Cloud County; 80 years ago, with higher water tables, they occurred 150 miles farther west to Decatur County. Oaks are rare west of Cowley, McPherson, and Jewell counties, as are Eastern Wood Pewees, which prefer oaks as breeding habitat. In western Kansas, often the only tree species present are cottonwoods, and the understory is restricted to grasses, indigobush, salt cedar (in flood plains), or sagebrush.

Much of the original forest in Kansas has been replaced by human communities and farmland. In these areas, control of natural fire has caused an expansion of secondary forest at the expense of bluestem prairie.

Grasslands

At least two-thirds of the state was originally grassland. Shortgrass predominated east to about Sheridan, Lane, and Meade counties. Buffalo grass and grama grasses predominated on upland sites; mixed grasses extended westward nearly to the Colorado border as fingers along rivers. Most of this area, known as the High Plains Physiographic Province, is now cultivated, and the remainder is much-degraded rangeland. As a result, birds requiring expanses of short grass (e.g., Mountain Plover, Chestnut-collared Longspur) have disappeared as regular breeding species. Mixed-grass prairie extended eastward though central Kansas, gradually merging into true tallgrass prairie from about Jewell, Rice, and Harper counties eastward. This prairie was quite variable with different combinations of short-, medium-, and tallgrass species. Shortgrass species predominated on the shallow soils of the uplands; tallgrass species, such as big bluestem, Indian grass, and switch grass, in moist areas; and mid-sized grasses, such as little bluestem and side-oats grama, elsewhere. A great variety of forbs (nonwoody flowering plants), various shrubs, and trees occurred in ravines and on "breaks." Dominant woody species included hackberry and skunkbrush.

Fully developed tallgrass prairie, dominated by big bluestem, switch grass and Indian grass, occurred on thick soils in lowlands, especially in the Flint Hills and eastward. Extensive areas, some of them in excellent condition, remain in parts of the Flint Hills. Lower streams are bordered by riparian woods. Characteristic breeding species here include the Greater Prairie-Chicken and the Upland Sandpiper, both of which occur in much smaller numbers in mixed-grass prairie. The Smith's Longspur is a regular transient, and after the annual burning by ranchers, flocks of Golden Plovers are a regular sight.

Sand-sage prairie occurred on the sandy soils south of the Arkansas and Cimarron rivers in southwestern Kansas. The largest area, now mostly replaced by irrigated farmland, was in southern Kearny and Finney counties and northern Gray County. Dominant grass species now are sand bluestem, little bluestem, and sand reed grass. The dominant woody species now found is sagebrush, followed by wild plum and tamarisk. Characteristic bird species are Lesser Prairie-Chicken, Brewer's Sparrow (locally), and Cassin's Sparrow.

Sand prairie, similar to sand-sage prairie except that it lacks sagebrush, is found on sandy soils south of the Arkansas River in central Kansas, chiefly in Edwards, Stafford, and Reno counties.

Grasses are taller, with big bluestem, little bluestem, switch grass, and sand reed grass dominant. Woody vegetation consists primarily of thickets of sandhill plum. The Bell's Vireo is a characteristic breeder in the thickets; the Mississippi Kite is common in planted windbreaks.

The Cedar Hills prairie extends northward from Oklahoma into the Red Hills physiographic province of south-central Kansas, from eastern Meade to western Harper counties. It is a heavily dissected, mixed grassland, characterized by red soil and scenic relief. Virginia junipers are scattered over the slopes, and small patches of woody growth, including hackberry, elm, soapberry, wild plum, and smooth sumac, occur in ravine bottoms and on north slopes. The Black-capped Vireo formerly nested here.

Wetlands

Wetlands occupy only a small area in Kansas, but they are of the utmost importance biologically. During pioneer days, they occurred extensively in flood plains, along major rivers, chiefly in eastern Kansas. Most of these marshes were drained or converted to other uses, but new marshes, usually small, have been formed by the impoundment of lakes and reservoirs or have been developed for waterfowl hunting. The best-known area is Cheyenne Bottoms, which was originally part of a 41,000-acre natural sink. During the 1950s, what was then the Kansas Fish and Game Commission acquired about half the area and now manages it for waterfowl. Like all natural marshes, it is at the mercy of a dependable water supply and thus faces an uncertain future. The most important locality in the central United States for migrating shorebirds, Cheyenne Bottoms is a major area for waterfowl, wading birds, and gulls. When conditions become unfavorable there, many birds move to nearby Quivira National Wildlife Refuge. Other important marshes occur in Republic, Cloud, Sumner, and Lincoln counties, among others.

In freshwater marshes, prairie cordgrass, sedges, and cattails dominate, and vegetation may be tall and dense. In salt marshes, saltgrass and seepweed dominate, but other grasses, sedges, spike rush, and various forbs may be important; vegetation is usually of low to medium height. These marshes are used by a great variety of birds, including waterfowl, wading birds, shorebirds, marsh wrens, and blackbirds, as long as open water exists. After the water freezes, these birds are largely replaced by sparrows, often huge roosts of blackbirds, and various raptors.

Disturbed Habitats

The Kansas landscape has altered dramatically since colonization by Europeans, causing changes in the distribution, numbers, and local composition of our bird-life. Although many species have been affected adversely, others have benefited from the changes. Today cropland covers more than half the state, making it our most extensive general habitat type. Most of this acreage is devoted to wheat, sorghum, and corn—hardly prime breeding habitat for most species, but very important for transient and wintering birds, from sparrows and longspurs to raptors and waterfowl. Redwings, Dickcissels, Horned Larks, Lark Buntings, and others nest in large numbers in the fallow fields.

Pasture and rangeland occupy about one-third of the state and are utilized by many of the prairie birds mentioned previously. Remaining habitat is chiefly in the form of plantings in towns, on farmsteads, and in windbreaks. Their importance is most noticeable in western Kansas, where the numbers of many familiar birds, such as robins, orioles, and swifts, have increased greatly since pioneer times. Unfortunately, with them come such immigrants as the House Sparrow and the European Starling. We suspect that the recent expansion of the House Finch is due in large part to feeding stations maintained by people.

Changes in bird-life typically follow changes in vegetation—that is, plant succession. As an example, Sharp-tailed Grouse were reported in Ellis County in the 1870s but were replaced by Greater Prairie-Chickens soon after settlement. As cultivation became more extensive, prairie-chickens were replaced by the introduced Ring-necked Pheasant. Recently, as more land is restored to grassland, the prairie-chicken is returning.

EXPLANATION OF SPECIES ACCOUNTS

Since this is a general work, we use a minimum of citations, many of which are available in most public libraries. We include citations where the reader is likely to question a comment or may wish additional detail. Other citations refer to published photographs or items of special interest to Kansas birdwatchers. Unless otherwise stated, our comments refer to birds and their activities *in Kansas*.

Names: Common and scientific names and the sequence of species follow the American Ornithologists' Union checklist (6th edition).

Maps: For each species, a small outline map indicates by symbols the counties in which a species has been reported. These reports may be specimens, literature records, or sight records. Obvious sighting errors are not included. These data were provided by many observers, chiefly members of the Kansas Ornithological Society, and are from files maintained either by Marvin Schwilling or by Ely.

Photographs: A photograph, often taken in Kansas, is provided for 178 of the 222 species treated in this book. The photographs are the work of 22 Kansas wildlife photographers, as well as the Kansas Department of Wildlife and Parks and the U.S. Fish and Wildlife Service. We are grateful to these individuals and agencies for allowing us the use of their photographs.

Status: This section is a general statement defining the occurrence of a species. If a species has been taken only a few times in the state, or if its status is still in question, additional detail is provided. Since this is a general work, our terms are defined broadly rather than quantitatively.

Regular:	Occurs in about the same numbers, in about the same areas each year
Irregular:	May vary each year in numbers or distribution
Local:	Present and/or breeds at only a few localities or is widely scattered over a larger area
Casual:	Occurs in very small numbers most years
Vagrant:	Occurs rarely but can be expected every few years
Accidental:	Far out of its normal range or movement pattern and not likely to appear in the near future

Indications of abundance refer to presence in proper habitat and are also qualitative:

Rare:	Only a few individuals seen in a season
Uncommon:	Small numbers present but found on most birdwatching trips
Common:	Easily found, usually in numbers
Abundant:	Present in large numbers, usually widespread and conspicuous

The status of a species is complicated by the fact that it may be resident, but the individuals present may be either permanent residents (e.g., House Sparrow), from both resident and migratory populations (e.g., American Crow), or from summering, wintering, and transient populations (e.g., Mourning Dove).

Period of Occurrence: We provide extreme dates of reported occurrence and main migration periods. Comments on variation from normal patterns and/or variation within the state are sometimes provided. Data are from files compiled and maintained by Ely.

Breeding: A brief life history is given for each regularly breeding species. Included are the basic data concerning nesting habitat, nest location and construction, egg colors, clutch size, incubation period, nestling period and, often, courtship and care of the young. This information is from basic sources such as Bent (various years), Palmer (1962, 1976) and Terres (1980). Breeding is reported only when an active nest, eggs or dependent young have been reported and documented. Both recent and historical accounts are included when available as are changes in status or distribution. Brief descriptions of downy young are provided for some species, especially waterfowl.

Habits and Habitat: Here we provide information on where the species is most likely to be found at various times of the year ecologically and (usually) geographically. We include interesting or unusual behavior and observations both from personal experience and from the literature.

Field Marks: For most species we provide no more than brief comments on identification, but where confusion with other species in Kansas is a definite problem we provide more specific comments. For difficult groups such as gulls, it is imperative that readers refer to one or more good field guides.

Food: The food preferences of each species are included. Data are from personal observation and the literature mentioned previously.

Adult Red-throated Loons (*Gavia stellata*). Photograph by Galen L. Pittman.

LOONS AND GREBES
Red-throated Loon
Gavia stellata (Pontoppidan)

Status: The Red-throated Loon is probably a vagrant. One specimen was taken by Capt. Joe R. White on the Marais des Cygnes River, near Ottawa, Franklin County, on 20 October 1925. There are several sight records from Shawnee and Johnson counties (Tordoff 1956) and Chase and Franklin counties. Three of the sight records in Johnson, Shawnee, and Riley 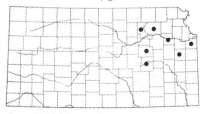 counties occurred on 10 April and from 8 to 18 May. There are four sight records from 13 to 27 October from Chase, Pottawatomie, and Shawnee counties. Look for this species, as well as the Arctic Loon, on large bodies of water during spring and fall migrations.

Pacific Loon
Gavia pacifica (Lawrence)

Status: The Pacific Loon, which only recently has been resurrected as a full species, is a casual visitor to Kansas. One female was shot in late

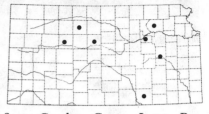

October or early November 1970 by a hunter on Wilson Reservoir, Russell County; the exact date is unknown. This bird was said to be with a group of six (Schwilling 1972). There are seven sight records from 15 August (Russell County) through 26 November from Cowley, Geary, Lyon, Pottawatomie, and Trego counties. There are two sight records from River Pond, Tuttle Creek Reservoir, Pottawatomie County, by L. K. Edmunds on 13 November 1965 and 23 October 1966 (Schwilling 1972). Another was recorded from 23 to 26 November 1976 on the Winfield City Lake, Cowley County, by David Seibel and others. This species was formerly considered to be the same as the Arctic Loon.

An adult Common Loon (*Gavia immer*). Photograph by David A. Rintoul.

Common Loon
Gavia immer (Brünnich)

Status: The Common Loon is an uncommon spring and fall transient throughout the state. Some birds have been observed as late as December when open water is present.

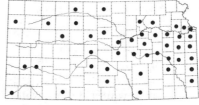

Period of Occurrence: These loons occur in March and April and during fall migration in September and October. One was found beside a road where it had hit a power line in Butler County on 16 December 1956.

Habits and Habitat: The Common Loon is usually found on large bodies of water. As Kansas now has numerous large impoundments, this species is recorded more frequently now than in the past. It probably overflew the state in former years. It usually dives when frightened and can swim long distances underwater. This loon is famous for its plaintive calls on the northern lakes where it breeds, but it is generally silent during migration and on its wintering grounds.

Food: This species feeds primarily on fishes but may take frogs, crayfishes, and, occasionally, vegetation.

An adult Pied-billed Grebe (*Podilymbus podiceps*). Photograph by Bob Gress.

Pied-billed Grebe
Podilymbus podiceps (Linnaeus)

Status: The Pied-billed Grebe is a common transient throughout the state. A few remain to breed in suitable habitat.

Period of Occurrence: Most migration falls within the periods from 1 March to 29 May and 25 August to 27 November. These grebes occur in winter if open water is present; Christmas counts have listed them frequently in late December to 9 January (Cowley County).

Breeding: Nesting records are reported from 13 counties, but most are from Barton and Stafford counties. The Pied-billed Grebe builds its nest from vegetation and anchors it to cattails or reeds. The birds are not colonial nesters, and nests are scattered in sloughs and on lake or pond edges. The nest, which may be as large as a bushel basket, floats on the water. Johnston (1964) lists 19 egg dates from 1 May to 30 June, with 15 May the average laying date. The number of eggs, which can range from 4 to 10, is usually 5 to 7. The young are precocious; they frequently ride on the back of a parent and cling there even when it dives.

Habits and Habitat: This species occurs on ponds, lakes, and, less frequently, rivers. When disturbed, it usually dives rather than taking wing. Grebes have the ability to "sink" out of sight when danger approaches. Unlike some of the other grebes and water birds, Pied-billed Grebes are usually solitary or in pairs and only occasionally flock.

Food: Pied-billed Grebes feed on small fishes, insects, crustaceans, and some vegetable matter (Bent 1919).

Horned Grebe
Podiceps auritus (Linnaeus)

Status: The Horned Grebe is an uncommon transient and rare winter resident throughout the state. It has been recorded from 44 counties.

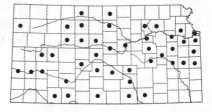

Period of Occurrence: Johnston (1965) gives an extreme spring arrival date of 24 February. The usual spring migration is from 14 March to 19 May and the fall migration from 3 October to 28 November. Since the building of major reservoirs in Kansas, this species has been recorded on several Christmas bird counts.

Habits and Habitat: The Horned Grebe occurs principally on lakes and reservoirs, but look for it also around marshes where there is enough water for it to take flight. Grebes must "run" along the surface for a considerable distance before attaining sufficient forward momentum to become airborne. They usually dive instead of taking flight when disturbed.

Food: Small fishes, aquatic insects, and crayfishes make up the main portion of their diet. They also eat some vegetable matter. McAtee and Beal (1912) found large numbers of feathers in the stomachs but gave no good explanation for their presence.

Adult Red-necked Grebes (*Podiceps grisegena*). Photograph by William J. Griffith.

Red-necked Grebe
Podiceps grisegena (Boddaert)

Status: Accidental. One example, shot by Logan I. Evans on the Kansas River east of Lawrence, Douglas County, on 29 October 1910, provides the only specimen record for Kansas. There are four sight records. Celia White observed one in Riley County. There were four on Pomona Reservoir in Osage County from 15 to 16 November 1985. L. Moore

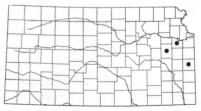

observed one in Wyandotte County on 13 January 1985, and L. Fox and Herb Moore saw one in Linn County in the spring of 1976. Look for this species on larger lakes and reservoirs.

An adult Eared Grebe (*Podiceps nigricollis*). Photograph by Ken Hollings.

Eared Grebe
Podiceps nigricollis (Brehm)

Status: The Eared Grebe is a common transient throughout the state and a rare breeder at Quivira National Wildlife Refuge and probably at Cheyenne Bottoms Wildlife Management Area.

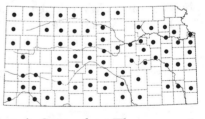

Period of Occurrence: The earliest arrival date is 5 April, and most birds have departed by mid-May. A few remain to nest. The return from the north begins in late July and early August, with peak numbers in September. There are several records from Christmas counts in late December and early January.

Breeding: The Eared Grebe, a colonial nester, attempted to breed in 1982 at Quivira National Wildlife Refuge where Ralph L. Bryant found 107 nests (Bryant 1983). Nest construction began on 28 June; each nest was a floating platform of vegetation. All were destroyed during a severe thunderstorm on 13 July. There are unconfirmed reports of nesting at Cheyenne Bottoms in 1982 and 1983. Subsequent breeding has not been recorded, but look for nests at Quivira Refuge and also at Cheyenne Bottoms.

Habits and Habitat: This grebe occurs on lakes, rivers, ponds, and marshes during migration. The winter records are principally from large impoundments that remain free of ice. Like the Horned Grebe, it usually dives when disturbed and swims great distances underwater before resurfacing.

Food: This species feeds primarily on water insects, tadpoles, frogs, and some water plants.

Adult Western Grebes (*Aechmophorus occidentalis*). Photograph by David A. Rintoul.

Western Grebe
Aechmophorus occidentalis (Lawrence)

Status: The Western Grebe is a rare transient in western Kansas and occasionally in the east; most records come from Cheyenne Bottoms Wildlife Management Area in Barton County. However, the species moves periodically into eastern Kansas, where several may flock on the larger reservoirs.

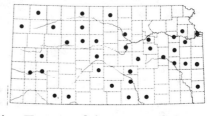

Period of Occurrence: This grebe has been reported from 36 counties. Twenty of those records have dates, in both spring and fall. Most records fall between 14 April–8 June and 12 October–28 November. There are midsummer records from Russell and Barton counties. It has been seen in winter to 5 January. Bent (1929) lists one record for Lawrence, Douglas County, on 3 November. Additional records are needed to clarify the temporal occurrence of this species.

Breeding: Although this grebe is not known to breed in Kansas, it breeds nearby in Colorado in colonies on marsh-fringed lakes.

Habits and Habitat: Western Grebes occur principally on larger bodies of water and at marshes and should be looked for at Cheyenne Bottoms and Quivira National Wildlife Refuge. Like other grebes, they dive readily when disturbed. These grebes usually occur in small flocks in migration.

Field Marks: The Western Grebe is quite large compared to the other grebes in Kansas and has a very long neck.

Food: Western Grebes feed primarily on fishes.

Clark's Grebe
Aechmophorus clarkii (Lawrence)

Status: The status of Clark's Grebe is unknown in Kansas, but it is probably a vagrant, possibly casual. There are no specimen records or other evidence except for sight records. The following have been recorded: Cheyenne Bottoms, Barton County, 30 August 1985; Phillips County, 19 October 1985; Trego County, 18 October 1986. All are by Scott Seltman. Until documentary evidence is available, this bird should be on the hypothetical list.

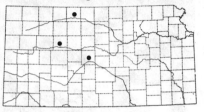

Adult American White Pelicans (*Pelecanus erythrorhynchos*). Photograph by Bob Gress.

PELICANS
American White Pelican
Pelecanus erythrorhynchos (Gmelin)

Status: The American White Pelican is an abundant to common transient at Cheyenne Bottoms and on large reservoirs; it is uncommon to rare elsewhere. It is casual in midsummer and during winter, and many of those sightings are of injured birds.

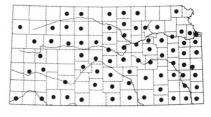

Period of Occurrence: Extreme dates for presumed migrants are from 4 March to 2 June and 8 September to 24 November. Migration peaks are in April and from late September to early October. In recent years, some birds have summered at Cheyenne Bottoms (there were 280 in 1968), but no nesting has been recorded. Occasional birds remain on the larger impoundments until midwinter or until there is no open water.

Habits and Habitat: This species prefers large bodies of water with shallow feeding areas. Both on land and on water, an American White Pelican is unmistakable because of its large size (10 to 17 pounds), its whiteness, and its huge bill. In flight the head is pulled back, but the

24

bill is still clearly visible. It is usually silent while in Kansas. At Cheyenne Bottoms, flocks spend much time resting on the duck-blind islands, and from a distance, they resemble snow banks. They feed, usually in groups, by swimming slowly in shallow water and dipping their head beneath the surface. The bird retains fishes in its pouch below the bill, squeezes out the water, then raises its head to swallow the fishes. Pelicans may drive fishes before them, and sometimes all the birds in a group will synchronize their dipping motions. Although ungainly on land, pelicans, with their 9-foot wingspread, are impressive in the air. They frequently fly in long, wavering, single-file lines following a leader; each bird changes course at the precise point where its precursor changed course. They may also soar for hours, sometimes spiraling upward until lost from view.

Field Marks: Adults in breeding condition have a knob near the tip of the upper mandible. Immatures are dusky-colored, especially around the head, and have paler, almost gray, pouches and bills.

Food: American White Pelicans eat almost entirely rough fishes such as carp but also feed on tadpoles, larval salamanders, and, occasionally, crayfishes.

An adult Brown Pelican (*Pelecanus occidentalis*). Photograph by Bob Gress.

Brown Pelican
Pelecanus occidentalis (Linnaeus)

Status: The Brown Pelican is a vagrant. Mark Goldsberry and Joe Lilly found an adult Brown Pelican at the Meade State Fish Hatchery on 21

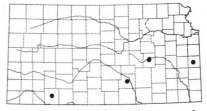

April 1985. The next day, Goldsberry and Tom Flowers found the bird at nearby Meade State Lake, approached to within 20 meters, and took photographs. On 23 April, Scott Seltman took additional photos (Williams 1985). It was last seen on 24 April. There is an early specimen from Linn County (June 1916), an early sight record from Sedgwick County (25 April 1910), and "a puzzling bird," possibly this species, reported from Pratt County (8 November and 6 December 1953). The most unusual Brown Pelican record, from Chase County, is a pelican which was roped on a farm pond by a cowboy about 1930; its feathers were used to stuff a pillow (Marvin Schwilling, pers. comm.).

Sight records need careful verification. A record from Barton County in 1970 was of an oiled, discolored American White Pelican. It is also important to try to ascertain whether a sighting is of a wild vagrant or an escapee from a zoo or aviary.

A family of Double-crested Cormorants (*Phalacrocorax auritus*). Photograph by Steve Burr.

CORMORANTS AND ANHINGAS
Double-crested Cormorant
Phalacrocorax auritus (Lesson)

Status: The Double-crested Cormorant is a regular spring and fall transient, especially in eastern and central Kansas. It breeds locally and is casual elsewhere in summer and in winter.

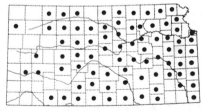

Period of Occurrence: Extreme dates for birds presumed to be migrants are from 3 March to 3 June and 8 August to 27 November. Migration peaks occur in mid-April and early October. Scattered birds appear on large bodies of water during summer and a few remain until midwinter when there is no more open water (e.g., there were 38 on Tuttle Creek Reservoir, 20 December 1975).

Breeding: There have been up to 23 nests at Kirwin Reservoir, Phillips County, since 1959. Glen Elder Reservoir, Mitchell County, has had as many as 220 nests since 1974, but there are now many fewer. A few birds nested at Cheyenne Bottoms, Barton County, in 1951, 1974, and 1975, and 43 nests were found in 1982. The nest is usually a compact platform of sticks in a tree over water, often in a Great Blue Heron colony. The nests at Cheyenne Bottoms were on the ground along interior earth dikes. The clutch is usually three to four pale blue eggs with a chalky outer layer. Dates for Kansas eggs are between 9 May and 20 June, and young are present from late June to early August. The young are naked and dark-skinned at hatching and develop black down in two weeks. First flight is at 5 to 6 weeks and they are independent at 10 weeks.

Habits and Habitat: Cormorants normally occur in flocks and prefer lakes or ponds with snags and dead trees. They usually swim low in the water with the beak angled upward. They perch upright, often with wings extended in a "drying" posture. They may resemble geese when they fly in lines or a V, but they have a different silhouette and faster wingbeats.

Field Marks: Immature birds are brown, and some individuals retain this color for two years. The crests are present only during the breeding season and are not often noticeable.

Food: Double-crested Cormorants feed almost entirely on fishes captured when they swim underwater. There have been flocks reported fishing cooperatively and in mixed feeding with pelicans. Salamander larvae and, less often, frogs, crustaceans, and perhaps some plant food are also eaten.

Olivaceous Cormorant
Phalacrocorax olivaceus (Humboldt)

Status: Olivaceous Cormorants occur casually in Kansas from 2 April to 10 September, with most sightings at Cheyenne Bottoms. Speci-mens have been reported from Douglas and Barton counties, and there are recent sightings in Linn, Pottawatomie, Riley, Sumner, and Stafford counties.

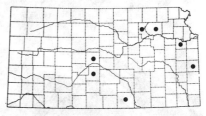

Field Marks: The species should be identified with care and, whenever possible, by direct comparison with Double-crested Cor-morants. The Olivaceous Cormorant is smaller and more slender; at close range, a narrow white border at the rear edge of the gular pouch may be seen. In breeding season there may be white filaments on the side of the head, and the pouch is dull yellow. Immature birds tend to be browner and paler, especially on the underparts.

An adult Anhinga (*Anhinga anhinga*). Photograph by Bob Gress.

Anhinga
Anhinga anhinga (Linnaeus)

Status: The Anhinga is a vagrant. Specimens have been taken in Rooks (1874), Meade (1888), and Barton (1933) counties, but only the first is extant. Recent sight records, between 16 April and 24 July and
on 1 September, are from Cowley, Greenwood, Linn, Osage,
and Phillips counties. Sight records need confirmation as some
purported Anhingas proved to
be cormorants.

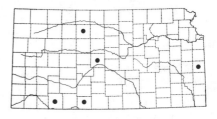

Field Marks: Anhingas differ from cormorants in being slimmer, with a small head, pointed bill, and long tail that may be spread in flight.

FRIGATEBIRDS
Magnificent Frigatebird
Fregata magnificens (Mathews)

Status: The Magnificent Frigatebird is a vagrant. There are two records; one, a specimen collected in Osborne County on 16 August 1880 and identified by Goss, is now lost. The other, of an adult female, was seen (and photographed) at Meade State Park on 16 and 17 June 1982 by mark Goldsberry, James Parker, and others (Parker et al. 1983). Mar- 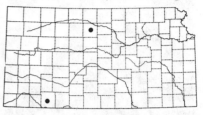 vin Schwilling and Jim Ptacek reported one, presumably the same bird, at a nearby fish hatchery on 23 July.

Field Marks: Frigatebirds are unmistakable because of their large size; long, narrow, angled, and pointed wings; long, deeply-forked tail; and long, straight, hooked beak. The frigatebird's normal habitat is maritime.

An adult American Bittern (*Botaurus lentiginosus*). Photograph by Ed and Jean Schulenberg.

HERONS
American Bittern
Botaurus lentiginosus (Rackett)

Status: The American Bittern is an uncommon, perhaps overlooked, transient in most of the state but is a common summer resident at Cheyenne Bottoms Wildlife Management Area and Quivira National Wildlife Refuge.

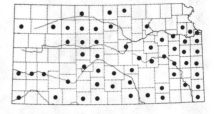

Period of Occurrence: The American Bittern is primarily a summer resident with extreme dates of 25 March and 21 December. The main population arrives 1 May and remains until 16 October.

Breeding: This bittern, a solitary nester, has been recorded nesting in six counties. It nests primarily in marshes, but nests have been found in heavy grasslands away from water. Nests are placed on the ground or on a platform of floating vegetation. Search for nests also in marshy areas or wet areas in grassy meadows. Five eggs, of a brownish-buff color, are the usual clutch. Incubation lasts approximately 29 days. The young leave the nest after two weeks and are apparently cared for by the female outside the nest.

Habits and Habitat: The American Bittern is found primarily in marshes among cattails or reeds but is seen frequently in pastures with heavy grass. It has also been observed in roadside ditches that have only a temporary water supply. This species is one of the more interesting herons in the state, because of its uncanny ability to hide among the cattails and, by pointing its bill straight up, become almost invisible. The striated plumage also blends in well with brownish cattails. While "skypointing," this bittern can rotate its eyes to look forward to watch for predators or prey. It feeds by patient stalking, with its bill horizontal and its eyes turned downward. A person familiar with its call may hear the bird more often than see it, for at night, its booming sound may be heard throughout the marsh—hence the nickname "thunder pumper."

Food: Fishes appear to be the primary food. Other items recorded are frogs, snakes, crayfishes, mice, clams, snails, and insects.

An adult Least Bittern (*Ixobrychus exilis*). Photograph by Frank S. Shipley.

Least Bittern
Ixobrychus exilis (Gmelin)

Status: The Least Bittern is an uncommon migrant and summer resident around marshes. It is common at Cheyenne Bottoms Wildlife Management Area and Quivira National Wildlife Refuge during spring migration. There are few nesting records.

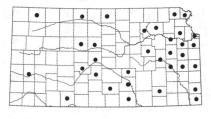

Period of Occurrence: There are few dates available, but the extreme dates are 9 April and 18 November (Linn County), with most of the sightings in May and June.

Breeding: The Least Bittern has been recorded breeding in Barton, Douglas, Johnson, Kingman, Linn, Lyon, and Pottawatomie counties, although it undoubtedly breeds in others. The nest is usually placed in marshes in cattails, just above the water, but sometimes may be placed on flood debris. The normal clutch size is four to five but may go up to seven; the eggs are greenish white. Much more information is needed on its nesting habits in Kansas.

Habits and Habitat: Like other bitterns, the Least Bittern is generally found in marshes, where it can be observed only by walking through cattails or, with patience, waiting for it to appear on the marsh edges to feed. Thompson flushed a dozen or more in an hour from cattails in the Quivira Refuge. Like its relative the American Bittern, the Least Bittern freezes when alarmed, with its bill pointed skyward and its yellow eyes rotated forward to follow the dangerous sound or object.

Food: Food consists mainly of small fishes, but anything small enough to swallow becomes fair game. This bird is also known to eat frogs, tadpoles, salamanders, insects, small mammals, and other small birds.

An adult Great Blue Heron (*Ardea herodias*). Photograph by Ed and Jean Schulenberg.

Great Blue Heron
Ardea herodias (Linnaeus)

Status: The Great Blue Heron is a common summer resident in the eastern half of the state and uncommon in the western half. It is normally a rare winter resident near open water, but in some warmer winters, it may be quite common along open stretches of rivers such as the Arkansas.

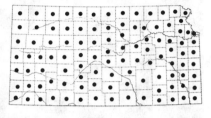

Period of Occurrence: Although a few birds winter in Kansas, the main population returns to the state in February and March and departs in October and November. Johnston (1965) lists the extreme dates as arriving 4 February and departing 29 November.

Breeding: This heron breeds colonially throughout the state. Colonies are usually located near water in trees, preferably Sycamores. The large nests, 3 to 4 feet across, are made of sticks placed at the end of branches. Colonies in Kansas range from just a few nests up to 200 to 300. Bent (1926) lists four eggs as the number most commonly laid, although clutch size may range from three to seven. The eggs are usually laid in March and April. Young remain in the nest or its immediate vicinity until they fly. Nesting trees are frequently killed by the excrement from the young. Some Kansas colonies have used the same immediate locality for years, and most of the Kansas colonies are well known.

Habits and Habitat: Great Blue Herons are usually found near ponds, lakes, streams, and temporary bodies of water. They stand quietly waiting for their prey or slowly stalk through the water catching the prey with a quick stab of the bill. They generally feed singly. They are the largest of the North American herons and are unmistakable. Their huge bills are dangerous weapons, and injured birds should be approached with caution, as herons, when cornered, tend to stab at a person's eyes. Herons are usually quite wary and will take wing quickly when approached. In urban areas where they are not bothered, they may become quite tame.

Food: Great Blue Herons feed primarily on fishes but will also feed on frogs, crayfishes, salamanders, and tadpoles; Audubon (1840) found lizards, snakes, birds, shrews, meadow mice, and young rats in their stomachs. They are, like most herons, opportunistic and will eat practically anything that moves that they can swallow.

An adult Great Egret (*Casmerodius albus*). Photograph by Ed and Jean Schulenberg.

Great Egret
Casmerodius albus (Linnaeus)

Status: The Great Egret is an uncommon migrant and rare breeder. Breeding records exist only for Cowley and Sedgwick counties.

Period of Occurrence: It has been recorded from 28 March to 9 October but is more common in late summer when southern birds augment the population.

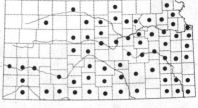

Breeding: This species should be looked for in Great Blue and Little Blue Heron colonies in Kansas. The first nesting records for Kansas were in Great Blue Heron colonies near Arkansas City in Cowley County. Apparently this species has nested sporadically in Cowley County since 1926 (Seibel 1978). Two nests were found there in 1963 and constitute the last known nesting in that rookery. Recently, the Great Egret has nested in Sedgwick County in the rookery south of Wichita. Four nests were found there in 1983 (Gress and Schaefer 1984), 12 in 1985, and 25 in 1986. Nests were found among those of the Little Blue Heron and Cattle Egret. With the sudden increase in numbers of herons nesting in Kansas, look for this species more closely. The nest is made of sticks in which two to five pale blue eggs are laid.

Habits and Habitat: Great Egrets are solitary feeders, rarely found in numbers except during the evening roosting period or in breeding rookeries. Their prime habitat is around ponds, lakes, and marshes, and they may occasionally be found along more open streams. They feed by stalking their prey and may "jump" to make the prey move so that it can be seen. This species was one of several hunted to near extinction in the United States 80 to 100 yeras ago for plumes that were used in the millinery trade.

Field Marks: This egret's large size and its yellow bill make it easy to identify.

Food: Great Egrets feed primarily on aquatic life such as fishes, molluscs, crustaceans, and aquatic insects; there are also records of mammals, small birds, turtles, and snakes being eaten. This heron is an opportunist and will eat almost anything.

An adult Snowy Egret (*Egretta thula*). Photograph by David A. Rintoul.

Snowy Egret
Egretta thula (Molina)

Status: The Snowy Egret is an uncommon migrant and rare summer resident.

Period of Occurrence: This species arrives in Kansas in early April and remains until October, with extreme dates of 4 April and 3 November. Most records occur after the breeding season in July and August and are probably of 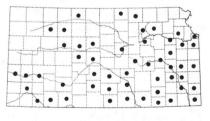 young birds that wandered from their more southerly breeding sites.

Breeding: The Snowy Egret has nested in Barton County at Cheyenne Bottoms Wildlife Management Area since 1965. In Finney County, two pairs nested in 1952, but that site no longer exists as the lake was drained and is now farmland. Six to eight pairs nested in Kearny County during 1955–56. Recent nesting (1983) has also occurred south of Wichita in Sedgwick County in the same rookery with the

Little Blue Herons, Cattle Egrets, and Great Egrets. Four birds nested in Reno County in 1982. This species should be looked for in any rookery where white herons breed. The nest is made of sticks and usually placed in the lower branches of trees, although there is nesting in reeds at Cheyenne Bottoms. The normal clutch size varies from three to five eggs, but there are occasionally six. The eggs are pale bluish green. The young leave the nest long before they can fly and scramble about in the trees.

Habits and Habitat: This species was one of those hunted nearly to extinction in the United States for its plumes, which were used in the millinery trade 80 to 100 years ago. Protection has brought its numbers back, and it continues to spread northward during the breeding season to areas formerly unoccupied by breeding colonies. The Snowy Egret occurs near marshes, streams, or lakes, where it feeds and nests. Like the Cattle Egret, it is occasionally seen in dry pastures feeding on insects around cattle. In Kansas it seems to prefer marshes or ponds, where it feeds mainly during the day and actively pursues its prey in short dashes in shallow water. The Snowy Egret frequently uses the "foot-stir" method to evict hiding prey which, when dislodged, is dispatched with a quick jab of the bill.

Field Marks: This species can be easily confused with the immature Little Blue Heron. It can be distinguished by its black legs, yellow feet, and uniformly black bill. The Little Blue Heron has a bluish bill tipped with black, and greenish legs. The Snowy Egret's black bill can be compared to the Cattle Egret's light yellow bill.

Food: Snowy Egrets feed primarily on aquatic animals such as frogs, fishes, crustaceans, and insects. It has also taken small lizards and snakes, including the venomous Cottonmouth, although this snake is not native to Kansas.

Mature (left) and immature Little Blue Herons (*Egretta caerulea*). Photograph by Ken Highfill.

Little Blue Heron
Egretta caerulea (Linnaeus)

Status: The Little Blue Heron is an uncommon transient and summer resident. Populations have been increasing rapidly since 1980.

Period of Occurrence: Record dates are 2 March and 19 December, but the average dates of arrival and departure are 6 April and 5 October. This species was formerly a postbreeding wanderer but is now a summer resident.

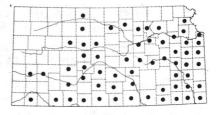

Numbers are augmented in late summer by arrivals from farther south.

Breeding: This heron has become a regular breeding bird since 1952. A large colony nests primarily in Black Willow trees on the edge of Hutchinson, Reno County. A recent colony has formed on the south edge of Wichita, Sedgwick County, and it is the largest heronry in the state. Several hundred Little Blue Herons nest there in a tree nursery. There are undoubtedly more undiscovered colonies in the state. A colony in Harper County moved after one year and has not been located again, although large numbers of birds have been seen in the area. Nests are usually placed in low shrubs, trees, and cattails. The nest is a typical heron nest made of sticks and is often destroyed by gale-force winds. The herons usually lay four to five eggs, but there may be as many as six. The incubation period is 21 to 23 days, and the young take about 30 days to fledge.

Habits and Habitat: The Little Blue Heron can be found around marshes, ponds, lakes, and streams. This heron is shy and will usually fly away, long before a person can get very close. They usually leave the rookery at daybreak and return at dusk to roost. They walk along the water's edge stalking their prey. The young are fed regurgitated food by the parents.

Field Marks: Usually more subadults than adults are seen in Kansas. Birds with intermediate molts showing both blue and white feathers are frequently seen. Young birds are totally white, which makes them easy to confuse with any white egrets that also occur in the state, frequently in the same rookery.

Food: Like all herons, this species is also opportunistic and takes a broad range of prey, including frogs, fishes, crayfishes, insects, snakes, lizards, and spiders, all of which are swallowed whole.

An adult Tricolored Heron (*Egretta tricolor*). Photograph by Bob Gress.

Tricolored Heron
Egretta tricolor (Müller)

Status: The Tricolored Heron is a rare summer resident at Cheyenne Bottoms Wildlife Management Area, Barton County. There are three specimen records: one each from Barton, McPherson, and Cowley counties (the latter two specimens have been lost). It has been recorded as well in Stafford and Sumner counties. No more than one or two pairs have been seen at one time; they are difficult to find.

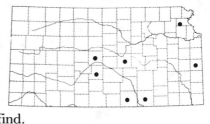

Period of Occurrence: There are so few records that little is known of the arrival and departure times, but extreme dates are 16 April and 12 September.

Breeding: The first nesting attempt at Cheyenne Bottoms in 1974 failed, but an attempt in 1976 was successful. The species has nested there most years since then, but not all nests have been successful. Look for it in breeding areas with Little Blue Herons and other egrets. The nest is a typical heron nest composed of sticks and is usually placed in low shrubs or cattails; some may be on the ground. The eggs are pale greenish blue and usually number three to four, but there may be as many as seven.

Habits and Habitat: Little is known about the Tricolored Heron in Kansas. Like the Mottled Duck, this species is found primarily along the Gulf Coast, but a few regularly come to Kansas to breed. Along the coastal United States, it feeds in fresh or salt water. It usually stands and waits for its prey, although at times it may stalk. Like the Snowy Egret, it has been observed to stir the water with its feet.

Food: This heron is omnivorous and eats practically anything small enough to swallow, including fishes, crustaceans, amphibians, snails, worms, and insects.

An adult Cattle Egret (*Bubulcus ibis*). Photograph by Bob Gress.

Cattle Egret
Bubulcus ibis (Linnaeus)

Status: The Cattle Egret is an uncommon transient and summer resident. It was first reported in the state on 26 April 1964, and it first nested in the state at Cheyenne Bottoms Wildlife Management Area, Barton County, in 1973.

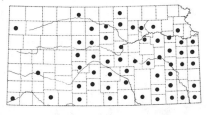

Period of Occurrence: Occurrence is not well documented, since this bird is new in Kansas. The earliest arrival date known is 6 March, and the last known departure record is 2 December. However, most birds arrive in mid-April and depart by mid-October.

Breeding: The first breeding records for this bird came from Cheyenne Bottoms, where nests were found on 8 July 1973. This species probably breeds in several areas in the state, but the best-known site is near Wichita, Sedgwick County, where nests were recorded in 1982. Another area that should be investigated is southeastern Kansas, where Rising (pers. comm.) saw hundreds flying southwest of Baxter Springs, Cherokee County. They probably belonged to a large colony in northeast Oklahoma. Many have been observed in Harper County, but no nests have been found.

Habits and Habitat: This heron, a native of Asia and Africa, is the success story of the century. Apparently a small flock found its way to southern South America and successfully bred; the species then expanded its range northward to the United States and Canada. It frequently feeds around cattle in pastures. During spring migration, it can also be found around ponds, lakes, and in wet meadows. In Kansas it is frequently found following tractors in open plowed fields, picking up freshly turned-over prey. It is exceedingly tame and may be approached quite closely. Several birds were observed near Cheyenne Bottoms, feeding in a roadside ditch in a mobile home park. While being photographed from a distance of ten feet, they still did not take wing.

Food: Cattle Egrets appear to eat mainly insects which they obtain in grassland and wet meadows. They follow cattle and at times stand on the backs of the cattle to look for insects. They have been observed eating toads unearthed by a tractor and also take fishes, crustaceans, frogs, and other animals small enough to swallow.

An adult Green-backed Heron (*Butorides striatus virescens*). Photograph by Bob Gress.

Green-backed Heron
Butorides striatus virescens (Linnaeus)

Status: The Green-backed Heron is a common summer resident around streams, lakes, and marshes.

Period of Occurrence: The main population of this bird arrives about 27 April and remains until 9 September. Extreme dates are 29 March and 30 October (Johnston 1965). There is one record for 18 December.

Breeding: The Green-backed Heron breeds throughout the state. Most nests are in trees, but Bent (1926) says they are also in bushes and even on the ground. Some have been found in woodland quite far from water. Although nests are usually placed singly, they are found occasionally in colonies. Tree nests are generally 10 to 12 inches in diameter and composed of sticks. Nests on the ground are normally made of reeds or cattails. Most eggs are laid in May, with a usual clutch size of four. Incubation lasts 21 to 23 days. The young remain in or near the nest until they fly.

Habits and Habitat: The Green-backed Heron, usually found along wooded streams where it stalks its prey, may also be found along the edges of ponds and lakes if trees are close by. Normally a wary bird that takes wing quickly when approached by humans, it has learned in urban areas to ignore people, particularly fishermen, and can be approached quite closely. Its greenish-brown coloration blends well into the shadows of the streams where it feeds, and it may not be seen until it takes wing with a loud squawk. Although it usually stands to wait for the prey to come by, several other techniques including wading slowly and, in Florida, placing food in the water to attract small fishes which it then captures have been observed. This species was formerly thought to be endemic to North America but is now considered conspecific with the other green herons and therefore cosmopolitan.

Food: This heron, which feeds primarily on small fishes, insects, crustaceans, and frogs, also takes most animals small enough to eat.

An adult Black-crowned Night Heron (*Nycticorax nycticorax*). Photograph by JoAnn S. Garrett.

Black-crowned Night Heron
Nycticorax nycticorax (Linnaeus)

Status: The Black-crowned Night Heron is a common transient statewide that is often overlooked. It is a local summer resident, especially in Barton County at Cheyenne Bottoms Wildlife Management Area, and in Stafford County at Quivira National Wildlife Refuge. It is casual in winter.

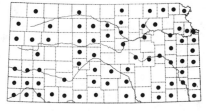

Period of Occurrence: This species is most numerous from 4 April to 17 June and from 30 July to 25 November. The extreme dates are 24 March and 2 January.

Breeding: There are breeding records for only seven counties, but it undoubtedly breeds throughout the state, particularly in the eastern part. The nest, which may be in trees or on the ground, is made of twigs and sticks, and is usually lined with grasses. The clutch size varies from three to five pale blue-green eggs. The incubation period is 24 to 26 days. The young may leave the nest in three weeks but remain close by for parental feeding. The nesting habitat ranges from marshes to trees near water, and even to shelterbelts far from water in western Kansas.

Habits and Habitat: These herons are seldom seen due to their nocturnal habits. They leave the rookeries at dusk, fly to the feeding area, and return in early morning. They stalk their prey. During the day, they can frequently be seen around the dike system at Cheyenne Bottoms, resting until dusk to feed. This heron is one of the few cosmopolitan species in Kansas.

Field Marks: In late summer, the young may be confused with those of the Yellow-crowned Night Heron, from which they may be distinguished by the buffy white spots on the back, longer wings, and darker brown streaking on the belly.

Food: This heron is also an opportunist, eating almost anything that moves that is small enough to swallow whole. Its diet includes fishes, frogs, tadpoles, snakes, salamanders, molluscs, crustaceans, marine annelids, insects, vegetable matter, and young birds and mammals.

An adult Yellow-crowned Night Heron (*Nycticorax violaceus*). Photograph by Bob Gress.

Yellow-crowned Night Heron
Nycticorax violaceus (Linnaeus)

Status: The Yellow-crowned Night Heron is an uncommon transient statewide and a local summer resident, especially at Cheyenne Bottoms Wildlife Management Area, Barton County.

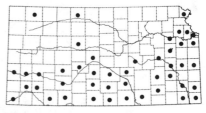

Period of Occurrence: This species usually arrives in Kansas in late April and stays until mid-October. The extreme dates are 3 April and 20 October.

Breeding: This heron nests locally in eight counties, but the largest numbers are at Cheyenne Bottoms where it is found in cattails. It is a more solitary species than the Black-crowned Night Heron and generally nests alone. Outside of Kansas larger colonies occur. The nest, a well-built structure of heavy twigs with a finer lining, is placed in trees, cattails, or shrubbery; it may be in marshes or sometimes in towns away from water. There are three to four bluish-white eggs in the clutch, sometimes five; the incubation period is about 24 to 26 days. Little more is known about the species. There are recent nesting records from Sim Park, Wichita, in Sedgwick County.

Habits and Habitat: The Yellow-crowned Night Heron is less gregarious than the Black-crowned Night Heron and usually feeds singly or with no more than one or two other birds. It is more diurnal than the latter species but sometimes feeds late in the evening. A single bird near Winfield (1984) was seen feeding during the day on a small pond every day for a month. Later in the season, it was accompanied by an immature bird.

Field Marks: See the species account of the Black-crowned Night Heron for identification of the immatures of both herons.

Food: This heron feeds largely on crustaceans such as crayfishes and seldom on fishes. However, like all herons, it is an opportunist and has been recorded eating frogs, molluscs, snakes, lizards, and many other things.

An adult White Ibis (*Eudocimus albus*). Courtesy U.S. Fish and Wildlife Service.

IBIS
White Ibis
Eudocimus albus (Linnaeus)

Status: The White Ibis is a casual summer visitor. There are no known Kansas specimens, but several photograph records exist. A summary of records follows: Barton County, 19 May to 21 June 1971, one adult, two birds on 19 July (Ed Martinez and Marvin Kraft), photographs taken; one bird until 29 July; 10 to 28 June 1974, one bird (Ed Martinez and Sebastian Patti); Douglas County, 16 to 17 August 1969, one immature on the sixteenth and two immatures on the seventeenth (Mrs. Bert Chewning and Mrs. J. H. Nelson); Harvey County, 26 August to 28 September 1977, one immature (Jane Hershberger); Stafford

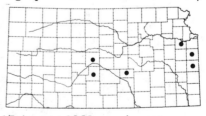

County, 2 to 14 May 1971, one adult photographed (Charles Darling and W. Dale); Miami County, August 1985, one unknown age (Jane Leo and Jane Lippencott). There are numerous Oklahoma records, and the species can be expected again in Kansas.

A juvenile White-faced Ibis (*Plegadis chihi*). Photograph by Ed and Jean Schulenberg.

White-faced Ibis
Plegadis chihi (Viellot)

Status: The White-faced Ibis is a rare spring and fall migrant and summer resident. It breeds regularly at Cheyenne Bottoms Wildlife Management Area and has bred recently at Quivira National Wildlife Refuge.

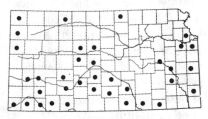

Period of Occurrence: This ibis has been recorded from 4 April to 20 October, but more data are needed.

Breeding: The White-faced Ibis has been a regular breeding bird at Cheyenne Bottoms since 1962. The only reliable breeding record prior to 1962 was of young photographed at Cheyenne Bottoms by Larry Nossaman in 1951. There are no older state breeding records, although the bird has been reported for many years. Goss (1886) reported it from Douglas County in the fall of 1879, and there are recent nesting records for Quivira Refuge, Stafford County. There seems to be a recent increase in the number of birds during the breeding season. A small flock "looked over" the Sedgwick County rookery but made no attempt to nest. The nest in Kansas is typically in cattails and is usually associated with heron species. The eggs are incubated for 21 days, and the young can fly at the end of six weeks.

Habits and Habitat: Ibis normally inhabit wetland areas, and this species is no exception. It has been observed feeding in temporary pools near Winfield, Cowley County, but it is more likely to be found in permanent marshes such as Cheyenne Bottoms or the Quivira Refuge. If one drives on the dikes in the summer at Cheyenne Bottoms, this bird will likely appear as it feeding in the waters near the dikes. It probes with its long bill to obtain its food.

Food: Very little is known about the food of the White-faced Ibis, but Palmer (1962) lists insects, newts, leeches, worms, molluscs, crustaceans, frogs, and fishes.

Roseate Spoonbill
Ajaia ajaja (Linnaeus)

Status: The Roseate Spoonbill is accidental, with only one record prior to 1986. That record, from Four Mile Creek near Douglas, Butler County, is the only known speci-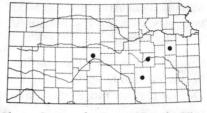men. The specimen was taken by Dr. R. Matthews on 20 March 1899 and became the property of a Mr. Gerald Volk of Wichita (Snow 1903); its present where-abouts are unknown. There was another sighting in April 1977 in Chase County by Jerry Horak. The bird was on the dam of a pond. In 1986, this species showed up at Melvern Reservoir, Osage County, on 24 August. On 26 August, there were two present which remained until 23 September (Charles Hall and Don Patton). On 2 September, a spoonbill was discovered at the Mallard Gun Club just north of Cheyenne Bottoms (Wayne Hoffman et al.), and it remained until 6 September. The species normally occurs along the Gulf Coast.

Adult Wood Storks (*Mycteria americana*). Photograph by Steve Burr.

Wood Stork
Mycteria americana (Linnaeus)

Status: The Wood Stork is a vagrant. One specimen, from 5 miles northeast of Goodland, Sherman County, was taken on 4 October 1913 by Willis Feaster and is now in the University of Kansas Museum of Natural History collection. There is a sight record from Ellis County, where Dr. Lewis Watson observed a Wood Stork on 26 March 1885 (Goss 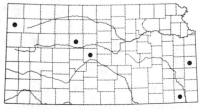 1886). A purported specimen, its whereabouts now unknown, from Chetopa, Labette County, was taken about 1877 by Albert Garrett and reported to Goss by Dr. George Lisle in 1883 (ibid.). Lisle reported seeing these birds on the flats east of Chetopa where the specimen was taken. In Barton County, Marvin Schwilling reported a bird at Cheyenne Bottoms on 22 May 1967, and in Linn County, one bird was observed at the Marais des Cygnes Wildlife Management Area from 17 to 23 July 1975 by Frank Wood, Ivan Sutton, et al. (Schwilling 1976).

Adult Greater Flamingos (*Phoenicopterus ruber*). Photograph by William J. Griffith.

FLAMINGOS
Greater Flamingo
Phoenicopterus ruber (Linnaeus)

Status: The Greater Flamingo is an accidental visitor to Kansas. There is one mounted specimen from Little Salt Marsh, Quivira National Wildlife Refuge, Stafford County. It was taken during the autumn of 1928 and is on display at the Kansas Department of Wildlife and Parks museum in Pratt. The specimen is one of two birds observed. Another record 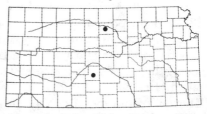 exists from Mitchell County, Lake Waconda (Glen Elder Reservoir); a photograph, taken on 11 November 1972 by Jerry Johnson, is on deposit at the University of Kansas Museum of Natural History.

Whether these are natural arrivals or zoo escapees, no one knows. However, both birds were in good color; until recently, captive birds were often white, because zoos were unable to adjust diet to maintain the salmon-pink color.

WHISTLING-DUCKS
Fulvous Whistling-Duck
Dendrocygna bicolor (Vieillot)

Status: The Fulvous Whistling-Duck is a casual visitor to Cheyenne Bottoms between 1 May and 9 November. There is no confirmed nesting from Kansas, but it may have attempted to nest at Cheyenne Bottoms in 1965 and 1967. There are also recent reports from Ford, Linn, Pottawatomie (specimen), and Pratt counties between 10 August and 28 November and from 13 to 20 April.

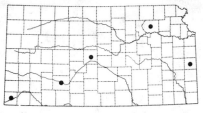

Black-bellied Whistling-Duck
Dendrocygna autumnalis (Linnaeus)

Status: The Black-bellied Whistling-Duck is a vagrant. There are three records. One was seen at Marais des Cygnes Wildlife Management Area, Linn County, by Marvin Schwilling on 20 September 1956. Roger and Jan Boyd saw a single bird at Quivira National Wildlife Refuge on 6 July 1980, and Ed, Jean, and Margaret Schulenberg photographed a 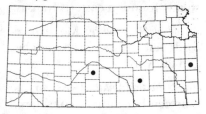 single bird there on 8 July. On 21 May 1982, Brad Williamson noted an apparently mated pair in Butler County.

SWANS
Tundra Swan
Cygnus columbianus (Ord)

Status: The Tundra Swan is a rare migrant and a casual winter visitor, chiefly found in eastern Kansas.

Period of Occurrence: Modern records fall between 1 November and 26 April.

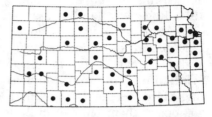

Habits and Habitat: Goss, in the nineteenth century, considered this bird a rare migrant in mid-March and October; 9 of 12 extant specimens prior to 1900 were taken between 7 March and 26 April. More recently, these swans have been reported mainly during early and midwinter. Most recent sightings have been of family groups on large reservoirs. The winter of 1971–72 provided one of the best swan flights in recent years, with sightings from six scattered counties; these included a flock of 15 in Lyon County on 19 and 20 December. Their arrival in an area also draws unwanted attention that often results in them being illegally hunted.

Field Marks: Swans are unmistakable because of their large size (they weigh 13 to 20 pounds), pure white wings, and very long necks. Immature swans are a dingier white than the adults. The Tundra Swan is best distinguished from the larger Trumpeter Swan by its head shape and posture (see next species).

Food: This species eats chiefly submerged aquatic vegetation such as pond weeds, which it takes while dipping from the surface of shallow water. Some seeds, shoots of grain, and perhaps animal food are also taken.

An adult Trumpeter Swan (*Cygnus buccinator*). Photograph by Ken Highfill.

Trumpeter Swan
Cygnus buccinator (Richardson)

Status: The Trumpeter Swan was probably a former transient during the nineteenth century, but no specimens or documented sightings exist from that period. Goss (1886) reported it as "rare. Arrives about the middle of March." Wintering birds from a captive "restoration" flock established near Haigler, Nebraska, apparently visited northwestern Kan-

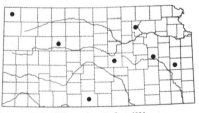

sas during the 1980s (Harold Burgess fide Marvin Schwilling, pers. comm.).

On 23 January 1985, a marked female and three immatures from a restoration flock near Minneapolis, Minnesota, arrived at South Lake, Garnett, Anderson County. Of the 29 birds of that flock (which migrated for the first time), 18 returned to Minnesota. The four Garnett birds departed on 22 February and reached Minnesota on the twenty-sixth. An immature Trumpeter Swan was also reported from Perry Reservoir on 28 February (Brecheisen and Brecheisen 1986).

In fall of 1985, 11 of the Minnesota birds migrated, and four sightings (not necessarily from that flock) were reported in Kansas. Three (one with a yellow neck collar) were in McPherson County on 24 November (Allan Jahn); one spent over a week (around 27 November) at Cedar Bluff Reservoir, Trego County (Scott Seltman);

a sick bird was found near Emporia, Lyon County, on 12 December (the first Kansas specimen); and four were reported in Barber County on 1 February 1986. There are also two reports for the winter of 1986–87, one from Morris County on 18 December and one from Saline County on 20 December. These observations suggest that the Trumpeter Swan may become a regular transient and/or winter visitor in Kansas.

Field Marks: The Trumpeter Swan, when at ease, has its neck kinked back basally, so that the neck appears to arise from its back (see Palmer 1976a).

An adult Greater White-fronted Goose (*Anser albifrons*). Photograph by Bob Gress.

GEESE
Greater White-fronted Goose
Anser albifrons (Scopoli)

Status: The Greater White-fronted Goose is a common transient statewide, is uncommon and local in winter, and is casual in summer.

Period of Occurrence: Extreme dates for presumed migrants are from 19 September to 27 November and 14 February to 22 May. Peak migrations are in mid-November and late February. A few flocks, notably at 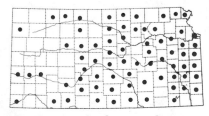 Cheyenne Bottoms, remain until all water is frozen. Summer stragglers are often injured or sick.

Habits and Habitat: Although Greater White-fronted Geese occur in large numbers at some localities, they are less familiar than Canada Geese to most people . They typically fly high, often in a V, and can be recognized by their high-pitched, laughing call. They often mix with flocks of smaller Canada Geese. Larger concentrations occur in Nebraska, as evidenced by the death toll from a fowl cholera outbreak in April 1975, when 15,000 died (Palmer 1976a).

Field Marks: On the ground or on water, they appear to be small, dark geese, and at close range, their speckled belly, pink bill, and white face (adults) are characteristic.

Food: Greater White-fronted Geese graze on grasses, millet, sedges, young wheat, and emergent aquatic vegetation; they glean waste grain from fields and grub for submerged roots.

An adult Snow/Blue Goose (*Chen caerulescens*). Photograph by Bob Gress.

Snow/Blue Goose
Chen caerulescens (Linnaeus)

Status: The Snow Goose is a common-to-abundant transient in the eastern third of the state and uncommon and irregular westward.

Period of Occurrence: Extreme dates for presumed migrants are from 8 March to 26 May and 14 August to 28 November. Migration peaks are in mid-March and mid-October. Large flocks in the northeast may remain on selected reservoirs until all open water freezes.

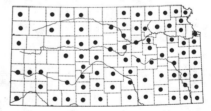

Habits and Habitat: Snow Geese often fly in long, diagonal, wavering lines, hence their name "wavies"; in winter, they may occur in huge concentrations. The call is high pitched and, when many birds are involved, can best be described as clamorous. Birds frequently have a reddish, ferrous stain about the head. Changes in climate and agricultural practices, as well as the establishment of reservoirs and a refuge system, have combined to cause radical shifts in the migratory habits and wintering areas of this species. Snow Geese typically migrate along narrow corridors rather than a broad front and tend to be abundant in some areas while rare elsewhere. One such corridor crosses extreme eastern Kansas en route to the Gulf Coast in Texas and Louisiana. It includes a major stopping point at nearby Squaw Creek National Wildlife Refuge in Missouri where numbers have been building since the 1960s. By 1961, some 5,000 birds were using nearby Brown County (Kansas) State Lake. Conditions there were ideal, and by 1974, over 300,000 birds were using the 62-acre lake; 200,000 overwintered. This tremendous concentration caused increased local crop damage, severe hunting problems, and the potential threat of disease; as a result, in 1975–76 the Kansas Department of Wildlife and Parks harassed the birds from the lake (Thompson 1985). Most returned to Squaw Creek National Wildlife Refuge, but some dispersed to larger water areas where conditions are more favorable for long-term management. Considerable numbers still visit northeastern Kansas each fall and winter. Other populations of Snow Geese winter in California and in the Chesapeake Bay area (Palmer 1976a).

Field Marks: Both white and blue birds are color morphs of the same species. Both forms occur throughout the state, often in the same flocks; the white morph predominates, often by a large proportion.

Food: Food is primarily seeds, stems and roots of grasses, sedges and aquatic plants, grains, and berries. In winter, much food is obtained by grazing the vegetation or grubbing for roots in water only a few inches deep.

Ross' Goose
Chen rossii (Cassin)

Status: Ross' Goose is a casual migrant and winter visitant that has been recorded from 18 October to 23 April, with most sightings during November. Occasional 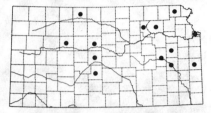 birds occur in the large concentrations of geese at Cheyenne Bottoms and on the larger reservoirs. A specimen was preserved from Brown County and others have been shot by hunters in Barton, Coffey, and Trego counties. Although the largest number of Ross' Geese occur with flocks of Snow Geese in eastern Kansas, most single white geese associated with small Canada Geese in the western half of the state are also of this species.

Field Marks: This species is the size of a Mallard, with a stubby bill, a reduced "grinning patch," and caruncles (warty protuberances) at the base of the upper mandible. Immatures are dusky and have a well-defined gray line through the eye. Birds are less likely to have a reddish, ferrous stain about the head than are Snow Geese.

Adult Brants (*Branta bernicla*). Photograph by Galen L. Pittman.

Brant
Branta bernicla (Linnaeus)

Status: The Brant is a casual transient and winter visitor, chiefly in the east. Occasional birds, usually singles, occur in the large concentrations of Canada Geese at the Cheyenne Bottoms, most often in February. Recorded dates of occurrence are from 9 November to 14 April. A flock of 15 was reported at Elk City Reservoir, Montgomery County, in December 1973.

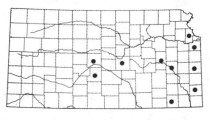

An adult Canada Goose (*Branta canadensis*). Photograph by Suzanne L. Collins.

Canada Goose
Branta canadensis (Linnaeus)

Status: The Canada Goose is a regular, common transient statewide, is casual in summer, and is locally common in winter.

Period of Occurrence: Extreme dates for birds presumed to be migrants are 29 September and 23 May. Main populations of small geese arrive first (by early October), peak by early November, then move south; they are replaced by large geese which remain until all water is frozen. These large geese return when there is open water in late January and depart before the arrival in late February or early March of most small geese.

Breeding: Native geese, now called "maxima," formerly bred along the Missouri River but were extirpated during the nineteenth century. Resident flocks (from commercial stocks of "maxima") were established at Kirwin Reservoir, Phillips County, where they first bred successfully in 1958, and at Cheyenne Bottoms where they first bred in 1962; their descendants still nest in both areas. Recent "wild" nesting has also been reported from Douglas, Linn, and Cowley counties. Nests, placed on artificial platforms or on small mounds of vegetation, are lined with down from the female. The four to six eggs are creamy white before becoming stained. The young, by two months of age, are almost indistinguishable from the adults.

Habits and Habitat: Geese, which usually pair for life, remain in family or larger groups except when they are nesting. A common sight during the nesting season is of a female incubating while the male stands guard, or of a family swimming single file, one parent leading, one "tailing." This bird is one of our best-known and most popular waterfowl. Migrating flocks usually fly low enough, especially during bad weather, to attract attention.

New, large reservoirs on the Missouri River in North and South Dakota now permit a high percentage of the "maxima" Canada Goose population to over-winter. Each year fewer birds migrate as far south as Kansas, as they are apparently altering their migratory habits. A project by the Kansas Department of Wildlife and Parks to establish resident flocks of "maxima" at the Marais des Cygnes Wildlife Management Area, Pratt Fish Hatchery, and Cedar Bluff Reservoir was undertaken in the fall of 1980 (Horak 1985).

Food: Canada Geese eat primarily natural grasses or cultivated cereals such as wheat, often at some distance from their resting areas. They obtain other food by dipping in shallow water—chiefly for aquatic plants, less often for invertebrates, and rarely for small vertebrates.

An adult male Wood Duck (*Aix sponsa*). Photograph by Bob Gress.

DUCKS
Wood Duck
Aix sponsa (Linnaeus)

Status: The Wood Duck is a common transient and a locally common summer resident in the eastern third of the state. It is an uncommon transient and summer resident westward and is casual in winter in the southeast.

Period of Occurrence: Extreme dates for presumed transients are from 9 March to 12 May and 28 August to 26 November. Main

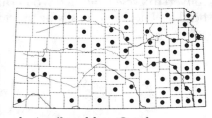

migration peaks are probably in early April and late October.

Breeding: Although most breeding records are from the eastern half of the state (and principally the eastern third), regular breeding occurs westward to Rooks, Ellis, and Kingman counties. The nest, which is placed in a natural cavity, an enlarged woodpecker hole, or an artificial nest box, is from 3 to 50 feet above the ground. Nest sites may be along wooded streams or around lakes, in woods, or in parks or shade trees in towns. Nesting is probably more frequent than now recorded; nesting birds are very secretive, and often the only indications of their presence are morning and evening flights in the vicinity of the nest. The cavity is lined with down and may contain 10 or 14 white to buffy-white eggs. The downy young are very dark brown above, with small whitish patches on the wings and on the sides of the rump. The face and underparts are yellowish white, and a black line extends from the eye to the nape.

Habits and Habitat: To see a pair of these ducks landing on tree branches while the female examines potential nest holes is an unforgettable experience. Nests are often near human habitation, but most are not noticed until the young have hatched. The young jump from the nest unassisted when coaxed by the female and follow her to water. When this route involves crossing streets, lawns, or highways, many ducklings fall prey to children, cats, and vehicles. Adult ducks prefer wooded ponds during the nesting season but at other seasons occur in marshes and other sites. Hunting and habitat destruction nearly exterminated the Wood Duck by the end of the nineteenth century, but it has since recovered over much of its range.

Field Marks: The male is very colorful and is unmistakable when in breeding plumage. At other times, he and the female may be recognized by the white face patch. In flight both sexes appear dark with white bellies and long square tails.

Food: Adults are primarily vegetarians, preferring duckweeds and seeds of various aquatic and terrestrial plants, including acorns. The young eat only insects during their first few days, then gradually convert to a vegetable diet. Wood Ducks feed chiefly by immersing the head and neck and rarely by upending.

An adult male (foreground) Green-winged Teal (*Anas crecca*). Photograph by Calvin L. Cink.

Green-winged Teal
Anas crecca (Linnaeus)

Status: The Green-winged Teal is a common, locally abundant transient statewide and occurs casually in summer, especially at Cheyenne Bottoms; it winters locally where open water permits.

Period of Occurrence: Extreme dates for presumed migrants are from 2 February through 29 May and 14 August through 25 November. Migration peaks are mid-March and early November. A few (as many as 75 in 1968) summer at Cheyenne Bottoms, but it is casual in summer elsewhere.

Breeding: Green-winged Teals nested at Cheyenne Bottoms in 1968 when three nests were found; eggs were present from 24 June to 6 August, and chicks from 10 July to 7 August. Like that of other puddle ducks, the nest is a bowl lined with vegetation and down. The 8 to 12 eggs range in color from cream to pale olive buff. The color of the downy young closely resembles that of Mallard young.

Habits and Habitat: This species is probably the least studied of the common puddle ducks. It usually occurs in flocks and in flight is recognized by the lack of color in its wing or body and its white belly. They typically fly like shorebirds, in a compact flock with much twisting, turning, rising, and descending. The flight, however rapid it appears, rarely exceeds 50 mph. This teal often feeds at night. The species is unusually mobile for a long period before migration, and family groups change their composition frequently. Unattached drakes and failed nesters of both sexes molt and migrate early. Females tend to winter farther south than males, and some pairing is delayed until the northward migration.

Food: Although food is mainly seeds of aquatic vegetation, the Green-winged Teal also eats sedges and grass, waste grain, insects, molluscs, and crustaceans.

An adult American Black Duck (*Anas rubripes*). Photograph by Bob Gress.

American Black Duck
Anas rubripes (Brewster)

Status: The American Black Duck is a rare transient and winter resident in the east and at Cheyenne Bottoms and is casual elsewhere. Sight records are chiefly from 21 October to 22 March. It has summered at Cheyenne Bottoms, where up to 50 birds occurred in 1963 and where a nest with three eggs was found on 7 July 1969. The American Black Duck is very similar to the Mallard in its habits, and the two frequently interbreed.

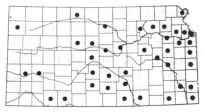

Field Marks: The sexes are similar; both resemble the female Mallard but are much darker, with silvery underwings which are conspicuous in flight. The speculum is a dark purplish blue, and the white borders are much reduced or missing.

Adult Mottled Ducks (*Anas fulvigula*). Photograph by Marvin D. Schwilling.

Mottled Duck
Anas fulvigula (Ridgway)

Status: The Mottled Duck is a spring to fall resident at Cheyenne Bottoms and is accidental elsewhere in the state. Its status is not easy to determine at Cheyenne Bottoms because of the small numbers and the difficulty of identification. A few specimens have been taken there, and others have been handled at hunter check-stations. The only other Kansas

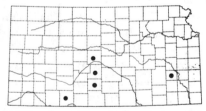

specimen record is a female taken in Woodson County by Goss on 11 March 1876. There are unconfirmed sightings during summer from Pratt, Clark, and Stafford counties. At least four were banded at Cheyenne Bottoms, and an adult male, banded 5 March 1968, was shot by a hunter near Jennings, Louisiana, on 17 December 1969. Marvin Schwilling estimated the total population at about 12 pairs in 1966. Local birds are presumed to migrate to the Gulf Coast when all open water freezes.

Period of Occurrence: The Mottled Duck has been reported at Cheyenne Bottoms from 15 February to 30 November.

Breeding: The nest, hidden in a dry place in a marsh or nearby field, is a bowl lined with vegetation and down. The seven to nine eggs are creamy to greenish white. At Cheyenne Bottoms, clutches have been found from 11 to 27 June, and broods from 23 June to 20 August.

Field Marks: This species, probably often overlooked among the large numbers of female Mallards, differs in having a green speculum that lacks the anterior white borders of the female Mallard.

Food: These ducks eat chiefly seeds of grasses and smartweeds, tubers and other aquatic plants, as well as insects and their larvae, molluscs, and other invertebrates.

An adult male Mallard (*Anas platyrhynchos*). Photograph by A. A. Tubbs.

Mallard
Anas platyrhynchos (Linnaeus)

Status: The Mallard is a regular, common-to-abundant transient statewide. It nests commonly at Cheyenne Bottoms and uncommonly but regularly elsewhere throughout the state. It is locally common in winter wherever open water occurs.

Period of Occurrence: Mallards are present most of the year throughout the state. Peak migration periods are in late February to early March and in late November.

Breeding: This species nests statewide in almost any wetland habitat, but it may nest in grasslands 1/2 mile or more from the nearest water source. The nest is usually near water in dense reeds or grass but may also be under dense weeds or bushes in prairie, pastures, or fields some distance from water. The nest is a hollow lined with vegetation and down. The eggs are greenish buff or pinkish white; the clutch size is usually 10 to 12. Extreme dates for 134 Kansas clutches are from 14 April to 17 July. The peak laying period seems to be in mid-May and early June. Downy young blackish brown above with yellow on the face and underparts, and spots on the back and wings have a dark line through the eye and a dark ear spot. Young birds have been reported from 23 May through July.

Habits and Habitat: The Mallard, our most adaptable and widespread duck, occurs practically anyplace that has some water. This is especially apparent in western Kansas where nearly every pond supports a pair in early summer. When the female starts incubation, only the male is seen, except when she joins him to feed. With luck, an observer might see the male escort the female to the vicinity of the nest, to which she suddenly veers while he returns to the pond. Later, the female and brood appear on the pond. Normally only the female incubates or cares for the young, which, when pursued, can dive proficiently and escape underwater.

Food: This species eats chiefly vegetable food, particularly seeds of sedges, grasses, smartweed, and other plant parts, either skimmed from the surface of the water or obtained by dipping. It also gleans grain from stubble fields, especially in the winter, and eats insects and other invertebrates in season.

Adult Northern Pintails (*Anas acuta*). Photograph by Bob Gress.

Northern Pintail
Anas acuta (Linnaeus)

Status: The Northern Pintail is a common-to-abundant transient statewide that nests locally and is casual elsewhere in summer. It is an uncommon, local winter resident where open water permits.

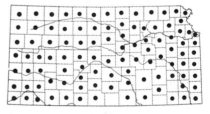

Period of Occurrence: The extreme dates for presumed migrants are from 8 February to 10 May and 5 September to 19 November. Migration peaks occur in early March and early November. Small numbers occur statewide in summer, and it may be locally common during some winters.

Breeding: Most nesting has been recorded from Cheyenne Bottoms and from western counties. The nest, the usual depression lined with fine vegetation and down, is typically near water but sometimes is found in a prairie or pasture at a considerable distance from water. The seven to nine eggs are olive-green to pale olive buff. Dates for 19 Kansas clutches range from 19 April to 3 July; the 21 brood records are from 23 May to 15 July. Downy young resemble Mallards but the brown is more earth-colored, and the buffy areas are largely replaced by white, especially underneath. There is a dark line through the eye and another from the bill to the ear.

Habits and Habitat: This slim, elegant creature is one of our best-known ducks. Pintails are early migrants in both spring and fall. In the spring, flocks frequent temporary shallow pools in flooded fields. In the fall, at Cheyenne Bottoms, birds may be so numerous when either at rest or feeding in shallow water that they can cover literally several acres almost shoulder-to-shoulder. The flight is graceful and rapid, and much of their courtship takes place on the wing. The usually silent males whistle frequently in the spring. Birds generally rest in the open but become secretive when they molt. The female has a very strong maternal instinct and uses a broken-wing display to divert potential nest predators. Pintails have a large breeding range in the Northern Hemisphere, and banded birds have flown great distances. For example, birds banded in New Mexico and California have been taken in Japan and on Palmyra Island in the central Pacific.

Field Marks: The adult male is unmistakable, and others can be identified by the long, slim neck and gray bill.

Food: The Northern Pintail eats primarily vegetation, including seeds of pondweeds, sedges, grasses, and smartweed. It also eats other plant parts, waste grains, and some animals such as molluscs, crustaceans, and insects.

Garganey
Anas querquedula (Linnaeus)

Status: The Garganey is probably accidental. It has been recorded in Kansas twice. Jay Newton saw a drake at East Lake, near Newton, Harvey County, on 29 March 1981. Another drake, found on a sewage pond near Oxford, Sumner County, by Walter Champeny on 21 April 1982, was photographed by Max Thompson on the twenty-third 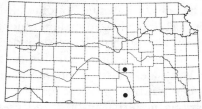 and remained until 1 May (Thompson et al. 1983). The recent increase in the number of Garganey sightings in the United States, including singles in Oklahoma in 1979 and 1982, suggests that the Kansas birds were wild rather than escapees from a zoo or aviary.

An adult male Blue-winged Teal (*Anas discors*). Photograph by Frank S. Shipley.

Blue-winged Teal
Anas discors (Linnaeus)

Status: The Blue-winged Teal is a common-to-abundant transient which nests commonly at Cheyenne Bottoms and uncommonly elsewhere. It is casual in winter.

Period of Occurrence: Extreme dates for transients are from 23 February to 24 May and 9 August to 20 November. Peak migrations are from early to mid-April and from mid-September to mid-October. It is regular to abundant in summer at Cheyenne Bottoms and occurs in smaller numbers statewide. It is rare to casual in the winter, especially in the east, but is not recorded every winter.

Breeding: The Blue-winged Teal is most numerous at Cheyenne Bottoms, where Marvin Schwilling estimated 4,000 young were produced in 1962. Most other nesting records are from the western half of the state. The nest a bowl with a grass and down lining is usually hidden in tall grass near water that may be only a temporary pond or pool. The 9 to 13 eggs are creamy tan with a slight gloss. The downy young are similar to Mallards but are sepia brown with the buffy areas replaced by yellow. Replacement nests have been found. Egg dates for 115 recent clutches were from 11 May to 18 July, with most found in mid-June; 57 broods were reported between 31 May and 15 August.

Field Marks: Breeding males are unmistakable; females and all other "dull-plumaged" birds may be recognized in flight by the light blue patch (which often appears whitish) on the forewing. In comparison with the Green-Winged Teal, the head and neck of this species are slenderer, and in flight it appears dark-bellied with a slower, more direct, less "maneuvering" flight. The breeding plumage is not assumed until at least November, after the birds have left Kansas.

Habits and Habitat: During the breeding season, Blue-winged Teals tend to be more pugnacious than most ducks, but they are highly sociable during the nonbreeding season and may flock in large numbers, especially along shorelines. They migrate late in the spring, early in the fall, and they winter southward through South America. One-way flights of 4,000 miles have been reported for banded birds. Like many other ducks, they have a "molt migration" before they fly to the staging areas where they start their fall migration. Blue-winged Teals appear to be more closely related to the shovelers than to Green-winged Teals. They tend to be primarily surface feeders and "tip" less than other puddle ducks.

Food: The species eats chiefly vegetation, primarily the seeds of aquatic plants, sedges, and grasses, but also their stems and leaves. They also glean waste grain from fields. Up to 20 percent of the diet may be animal food, largely molluscs (especially snails), crustaceans, and insects.

Adult Cinnamon Teal (*Anas cyanoptera*). Photograph by C. L. Cink.

Cinnamon Teal
Anas cyanoptera (Vieillot)

Status: The Cinnamon Teal is a rare but regular transient at Cheyenne Bottoms, where it nests casually, and is irregular to vagrant elsewhere in the state.

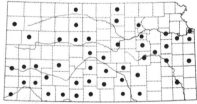

Period of Occurrence: Extreme dates for nonbreeding birds are from 21 February to 29 May and 22 August to 22 October. They are casual in winter. A few summer at Cheyenne Bottoms, where at least seven territorial males were seen in 1962, and they probably breed there during most years. They are casual elsewhere in summer.

Breeding: The only confirmed breeding record is of a brood of seven young at Cheyenne Bottoms on 13 June 1969. Territorial birds were seen regularly in the summer from 1962 through 1964. On 3 June 1885, in Meade County, Goss (1886) shot the female of a pair, recording that she had "several well developed eggs in ovary."

Habits and Habitat: This species largely replaces the Blue-winged Teal west of the Rockies and is at best a rare bird in Kansas. The Cinnamon Teal very closely resembles the Blue-winged Teal in its habits but perhaps occurs more often in pairs or smaller flocks.

Field Marks: Males in the spring are unmistakable, but the females, the young, and the eclipse males are indistinguishable in the field from Blue-winged Teals, as the paucity of fall records attests. In the hand, the bill of this species is more constricted basally.

Food: The Cinnamon Teal has the same diet as the Blue-winged Teal.

An adult male (foreground) Northern Shoveler (*Anas clypeata*). Photograph by Frank S. Shipley.

Northern Shoveler
Anas clypeata (Linnaeus)

Status: The Northern Shoveler is a common-to-abundant transient statewide, is casual in summer, and rare in winter.

Period of Occurrence: Extreme dates for presumed transients are from 1 March to 5 June and 31 July to 8 December. Migration peaks are in mid-April and early November. Breeding has been recorded from Barton, Finney, 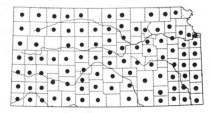 and Seward counties, and there are numerous midsummer records elsewhere, especially in the west. Only a few birds winter.

Breeding: The two dated sightings of broods in Kansas are on 11 and 13 July. The nest is the usual depression lined with vegetation and down and may be near or distant from water, carefully hidden or barely exposed. The 7 to 14 eggs are greenish buff. Downy chicks resemble Blue-winged Teal chicks, but the brown areas are darker, the yellow areas more dusky, and the spots less well defined.

Habits and Habitat: Most food is obtained by straining the surface or by immersing the head and neck; relatively little upending occurs.

Northern Shovelers usually occur in small flocks during spring migration but form much larger congregations in the fall. They migrate late in the spring and early in the fall at about the same time as the Blue-winged Teal. The flight is swift, erratic, and teal-like. Females may sometimes have two mates.

Field Marks: In any plumage, the shoveler is easily recognized by its large sloping head and oversized bill. The bill, edged with a row of long bristles or lamellae which give it a comblike appearance, is the most specialized of any Kansas duck. It serves as a sieve to remove edible particles from the surface layer of water and at times from the upper mud layer under shallow water.

Food: About 70 percent of the diet is plant food, chiefly seeds of sedges, smartweeds, and pondweeds, and other plant parts strained from the surface of the water. The remaining 30 percent, which is high for a puddle duck, is primarily insects and their larvae, snails, and other invertebrates.

An adult male Gadwall (*Anas strepera*). Photograph by Frank S. Shipley.

Gadwall
Anas strepera (Linnaeus)

Status: The Gadwall is a common transient statewide, is a rare summer resident, and is rare to uncommon in winter. The breeding range is said to be decreasing in the central prairies but expanding in the north and in Kansas.

Period of Occurrence: Extreme dates of presumed transients are from 5 February to 4 June and 3 August to 30 November. Migra-

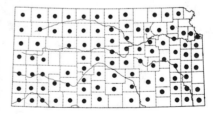

tion peaks are in late March to early April and in late October. Small numbers remain in winter until all water is frozen. It is casual in summer and nests locally in the western half of the state.

Breeding: Nesting has been documented for Barton, Ellis, Meade, Russell, and Trego counties. The nest, a bowl lined with vegetation and down, is placed in a dry spot in a marsh or a nearby field, or in an upland pasture or "draw" near a pond; it is usually well hidden in dense vegetation or under a bush. The 8 to 12 eggs are creamy white. Downy young resemble Mallards but are paler brown with creamy buff replacing the yellow and a less distinct eye line and ear spot.

Habits and Habitat: Gadwalls usually occur in small flocks and are less sociable than Mallards and Northern Pintails. They are usually inconspicuous, often misidentified, and are probably more numerous than casual records would suggest. Gadwalls typically fly in small, compact flocks and have a direct flight. They tend to feed more in open water than most puddle ducks. Gadwalls can dive for food when necessary, but that is not their regular practice. Like Pintails, Gadwalls occasionally undertake long, overwater flights. "Molt migrations" are also characteristic.

Field Marks: The Gadwall is the only species of puddle duck with a white speculum. On the water, males appear dark gray with a black rear and females resemble female Mallards. In the hand, a dense mane of feathers is conspicuous in breeding plumage on the head of males.

Food: The species eats primarily vegetation, including a higher proportion of underwater parts of aquatic vegetation than most puddle ducks eat. Pondweeds are a dominant food, but seeds of grasses and sedges are important. Waste grain in fields is eaten at times, especially in winter, and some animal food is consumed.

Eurasian Wigeon
Anas penelope (Linnaeus)

Status: The Eurasian Wigeon is included on the hypothetical list on the basis of five or six sightings from Barton, Coffey, Crawford, Johnson, Riley, and Shawnee counties from 21 March to 22 April and on 1 June. On 21 March 1981, a single male on the river outlet just below the dam at John Redmond Reservoir, Coffey County, was watched for some time by six experienced birders.

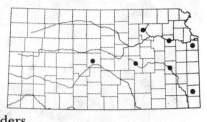

Field Marks: In the hand, this species differs from the American Wigeon by its mottled, rather than white, axillars. In the field, males in breeding plumage have a rusty brown head and pale forehead and crown, but females and males in nonbreeding plumage closely resemble the female American Wigeon, and accurate field identification is unlikely.

An adult American Wigeon (*Anas americana*). Photograph by Bob Gress.

American Wigeon
Anas americana (Gmelin)

Status: The American Wigeon is a common-to-abundant transient statewide, especially at Cheyenne Bottoms where it has bred once. It is casual elsewhere in summer and uncommon to locally common in winter, depending on water conditions.

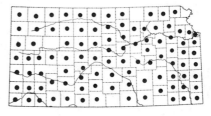

Period of Occurrence: Extreme dates for presumed transients are from 30 January to 6 June and 4 September to 29 November. Migration peaks are from mid-February to mid-March and from mid-October to mid-November. It may occur locally at any time.

Breeding: The nests reported from Cheyenne Bottoms in 1963 were later determined to be those of Gadwalls. However, a deserted wigeon nest with three eggs was found there on 23 June 1973. The nest is the usual depression lined with vegetation and down. The 7 to 12 eggs are white to cream-colored. The downy young is dark brown above, especially on the crown and back, the face is reddish with a small dark streak behind the eye, and the underparts and spots on the back and wing are brownish yellow.

Habits and Habitat: Identification on the water is easy from a distance due to the buoyant posture and contrasting markings of the species. The call of the male is a pleasing whistle. The American Wigeon prefers open water and is most common in areas with a permanent water supply. Especially in winter, it parasitizes coots and diving ducks, either by filching food secured by the former or by snatching the latter's food fragments that come to the surface. It spends much time on land and is considered the most terrestrial member of its genus.

Field Marks: In flight the white patch on the leading edge of the male's wing is characteristic.

Food: The species consumes almost entirely vegetation and takes the stems and foliage of aquatic plants, sedges, and grasses, and the seeds of various aquatic and marsh plants. It grazes frequently and has become a pest in some truck-farm areas. A small amount of animal material, chiefly snails and insects, is also eaten.

An adult female Canvasback (*Aythya valisineria*). Photograph by David A. Rintoul.

Canvasback
Aythya valisineria (Wilson)

Status: The Canvasback is an uncommon transient statewide. It nests occasionally at Cheyenne Bottoms and is casual in summer elsewhere. It is casual in winter.

Period of Occurrence: Extreme dates of presumed transients are from 9 February to 9 May and 6 October to 22 November. Migration peaks are in early to mid-March and in late October. A few winter on larger reservoirs when open water remains.

Breeding: Nests with eggs have been documented at Cheyenne Bottoms during five summers (from 17 June to 11 July), and it probably has nested in other years. Two large, downy young were reported at Quivira National Wildlife Refuge in 1980. The nest is a bulky, well-built structure of reeds or sedges lined with down and placed near or over water in a marsh. The seven to nine large eggs are an unusually dark grayish olive to greenish drab. The downy young differs from downy Redheads in having darker upperparts and a dark, sloping forehead.

Habits and Habitat: The Canvasback usually remains in flocks of its own species. It is one of our fastest flying ducks and in flight appears longer and slenderer than other divers. Flocks are usually V-shaped, and flight is direct, powerful, and often close to the water. When it was hunted for market, "can" was considered the king of ducks for its taste and was the choice of the epicure. Its numbers were greatly reduced by drainage of the small ponds that it prefers on its breeding grounds, droughts, and overhunting, and even today the species remains much diminished.

Field Marks: The sloping forehead and bill shape are the best identification characteristics after four to five weeks of age. Males also appear much whiter above than Redheads, even in flight.

Food: About 80 percent of its food is vegetation, which it obtains chiefly by diving. Where present, wild celery is considered the favorite item; elsewhere, roots and underwater parts of pondweeds, grasses, and sedges predominate. The animal food is chiefly molluscs (in Kansas, snails) and insects.

An adult Redhead (*Aythya americana*). Photograph by Bob Gress.

Redhead
Aythya americana (Eyton)

Status: The Redhead is a common transient statewide, is uncommon in winter, and is rare to casual in summer.

Period of Occurrence: Extreme dates for transients are from 8 February to 20 May and 26 September to 5 December. Migration peaks are in mid-March and from mid-October to mid-November.

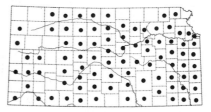

Breeding: Redheads were first recorded nesting at Cheyenne Bottoms about 1928 and since 1962 have bred there regularly; peak numbers were in 1972. Thirty recent clutches were found between 15 May and 11 July, and seven broods from 11 June to 23 July. Summering birds reported elsewhere may have been injured. The nest is placed in a marsh near or over water and is a substantial bowl of reeds lined with down. The 10 to 15 eggs are pale olive buff to creamy buff. Downy young are pale olive brown above and yellow below. The nail at the tip of the bill is broad.

Habits and Habitat: Redheads are highly gregarious and often occur in huge rafts on open water, especially on the larger reservoirs. Birds may move closer to shore at night to feed. The flight is rapid with much wheeling and turning. Most feed by diving in shallow water (less than 6 feet) and feeding birds may upend in even shallower water. Some females are partially parasitic (some are completely parasitic) and lay eggs in nests of their own species or of other species, and then nest normally (Palmer 1976b).

Field Marks: Both sexes are best recognized in profile by the round, abrupt forehead. Males appear dark-backed (gray) with reddish heads; females lack a distinct white facial patch or an eye ring.

Food: The Redhead eats about 90 percent vegetation, chiefly bulbs, stems, and leaves of aquatic plants such as pondweeds and smartweeds, and also algae. Aquatic insects predominate among the animal food consumed.

An adult Ring-necked Duck (*Aythya collaris*). Photograph by A. A. Tubbs.

Ring-necked Duck
Aythya collaris (Donovan)

Status: The Ring-necked Duck is a common spring transient statewide, uncommon in fall, and casual in winter.

Period of Occurrence: Extreme dates for transients are from 8 February to 31 May and 3 October to 26 November. Migration peaks occur in late March and in late October to early November. Small numbers are reported during some winters. The only summer records are for Pratt and Russell counties on 15 and 19 June respectively.

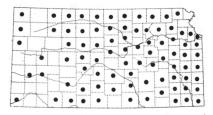

Habits and Habitat: The Ring-necked Duck is possibly often overlooked in fall. It is alert and lively, like the Redhead, but usually occurs in smaller flocks and tends to frequent smaller expanses of water. It is a fast, erratic flier. Birds are said to choose their favorite ponds or areas in a marsh and to return to them consistently.

Field Marks: The chestnut collar ("ring") is rarely seen. Both sexes have a double white ring around the bill, which is a better field mark.

In addition, males are black-backed and in spring have a crested head and a white crescent before the wing. The female has a white eye ring and often faint white near the bill.

Food: About 80 percent of the diet is aquatic vegetation obtained by diving. Pondweeds, sedges, grasses, and smartweed are favorites. The remaining portion of the diet is animal, chiefly insects and snails.

An adult male Greater Scaup (*Aythya marila*). Photograph by David A. Rintoul.

Greater Scaup
Aythya marila (Linnaeus)

Status: The status of the Greater Scaup in Kansas is uncertain, due to its similarity to the Lesser Scaup. Sight records from 13 counties cover the periods 27 October to 16 April and 3 July to 23 September. A few specimens have been taken in Barber, Barton, Clay, and Douglas counties in August, November, and April. It is probably a rare but regular transient and a winter resident.

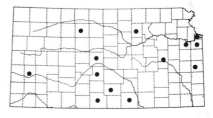

Field Marks: It is difficult and sometimes impossible to distinguish the two scaups in the field. The best field mark (when visible) for the Greater Scaup is its longer white wing stripe, which extends into the primaries. In perfect light, the greenish sheen to the head is a useful identifier. In the hand, the nail on the bill is more than 7 mm wide.

An adult female Lesser Scaup (*Aythya affinis*). Photograph by David A. Rintoul.

Lesser Scaup
Aythya affinis (Eyton)

Status: The Lesser Scaup species is a common transient statewide and occurs casually in winter and in summer.

Period of Occurrence: Extreme dates for presumed transients are from 5 February to 29 May and 3 September to 5 December. Migration peaks are in late March and mid-October. There are scattered midsummer re-cords. Some remain locally until all open water freezes.

Breeding: The Lesser Scaup was reported breeding in Cowley County about 1928, but there is no recent documentation. Some birds spent the summer of 1954 in Sedgwick County, and there are scattered midsummer records statewide. Lesser Scaup mature slowly, and few, if any, are sexually mature before they are two years old. Some of these nonbreeding birds remain south of the breeding grounds during their first summer. The nest is a hollow lined with sparse vegetation and down, often some distance from water. The 9 to 11 eggs are greenish to olive buff. Downy young are brownish black above and on the breast, with indistinct wing and rump patches. They are buffy yellow below and on the face, with dark lines through and below the eyes.

Habits and Habitat: Lesser Scaup are medium to small divers that sit low in the water and fly in compact flocks with an irregular, darting flight. They usually form large rafts on the water when resting. They utilize small ponds as well as larger expanses of water and seem to prefer individuals of their own species. Scaups are very active ducks and spend a great deal of time diving, especially during the morning. Like many other divers, the female voids a malodorous liquid on the eggs and nest when flushed (Palmer 1976b).

Field Marks: From the side, males in breeding plumage appear distinctly bandeddark at either end and light in the middle and in good light the violet head is iridescent. Females are brown, usually with a distinct white patch at the base of the bill. The white wing patch is restricted to the secondaries, and the width of the nail on the bill is 7 mm or less.

Food: About 60 percent of the diet is the seeds and other parts of pondweeds, other aquatic plants, sedges, and grasses. The remainder is animal food, chiefly amphipods, snails and other molluscs, and insects. Immatures take more animal food. In some areas, adults may feed predominantly (up to 90 percent) on invertebrates.

Adult Common Eiders (*Somateria mollissima*). Photograph by Galen L. Pittman.

Common Eider
Somateria mollissima (Linnaeus)

Status: The Common Eider is a vagrant, known only from a single specimen taken on the Kansas River near Lecompton, Douglas County, on 3 November 1891.

An adult King Eider (*Somateria spectabilis*). Photograph by Galen L. Pittman.

King Eider
Somateria spectabilis (Linnaeus)

Status: There is a single specimen of the King Eider, a vagrant species, which was taken on the Kansas River near Lawrence, Douglas County, on 27 November 1947.

An adult Oldsquaw (*Clangula hyemalis*). Photograph by Galen L. Pittman.

Oldsquaw
Clangula hyemalis (Linnaeus)

Status: Oldsquaws are rare transients and winter visitors.

Period of Occurrence: There have been scattered sightings throughout the state from 31 October to 18 April; most sightings have been in November.

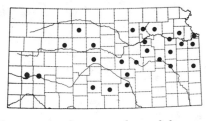

Habits and Habitat: The name is derived from the garrulous calling within large flocks, but individuals are relatively silent here. Oldsquaws winter primarily on salt water and on very large lakes.

Field Marks: In flight, the Oldsquaw is our only white-headed or extensively white-bodied duck with all dark wings. Males have two distinct plumages, plus the eclipse plumage, so individuals may be quite variable. Most Kansas Oldsquaws are immature or first-year birds and usually are brownish with some white on the face, breast, and underparts.

Food: Food is almost entirely animal and is obtained by diving, often to considerable depths.

Black Scoter
Melanitta nigra (Linnaeus)

Status: The Black Scoter is a rare fall transient that has been recorded from 22 October to 27 November and on 18 March. There were only 2 documented records prior to 1956, but 15 additional records of about 23 individuals were reported by 1984. Sightings have been reported from 13 counties in eastern and central Kansas. Most scoter sightings have been

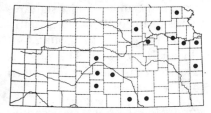

at Cheyenne Bottoms and on the larger reservoirs. The dramatic increase in the number of sightings since the 1950s is perhaps due to the construction of large impoundments and to the increased number and proficiency of birdwatchers.

Field Marks: Since most scoters seen in Kansas are immature, problems of identification abound. In the hand and at close range, the shape of the bill and head and the head pattern are useful (Schwilling 1977). All scoters are dark-colored, heavy-bodied, diving ducks. This species is the most "ducklike" of the scoters, with its high forehead, rounded head, and thin bill. Males in breeding plumage are completely black; in other plumages, the light, whitish cheek and foreneck and the dark crown are useful field marks. In flight, the wings show a silvery sheen from below. On the water, birds tend to rest with their bill held horizontally or tilted upward.

Food: Black Scoters feed entirely on animal food (chiefly molluscs) obtained by diving.

Surf Scoter
Melanitta perspicillata (Linnaeus)

Status: The Surf Scoter, a rare fall transient, has been reported from 17 October to 29 November; it is casual in spring (19 April). There

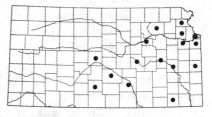

were 8 specimens and 2 sight records prior to 1956 and an additional 17 records of about 23 individuals by 1980. The records
are from 16 counties in eastern
and central Kansas.

Field Marks: Males in breeding
plumage have a white nape and forehead. The completely dark wing, two whitish facial patches, and elongated head which slopes down to the bill are useful aids to identification. Both White-winged and Surf Scoters usually rest with the bill tilted downward.

White-winged Scoter
Melanitta fusca (Linnaeus)

Status: The White-winged Scoter is a rare fall transient, recorded from 22 October to 22 December, which is casual both in winter (23 February) and in spring (15 April to 8 May). There were 9 specimens and 2 sight records prior to 1956 and an additional 29 reports of about 36 individuals were made by 1980. This species is the most common and most widespread scoter in the state, with sightings from 18 scattered counties.

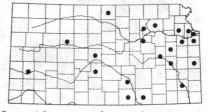

Field Marks: When visible, the white wing patch is diagnostic in any plumage. Other useful field marks are the white eye patch of the male in breeding plumage, the basally wide bill, the whitish patch between the eye and the bill, and whitish ear patch.

An adult male Common Goldeneye (*Bucephala clangula*). Photograph by David A. Rintoul.

Common Goldeneye
Bucephala clangula (Linnaeus)

Status: The Common Goldeneye is an uncommon transient and winter resident.

Period of Occurrence: Common Goldeneyes are usually present from mid-December to mid-March, with extreme dates of 4 November and 4 May. Some winter on the larger reservoirs while water remains open. A

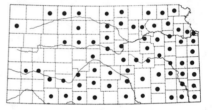

crippled bird spent the summer of 1921 in Pratt County.

Habits and Habitat: The flight is strong and swift, and there is a characeristic whistling sound produced by the wings. It is a superb diver. Goldeneyes are most often seen in flocks on the larger bodies of water in early winter through early spring. On the breeding grounds, the goldeneye, like our Wood Duck, nests in a tree cavity.

Field Marks: The male is medium-sized with a black head and back and a white body. In flight it displays more white than other divers. The round white patch between the eye and the bill and the green gloss on the head are distinctive. The female is chunky with a dark head, white collar, and a relatively gray body.

Food: About 75 percent of the diet is animal food, chiefly crustaceans, insects, molluscs, and some fishes. The remainder is primarily seeds of many kinds, tubers and leaves of pondweeds, and other submerged plants.

Barrow's Goldeneye
Bucephala islandica (Gmelin)

Status: The Barrow's Goldeneye is an accidental visitor, with three sight records from Scott, Stafford, and Trego counties during the period 4 October to February.

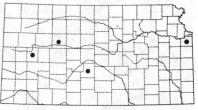

Field Marks: Males can be iden-
tified by the purple gloss on the head and the crescent-shaped white patch between the eye and the bill. Its bill is shaped differ-
ently from that of the Common Goldeneye. Identification of females and nonbreeding males, unless they are associated with a male in breeding plumage, is probably impossible in the field. It may be impossible to distinguish even museum specimens of females from the Common Goldeneye.

Adult Buffleheads (*Bucephala albeola*). Photograph by Mike Blair, courtesy Kansas Department of Wildlife and Parks.

Bufflehead
Bucephala albeola (Linnaeus)

Status: The Bufflehead is a regular but uncommon transient and is casual in winter.

Period of Occurrence: Extreme dates are from 19 September to 8 December and 10 February to 24 May. Main migration peaks are in mid-November and from late March to early April. A few remain on the larger reservoirs until no open water remains.

Habits and Habitat: According to Kortright (1942), it was formerly called "buffalo-headed" because of its disproportionately large head. It is an active bird with a swift flight and very rapid wingbeats, and it flies low over the water. It is a buoyant swimmer, an excellent diver, and can rise almost vertically from the water. It is a late migrant in both spring and fall. Courtship is often observed in the spring. Males are then very active and aggressive; they display in small groups on the water with much posturing, diving, and chasing. As pair formation develops, intruding males are attacked when they approach.

Field Marks: The Bufflehead is a small, nearly teal-sized diver, easily identified by the large white patch from ear to nape on males in breeding plumage or the white patch behind the eye on females and young males. A white wing patch is conspicuous in flight.

Food: About 75 to 90 percent of the diet is animal food obtained by diving. Invertebrates (crustaceans, molluscs, and insects) predominate, and some fishes are taken. Seeds and stems of aquatic plants compose the remainder of the diet.

An adult male Hooded Merganser (*Lophodytes cucullatus*). Photograph by Ed and Jean Schulenberg.

Hooded Merganser
Lophodytes cucullatus (Linnaeus)

Status: The Hooded Merganser is a transient, is rare in the west, and is uncommon in the central and eastern parts of the state. It breeds locally and is casual in winter. It was formerly more common and widespread.

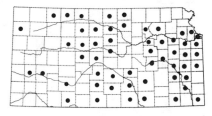

Period of Occurrence: The extreme dates for presumed transients are from 16 February to 14 June and 10 October to 30 November. A few occur at other seasons.

Breeding: The Hooded Merganser was formerly a rare breeder in the east. It has recently bred twice at the Marais des Cygnes Wildlife Management Area, Linn County, once at the Neosho Wildlife Management Area, Neosho County, and once at the Quivira National Wildlife Refuge, Stafford County. In Linn County, a clutch of 11 eggs found 3 April 1968 hatched 9 young on the thirtieth, and a brood of about 10 young about a week old was seen on 21 April 1985. The Neosho County sighting was a brood of 3 young, first seen on 18 May 1966. The brood at Quivira National Wildlife Refuge was seen in June 1986. The nest is typically in a tree cavity or a nesting box. The 8 to 12 eggs are pure white. Downy young are sepia with white spots on the wings and sides and a white chin, throat, and foreneck. The sides of the head below the eye are buffy brown, the upper breast is grayish brown, and the remaining underparts are white.

Habits and Habitat: Like the Wood Duck, this species was seriously reduced in numbers during the late nineteenth century as a result of deforestation and overhunting. It is making a comeback today but at a slower rate than the Wood Duck. Its acceptance of artificial Wood Duck nest boxes could aid its return as a regular breeder, at least in southeastern Kansas. It prefers quiet waters usually streams, marshes, ponds, or reservoirs with nearby trees, preferably trees standing in water. It usually occurs singly or in small groups and is normally silent. It swims buoyantly and swiftly, dives well, and rises vertically from the water without pattering. The flight is rapid, often with swift changes of direction.

Field Marks: The male in breeding plumage is unmistakable, especially if its fan-shaped crest is erect. Females and other males are small, dainty, thin-billed ducks with thin crests and brown backs.

Food: About 96 percent of the diet is animal food, about half being small fishes, and the remainder being frogs, crustaceans, and insects all obtained by diving. Much of the plant food is probably taken incidentally.

Common Merganser
Mergus merganser (Linnaeus)

Status: The Common Merganser is a common transient and winter visitor, especially on larger bodies of water.

Period of Occurrence: Most migrants arrive in early November, remain until all open water freezes, and then move southward. They return when there is open water and depart northward by late March. Extreme 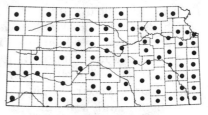 dates, including those of stragglers, are 22 August and 8 June.

Habits and Habitat: Mergansers can be recognized by their long, slim, loonlike appearance, and especially their long, thin bill, head, and neck. Flying birds appear even longer and slimmer. The Common Merganser prefers fresh water and is the merganser regularly seen in Kansas, where it prefers the larger, deeper bodies of clear water. It usually dives from the surface after a short jump forward but can sink slowly beneath the surface like a grebe. Most of its time is spent on open water, often in large rafts. It typically needs a long run for take-off, but, once airborne, the flight is swift, strong, and direct. It frequently scans for prey with its bill and face beneath the surface of the water.

Field Marks: Males in breeding plumage can be distinguished from a distance by the white breast and the considerable amount of white in the overall plumage, which are especially visible in flight. The sharply defined white throat patch, sharp demarcation between foreneck and breast, and the gray mantle are useful field marks for the female. (Also see next species.)

Food: The diet consists almost entirely of whatever animal food is most available locally. Fishes, usually small rough fishes sometimes up to a foot or more in length, predominate with molluscs and crustaceans eaten less frequently. Any plant food is probably taken incidentally.

An adult Red-breasted Merganser (*Mergus serrator*). Photograph by Steve Burr.

Red-breasted Merganser
Mergus serrator (Linnaeus)

Status: The Red-breasted Merganser is apparently a rare spring and fall transient that is often confused with the Common Merganser.

Period of Occurrence: Extreme dates for sight records are from 3 March to 15 May and 29 October to 25 November. There is one midsummer record, 22 June in Osage County. Johnston (1965) reported the species to 8 December.

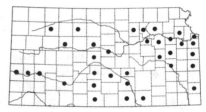

Habits and Habitat: This merganser is essentially a marine and coastal species, but a few birds probably occur in Kansas each year. Although sightings have been statewide, most were at Cheyenne Bottoms or on the larger reservoirs.

Field Marks: The male in breeding plumage is easily identified by its dark breast; females and males in other plumages have a poorly defined white throat, little contrast between the neck and the breast, and a browner mantle, giving them an overall dingier appearance. In the hand, the nostril is near the base of the bill, and the feathering at the base of the upper mandible extends farther forward than on the lower mandible.

Food: The diet is almost entirely animal, chiefly fishes, obtained by diving.

An adult female Ruddy Duck (*Oxyura jamaicensis*). Photograph by David A. Rintoul.

Ruddy Duck
Oxyura jamaicensis (Gmelin)

Status: Ruddy Ducks are regular but uncommon transients statewide. They breed locally but are casual elsewhere in summer and in winter.

Period of Occurrence: The extreme dates for birds presumed to be transient are from 25 February to 21 June and 31 August to 8 December. Migration peaks occur from late March to late April and in early November. This species 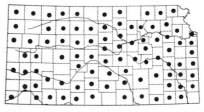 breeds regularly at Cheyenne Bottoms and has bred in Ellis (prior to 1888), Grant, Sedgwick, and Stafford counties. There are scattered midsummer records elsewhere. A few remain in some winters until all open water is frozen.

Breeding: Nests were found at Cheyenne Bottoms in 1929 and occasionally since 1962, but Ruddy Ducks probably breed there every year. Twenty-two clutches were observed between 30 May and 30 July (most in mid- and late June), and 10 broods were seen between 11 June and 18 August. The nest, a platform of vegetation lined with down, is placed in thick cover over shallow water. The 5 to 10 eggs are dull white and are very large in proportion to the small female. Ruddy

Ducks are occasionally parasitic. The male does not incubate but remains with the female and helps to care for the brood. Downy young are sooty brown tinged with gray, are grayer on the face, and have a dark streak across the cheek. Patches on the lower breast, belly, and back are pale gray.

Habits and Habitat: The Ruddy Duck is a short, squat duck with a thick neck; the male's neck has an inflatable tracheal pouch and is especially thick. Courtship is spectacular with much male posturing; during display, males cock the long, stiff tail up over the back. This duck is grebelike, with short, narrow wings and large legs placed far back on the body. When approached, it frequently dives or sinks slowly beneath the water rather than flying. The flight is swift and "buzzy" with very rapid wingbeats. On land, adults walk with difficulty, and even the downy young scoot along on their bellies.

Field Marks: The male in breeding plumage is unmistakable, with its brilliant rust pattern, white cheek, and bright blue bill. In other plumages the light cheek patch (the female's is crossed by a dark streak) and the general shapes of the body and bill are diagnostic.

Food: About 75 percent of the diet is vegetable, chiefly seeds of aquatic plants strained underwater from the mud bottom. Some food is also skimmed from the surface. Animal food consists chiefly of insect larvae with some molluscs and crustaceans.

Black Vulture
Coragyps atratus (Bechstein)

Status: The Black Vulture was possibly a former local resident but is now a vagrant. According to George Lisle, it was quite common and bred at Chetopa, Labette County, 15 to 20 years prior to 1883; he saw three there in the fall of 1882 and a nest with two eggs in 1858 (Goss 1891). A specimen, since lost, was taken at Ellis, Ellis County, on 27 March 1885.

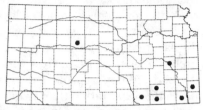

There are several unconfirmed recent sight records from Elk, Cowley, and Chautauqua counties from July or August to September.

Field Marks: Look for it in southeastern Kansas. It can be distinguished from the Turkey Vulture by its short, square tail and its broad, short wings with white patches. In flight it flaps its horizontal wings frequently and then resumes gliding or soaring.

An adult Turkey Vulture (*Cathartes aura*). Photograph by Bob Gress.

Turkey Vulture
Cathartes aura (Linnaeus)

Status: The Turkey Vulture, a common transient and summer resident especially in the east, also occurs occasionally in winter.

Period of Occurrence: Birds usually reach east and south Kansas in mid-March and the west and north up to a month later. Most birds depart by 15 October with stragglers remaining into November. Extreme dates for nonwintering birds are 29 February and 21 November. There are scattered records from 8 December to 22 January.

Breeding: Although this vulture is widespread throughout the state during summer, only twenty counties have documented breeding records. Eggs have been reported from 7 to 31 May and young from 6 June to 14 August. Johnston (1964) reported nesting by 21 April. Eggs are laid without benefit of a nest in a cave, hollow stump, abandoned building, fruit cellar, or similar place. The one to three (usually two) eggs are dull white with brown blotches and spots. At hatching, the young are helpless and covered (except for the black face) with long white down. They remain in the "nest" for 8 to 10 weeks. Adults carry food in the crop and feed the young by regurgitation. The young also reach into the gullet of the adult to obtain food. Young birds often disgorge their stomach contents when they are disturbed.

Habits and Habitat: Vultures may occur over any habitat but tend to concentrate where ridges or rock outcrops provide updrafts and perches, as at Scott County Lake and Cedar Bluff Reservoir, Trego County. They are clumsy on land but graceful in the air, soaring with a characteristic slight dihedral of the wings and a slight teetering or rocking motion. The wingbeats are deep, slow, and deliberate. When they are not nesting, vultures frequently congregate at favorite roosting sites, which are often dead trees, and in early mornings can be observed spreading their wings toward the sun. Vultures are silent except for hissing, a low grunt, and a snapping of the beak, the last made especially by the unfledged young. Vultures were more common (or at least more visible) during the nineteenth century, when they concentrated at slaughterhouses and open garbage pits. The loss of this abundant food supply has been partially offset by animals killed by vehicles on roadways. Some recent studies have shown that vultures locate carrion by means of smell.

Food: The usual food is carrion, either freshly killed or badly decomposed. Other reports (Bent 1937) mention them eating tadpoles in a drying pond, taking living young herons in a colony, and once, when hard-pressed for food, even eating pumpkins!

An adult Osprey (*Pandion haliaetus*). Photograph by David A. Rintoul.

OSPREYS
Osprey
Pandion haliaetus (Linnaeus)

Status: The Osprey is a rare-to-uncommon transient, chiefly around large bodies of water and rivers. It is reported occasionally in winter where open water persists.

Period of Occurrence: The Osprey is most common from early April through mid-May and from mid-September through October. Extreme dates are from 1 March to 6 June and 1 September

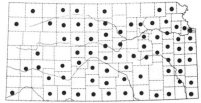

127

to 19 November. It is an occasional visitor in summer and during winter.

Habits and Habitat: The well-known "fish hawk" has one of the widest global distributions of any bird. In Kansas, it is most regular at the larger reservoirs and rivers, but individuals appear also at farm ponds and along small, open streams. Its flight is powerful and sustained, and it commonly soars. The wings, which are usually partially flexed at the wrist, present a distinctive flight profile. It hunts by flying or hovering 30 to 100 feet above the water. When it sights a fish near the surface, the Osprey drops downward with half-closed wings, extends its feet, and enters the water with a great splash. It then labors upward and shakes its plumage, which is waterproof. After a successful dive, it carries the fish, head foremost, to a convenient perch for a leisurely meal. The long, curved claws, sharp projections on the soles of the feet and toes, and a "reversible" outer toe which allows an X-shaped grip are specializations for handing slippery prey.

The Osprey was once common along the Atlantic coast and in some places nested in colonies. The adverse effects of civilization, especially the use of organic pesticides that resulted in eggshells too thin to support the weight of an incubating bird, made the Osprey a rare bird in most areas. However, recent restrictions on the use of DDT and related compounds have resulted in greatly improved nesting success. In some areas, Ospreys now utilize man-made platforms on poles erected for their use. Where Bald Eagles and Ospreys occur together, the eagles frequently harass the Ospreys to obtain the fishes that the latter have captured.

Food: Under most conditions, food is entirely fishes, chiefly various species of slow-moving "rough fishes." Game species are also taken, especially at concentrations such as fish hatcheries. There are rare reports of Ospreys taking turtles, snakes, frogs, and even young ducks.

An adult American Swallow-tailed Kite (*Elanoides forficatus*). Photograph by Marvin D. Schwilling, courtesy Kansas Department of Wildlife and Parks.

KITES
American Swallow-tailed Kite
Elanoides forficatus (Linnaeus)

Status: The American Swallow-tailed Kite, formerly "an irregular summer resident in east, some seasons common, others rare" (Goss 1891), was extirpated and is now a vagrant. It has been recorded west to Riley and Greenwood counties.

Period of Occurrence: The four specimens and few available sight records from the nineteenth century span the period January to 1 September. The recent sighting was 6 September 1972. According to Goss, birds arrived in late April or early May, and few remained until fall.

Breeding: The only published breeding record is of a nest near Neosho Falls, Woodson County, 27 April–July 1876 (Goss 1891). Several pairs were seen near Topeka, Shawnee County, in May 1871 by Allen (1872). The nest near Neosho Falls, in the top of a huge hickory, was two-thirds completed on 18 May. Nests are of sticks, twigs, and strips of inner bark and are placed high in a treetop, usually 75 to 200 feet above ground. The two to three eggs are creamy white with irregular, bold markings of brown and lavender. Both sexes build and defend the nest, incubate the eggs, and care for the young. In the summer of 1982, the Kansas Department of Wildlife and Parks, using the ("Chickadee Checkoff") tax refund donations, sponsored a reintroduction program by fostering chicks in Mississippi Kite nests. One of two chicks fledged successfully.

Habits and Habitat: This spectacular species once nested north to Minnesota and Wisconsin but is now confined to the southeastern United States. Individuals do wander, however, and one was seen near Topeka on 6 September 1972. The flight is swallowlike and is unmatched by that of any other North American raptor in its grace and elegance. The species hunts and devours much of its prey while on the wing. It drinks and bathes by skimming the water. Unfortunately, very little information was recorded concerning the Kansas population.

Field Marks: This kite is unmistakable, due to its white head, body, and underwings, black back, long pointed wings, and deeply forked tail.

Food: The food is chiefly large flying insects, frogs, snakes, and lizards.

An adult Mississippi Kite (*Ictinia mississippiensis*). Photograph by Galen L. Pittman.

Mississippi Kite
Ictinia mississippiensis (Wilson)

Status: The Mississippi Kite is a common summer resident in south-western and south-central Kansas. It occurs casually and occasionally breeds north and east to Phillips and Wyandotte counties.

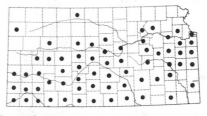

Period of Occurrence: The species is usually present from early or mid-April to late September with extreme dates of 14 March and 29 October. The few winter records are doubtful and need confirmation.

Breeding: The Mississippi Kite breeds chiefly in those counties bordering on, or south of, the Arkansas River and casually or locally north to Ellis County, where it has been regular since the 1960s, and Douglas

County, where it nested in 1906. Kites are gregarious and may nest in loose colonies in hedgerows, windbreaks, or riparian areas. In Kansas, increasing numbers of birds are nesting in towns. Nest building, incubation, and care of the young are shared by both sexes. The nest, a flimsy structure of coarse twigs lined with finer twigs bearing fresh leaves, is placed in a crotch of a tree from 10 to 30 feet above the ground; its material is usually taken from live trees. The usual clutch is two plain bluish-white eggs. The peak of egg laying is probably in late May. The young, which are covered with white down when they hatch, fledge in about five weeks. Often only one young is raised, but Parker (1979) notes that more are raised under optimal conditions. The same nest may be refurbished and used for several years. Year-old birds may nest while retaining the barred tail feathers of their juvenal plumage, and nonbreeding immatures may visit active nests.

Habits and Habitat: Kites are named for their ability to hang motionless in the air and to drift back and forth as if suspended on a string. Their flight is buoyant and very maneuverable, and they capture and eat much of their food on the wing. Some individuals become so tame that they snatch food tossed to them by observers on the ground. Birds nesting in towns prefer parks, golf courses, and residential areas. The birds are sometimes killed in populated areas because their aggressive behavior is not understood as nest defense. Nevertheless, kite numbers seem to be increasing. After breeding, many birds disperse northward, and flocks of up to 120 birds have been seen returning southward over Hays in early September. Birds in juvenal plumage are heavily streaked below and are sometimes mistaken for Sharp-shinned Hawks.

Food: These kites eat chiefly cicadas and grasshoppers taken either on the wing or snatched from vegetation. They also eat frogs, snakes, an occasional bird or small rodent, and even road-killed box turtles (Parker 1979).

An adult Bald Eagle (*Haliaeetus leucocephalus*). Photograph by Mike Blair, courtesy Kansas Department of Wildlife and Parks.

HAWKS AND EAGLES
Bald Eagle
Haliaeetus leucocephalus (Linnaeus)

Status: The Bald Eagle is an uncommon transient and winter visitor, chiefly near open water.

Period of Occurrence: Most sightings are between mid-October
and mid-March, with extreme
dates of 5 September and 8 May.
Summer records need verification.

Breeding: The Bald Eagle builds
a huge nest of sticks and weeds lined with dried grass. It is typically in
a large tree 50 or more feet above ground. It usually lays two eggs
(one to three), which are pure white, are often stained by the nest
lining, and are small for such a large bird. Both sexes share the
incubation period of about 35 days. Young leave the nest in about
three months. Bent (1937) described the "great nest" near Vermil-
ion, Ohio, which was occupied for at least 35 years before being
blown down by a storm in 1925. It measured 12 feet in depth and 8½
feet across at the top. The nest was placed 81 feet above ground in a
shagbark hickory tree.

There are vague unverified references to Bald Eagle nestings
during pioneer days but no recent reports of successful ones. However, Bald Eagles occasionally build nests in Kansas, and their recent
nesting in east-central Oklahoma suggested that they might be successful here soon. From 1957 to 1962, H. A. Stephens (1966)
checked eagle nests at 12 Kansas localities and saw Bald Eagles
associated with several; he saw one carrying a stick. The nests were
apparently built during late winter, but no eggs were ever seen.
Another was built in flooded timber at the Neosho Wildlife Management Area, Neosho County, during the winter of 1965–66.

In late March or early April 1989 a nesting attempt was reported
by John Burghart and sons, who found a nest attended by adults on
the Deer Creek arm of Clinton Reservoir in Douglas County. State
and federal officials confirmed the nesting (photos by Mike Blair)
and cordoned off the nest to prevent disturbance of the nesting pair.
At this writing the nest contents have not been determined, but
dozens of visitors have observed the birds from an observation point
several hundred yards distant. Even if this attempt proves to be a
"practice run" by a young pair, as some suggest, it bodes well for
future nesting in Kansas.

Habits and Habitat: Bald Eagles are seen regularly over most of the
state with winter concentrations of 30 or more birds at the larger
impoundments, particularly at Glen Elder Reservoir, Mitchell
County; there they find large concentrations of waterfowl and a
plentiful supply of fishes. Wintering eagles have either become

more common in Kansas recently or their concentrations at reservoirs are more visible. Winter roosts require, in addition to food, large trees to perch on, a sheltered roost site, and minimum human disturbance. The midwinter Bald Eagle inventory, taken annually in early January by the Kansas Department of Wildlife and Parks and volunteers, has averaged over 300 individual birds since 1980. In western and central Kansas both eagle species use the same roosts, but Bald Eagles tend to concentrate most of their hunting activities along waterways, and Golden Eagles search for prey in open prairie land.

Field Marks: Although white-headed Bald Eagle adults are unmistakable, immatures are often confused with immature Golden Eagles and sometimes even with the larger hawks and Turkey Vultures. The large, thick bill ("Roman nose") and flat flight profile aid in identification.

Food: In Kansas, they feed primarily on dead or injured waterfowl, dead or dying fishes, and carrion. Bald Eagles concentrate both at fish kills and at dead livestock.

An adult Northern Harrier (*Circus cyaneus*). Photograph by Mike Blair, courtesy
Kansas Department of Wildlife and Parks.

Northern Harrier
Circus cyaneus (Linnaeus)

Status: The Northern Harrier is a common transient and winter
resident and an uncommon and local summer resident.

Period of Occurrence: This mainly
migratory species occurs year-
round locally but is most numerous and widespread from early
September to late April. It is
probably declining in numbers as
a breeding species in Kansas.

Breeding: The nest, found on the ground in a field, in grassland, or in a
marsh, is composed of sticks, weeds, and grass. In dry areas it may be
only a shallow depression, but in wet areas it is built up to as much as
18 inches above ground level. In Kansas, many nests in alfalfa or

wheat fields are destroyed when the harvest may either expose the nests or kill the young. The usual four to six (but up to nine) eggs are dull white or pale bluish white and are usually unmarked. Incubation is largely by the female, may begin with the laying of the first egg, and lasts about 24 days. The male brings food to the female and the exchange often takes place in the air near the nest. The young have pure white down, tinged with buff above at hatching, and fledge at four to five weeks. Both parents are aggressive in nest defense and dive close to intruders. Courtship includes a spectacular aerial display, involving a rapid, irregular flight by the male who dives on, then rises over, the female and sometimes performs complete loops or a tumbling display. He usually calls while displaying.

Habits and Habitat: Long-called the "Marsh Hawk," this species is one of the better-known Kansas raptors. It is an open-country bird which systematically patrols fields, fence lines, roadsides, and draws, seeking prey which it captures during a short pursuit or a sudden pounce from above. It rarely perches more than a few feet above ground. During migration, however, individuals fly much higher, with steady wingbeats, and may even soar high overhead. It is the only hawk in Kansas with an owl-like facial disk.

Food: Diet varies with locality and circumstance. Small rodents, especially voles and cotton rats, young rabbits, and ground-nesting birds usually predominate as food. Frogs, snakes, lizards, and large insects, especially grasshoppers, are important food as well.

An adult Sharp-shinned Hawk (*Accipiter striatus*). Photograph by Galen L. Pittman.

Sharp-shinned Hawk
Accipiter striatus (Vieillot)

Status: The Sharp-shinned Hawk is an uncommon transient and winter resident that is casual in summer. It has bred in northeastern Kansas.

Period of Occurrence: Sharp-shinned Hawks are most common during April and October. Extreme dates for nonbreeding birds are 1 August and 9 June, but there are a number of mid-summer records throughout the state.

Breeding: These hawks have bred here on several occasions. One nest in Pottawatomie County was observed from 30 April to June 1954, but its contents could not be seen. Johnston (1960) reported nesting in Cloud County in 1938. The main breeding range is in the northern United States and Canada, especially in coniferous forests. The nest is the usual structure of sticks, often placed on a branch near the trunk, from 20 to 60 feet above ground. The three to five eggs are white or bluish white, handsomely marked with rich brown. Incubation lasts 21 to 24 days and is undertaken primarily by the female.

Habits and Habitat: The Sharp-shinned Hawk is our most regularly seen and common accipiter. It may occur wherever there are trees and small birds, from isolated farmyards to city parks to extensive woodlands. In its habits, it is a smaller version of the Cooper's Hawk and, like it, is a bold and efficient predator. Individual hawks may learn that bird-banding stations and feeders are easy hunting grounds and may haunt them until physically removed. Sudden silence in an area, with the local sparrows hiding in the midst of the densest shrubbery, usually indicates the presence of a Sharp-shinned Hawk perched nearby. It captures prey by a quick strike from a hidden perch or by extended pursuit, even throwing itself against bushes in an attempt to capture or flush birds hiding within. On one occasion, Ely watched a Sharp-shinned Hawk repeatedly dash itself against a hawthorn thicket, from which a bloody but still defiant flicker was screaming incessantly. Others have reported this species bounding along the ground in pursuit of small birds. Sometimes Sharp-shinned Hawks are killed when, while pursuing prey, they hit plate-glass windows. Prey is typically plucked before it is eaten.

The Sharp-shinned Hawk was once abundant but its numbers have declined drastically throughout the eastern part of its range. Large concentrations can still be seen during fall migration as they funnel through such favored points as Point Pelee, Ontario, Hawk Mountain, Pennsylvania, and Cape May, New Jersey.

Food: The diet consists almost entirely of small birds.

An adult Cooper's Hawk (*Accipiter cooperii*). Photograph by David A. Rintoul.

Cooper's Hawk
Accipiter cooperii (Bonaparte)

Status: The Cooper's Hawk is an uncommon transient and winter resident statewide. Small numbers nest, chiefly in the east.

Period of Occurrence: The extreme dates for nonbreeding birds are 5 August and 21 May. It is a local summer resident.

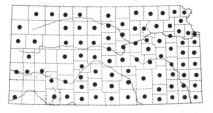

Breeding: Johnston (1964) gives the modal date of egg laying as 25 April. Clutches have been re- ported between 26 April and 11 June, and recently fledged young have been reported as late as 17 June. The nest is in a tree crotch usually 15 or more feet from the ground; it is built of sticks and lined with bark. The clutch is usually four (three to six) bluish-white eggs which are sometimes lightly marked with buff. Both sexes line the nest and incubate. Most nests in Kansas are in deciduous trees in riparian areas. The young are covered with white down and typically fledge in five to six weeks. Adults are usually wary near the nest, at least until the young are partially grown.

Habits and Habitat: Most bird books describe the Cooper's Hawk as a "bloodthirsty villain" or use similar terms to describe its efficiency as a predator. It feeds largely on birds up the size of meadowlarks and robins and is probably the raptor most appropriately called a "chicken hawk." It is a woodland bird and thus was probably never common in Kansas. Its status even today is difficult to determine, because it is so easily confused with the female Sharp-shinned Hawk in the field. Both species are secretive, and one usually gets only a brief view of a bird as it darts among trees or across a clearing. It captures prey either after a stealthy approach and sudden pounce or after active pursuit in which every twist and turn of its flying prey is duplicated. The short, rounded wings and long tail are well adapted for fast, intricate maneuvering through thick vegetation. Its flight is typically four to five quick wingbeats alternating with a short sail, and it is rarely seen in the open except during migration.

The breaking up of dense stands of forest during the nineteenth century briefly caused a population increase, but subsequent shooting, pesticides, and habitat loss resulted in a drastic decline.

Food: About 85 percent of the diet is small and medium-sized birds. The balance is chiefly small mammals (squirrels, rabbits, and rodents) with occasional snakes, lizards, frogs, and, rarely, large insects.

An adult Northern Goshawk (*Accipiter gentilis*). Photograph by Steve Burr.

Northern Goshawk
Accipiter gentilis (Linnaeus)

Status: There are scattered records for the Northern Goshawk throughout the state, especially in the northeast, making it a rare, irregular winter visitor.

Period of Occurrence: Specimens and confirmed sight records are from 3 October to 24 February. Extreme dates for unconfirmed sight records are 7 September and 23 April.

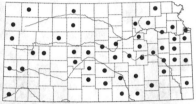

Habits and Habitat: This species is primarily a bird of boreal forest, but occasionally it irrupts into the Great Plains during winter. A major invasion reached Kansas during 1916–17, when 10 specimens were taken in Douglas and Shawnee counties. In 1973–74, there were five documented sightings, and in 1982–83, there were many.

The Northern Goshawk prefers wooded areas where it hunts below treetop level, surprising its prey and capturing it after quick pursuit. It also rests quietly in thick growth and awaits its prey. It is a very powerful species which feeds on various vertebrates as large as grouse, ducks, and rabbits. It has long been a favorite of falconers. It is also noted for its fierce defense of its nest.

Food: In the far north, the Goshawk's major foods include ptarmigan, grouse, lemmings, and hares. In Kansas, it probably feeds mainly on squirrels, cottontail rabbits, rodents, and medium-sized birds such as crows, ducks, and at times, domestic poultry. Snakes and terrestrial invertebrates are uncommon food items.

An adult Harris' Hawk (*Parabuteo unicinctus*). Photograph by David A. Rintoul.

Harris' Hawk
Parabuteo unicinctus (Temminck)

Status: The Harris' Hawk is normally a winter straggler (there are five records), and one nest was found in 1963. The additional Kansas records are of specimens from Douglas and Sedgwick counties in December 1918, of one found dead in Mitchell County on 7 January 1963, and of one seen regularly from 11 December 1972 through 7 January 1973 at Cheyenne Bottoms, Barton County.

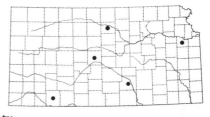

Period of Occurrence: Nonbreeding birds have been reported between 11 December and 7 January, and the breeding birds to at least 28 May.

Breeding: The only recorded breeding for Kansas (Parmelee and Stephens 1964) was at Meade State Park, Meade County. During the first week of January 1962, an adult female was trapped near the pheasant-rearing pens; that fall, a second bird was trapped and released unharmed. Parmelee and Stephens saw three birds there on 21 December 1962 and two on 8 February 1963. Copulation was observed on 29 and 30 March and on 13 April. The nest, with an incubating female, was found in the top of a cottonwood; it contained three eggs on 21 April, a downy chick on 28 May, and was destroyed by a storm on 6 June. The species has not been reported breeding in Kansas since.

The usual breeding range is from the southwestern United States and central Texas, south into South America. The nest, typically a small, compact structure of sticks lined with finer materials, is built from 5 to 30 feet above ground in a low tree or cactus. The three to four eggs are white, sometimes faintly marked with brown.

Habits and Habitat: The species normally inhabits semi-open grassland, desert, chaparral, and water courses. It resembles the Red-tailed Hawk in many respects, often soaring and resting on conspicuous perches. However, it spends more time on the ground and is a more aggressive hunter. The fast, powerful flight through vegetation has been likened to that of an accipiter. The species is apparently migratory, since large flocks congregate in the fall.

Food: The Harris' Hawk eats primarily small mammals, including ground squirrels and rabbits, snakes, lizards, and, rarely, birds.

An adult Red-shouldered Hawk (*Buteo lineatus*). Photograph by Bob Gress.

Red-shouldered Hawk
Buteo lineatus (Gmelin)

Status: The Red-shouldered Hawk is a local, uncommon summer resident and transient in the eastern quarter of the state. It is rare in winter and casual westward. Most sightings in the western two-thirds of the state need confirmation.

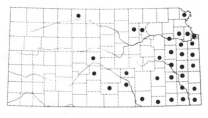

Period of Occurrence: The species is most common from early April to mid-October. The extreme dates for transients are 11 February and 16 November, and there are a few winter records.

Breeding: At present, most breed in riparian forest in southeastern Kansas; smaller numbers breed in the northeast. The nest, a well-built structure of sticks that is lined with bark and usually decorated with sprigs of fresh leaves, is placed in a tree crotch 20 to 50 feet above ground. The nest is usually in lowland woods and may be used several years in succession. The three to four eggs are white marked with brown and are laid in late March or early April. Both parents incubate. The young, which are covered with white down, fledge in five to six weeks. There may be renesting if eggs are destroyed during the early stages of incubation, but only a single brood is raised each season.

Habits and Habitat: This species is infrequently seen in Kansas due to its restricted breeding habitat and usually secretive nature. Its most favored places are the Marais des Cygnes Wildlife Management Area in Linn County, where it nests regularly, and along wooded streams in Cherokee County. Population numbers are declining nationally.

This is a noisy hawk during its courtship period in March and early April. The "kee-you" call given by Blue Jays throughout Kansas is thought to be an imitation of the Red-shouldered Hawk's call. The hawk frequently soars above the forest canopy, sometimes probably hunting in this manner. At other times, it hunts by sitting quietly on a favorite, often secluded, perch and pouncing on nearby prey. In general, its habits are similar to those of the more common Red-tailed Hawk.

Food: Up to 65 percent of its food is small rodents, and it also eats frogs, snakes, and smaller numbers of birds. Large insects and other invertebrates may be important comestibles locally.

An adult Broad-winged Hawk (*Buteo platypterus*). Photograph by Galen L. Pittman.

Broad-winged Hawk
Buteo platypterus (Vieillot)

Status: The Broad-winged Hawk is a regular transient statewide, uncommon in the east to rare in the west. It is a local and rare summer resident in the northeast.

Period of Occurrence: Most migrate during April and May, with a peak in late April, and during September and October, with a peak in late September. Extreme dates are 6 April and 14 October.

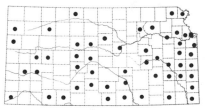

Breeding: Johnston (1964) reported four nesting records for eastern Kansas in swampy woodland; a few birds probably nest during most years. The nest, of sticks lined with bark and usually ornamented with sprigs of green leaves, is placed in a crotch from 20 to 40 feet above ground. The two to three eggs are white or bluish white, with varying amounts of brown and lavender markings. Incubation lasts from 21 to 25 days, and the newly hatched young are covered with buffy-white down. The young fledge in five to six weeks.

Habits and Habitat: In Kansas, most Broad-winged Hawks are seen during migration when they are silent and unsuspicious. With the possible exception of some young Swainson's Hawks, this species is our tamest hawk. Bent (1937) relates two instances in which incubating birds were lifted from their nests without protest. In western Kansas, where migrating individuals often rest in the shade trees of parks and along residential streets, birds can sometimes be approached to within a few meters. The species is widespread across Kansas, but does not form the huge flocks, or "kettles," of migrating birds that pass favored concentration points in the eastern United States (e.g., at Hawk Mountain, Pennsylvania) and in Central America. It hunts primarily while perched quietly or while flying below the forest canopy.

Field Marks: When they soar, adults are easily identified by the compact silhouette and the broad white bands on the tail.

Food: During late summer and fall, the major food of the species is large insects, such as cicadas, grasshoppers, and large caterpillars. A few small mammals, small birds, reptiles, and amphibians are also eaten.

An immature Swainson's Hawk (*Buteo swainsoni*). Photograph by Roger Boyd.

Swainson's Hawk
Buteo swainsoni (Bonaparte)

Status: Swainson's Hawk is a common transient and summer resident in the west that becomes less common eastward.

Period of Occurrence: Swainson's Hawk is most abundant from early April through September. Johnston (1965) gives median arrival and departure dates of 12 April and 12 October, respectively. Extreme dates are 2 March

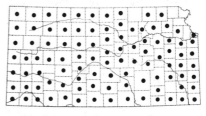

(doubtful) through 2 November. Midwinter sight records are of doubtful credibility.

Breeding: Nest building begins within a few days of the spring arrival and proceeds rapidly. The peak of laying is in late April. Most nests are built 15 to 40 feet above ground in trees along roadsides, in open prairie, or in farmyards, often near houses; nests are less commonly built on rock outcrops and on the ground. They are constructed of sticks and large weed stems and may be quite loose and bulky. The two to three eggs are dull white with scattered brown markings. Smaller birds frequently nest near Swainson's Hawk nests, and at least six different species have nested within the sides of nests themselves.

Habits and Habitat: In Kansas, this species largely replaces the Red-tailed Hawk in open country with scattered trees. Except when molested, individuals are usually tame and unsuspicious and often allow a close approach while perched along a roadside. Immature birds may sometimes be approached to within a few meters. The species frequents cultivated areas as well as rangeland; small flocks are regularly attracted to fields being prepared for planting, where they capture rodents, large insects, and other prey disturbed by the machinery. It has the most extensive migration of any hawk and regularly winters in Argentina. In earlier times, but no longer, huge spiraling flocks or "kettles" were a common sight during migration. A concentration of "thousands" seen in Wabaunsee County in October 1957 was one of the few reported since the 1930s. As the hawks move southward they congregate, and the entire population funnels through Central America in a few huge flocks. In 1947 and 1949, huge flocks alighted overnight in southern Mexico, causing near panic among rural residents (Alvarez del Toro 1971). Such flocks seldom feed while migrating.

Food: The major foods are small mammals (chiefly mice and ground squirrels), large insects (mainly grasshoppers), lizards, and frogs. One hawk's stomach contained 106 grasshoppers. Several observers (Bent 1937) have seen them taking and eating insects while in flight, but more often they hop around on the ground, which reminded one observer of a flock of Turkeys.

Red-tailed Hawk
Buteo jamaicensis (Gmelin)

Status: The Red-tailed Hawk is most common in eastern Kansas and becomes progressively less common to the west, where it is largely restricted to watercourses. Its numbers are greatly augmented during migration and in winter by individuals from farther north and west.

Period of Occurrence: In most areas, the species is present all year.

Breeding: Red-tailed Hawks are early nesters, and many nests are occupied by mid- or late February. Johnston (1964) gives 5 March as the modal date for egg laying. The nest is a large structure of sticks lined with strips of bark. It is usually placed in the crotch of a large tree from 20 to 50 feet above ground. Red-tailed Hawks may also nest on rock ledges and cliff faces. A nest may be used more than once. The two to three eggs are white, or bluish white, with sparse brownish spotting. Most incubation is by the female, but the male brings her food and shares the care of the young. The incubation period is about 28 days, and the young fledge in four to five weeks.

Habits and Habitat: This species is the most common and widespread large hawk throughout the eastern half of the state. Its habit of using utility poles along highways and roads as hunting perches increases its visibility and apparent abundance. Such birds usually feed on the small mammals and reptiles which occur along roadsides, but various road-killed vertebrates are also scavenged. Early in the nesting season, the birds are very noisy and spend much time soaring lazily in circles.

Field Marks: From below, soaring adults are easily identified by wing shape, their light underparts, and their red-brown tail. During winter, the numerous hawks migrating from more northern localities present major identification problems. Some melanistic individuals appear jet black from a distance, while others (of the race *krideri*) are so pale that they appear almost white. Many hawks, especially immatures, are intermediate in color. These "nontypical" individuals occur chiefly in the western half of the state and are good examples of polymorphism. The color pattern is determined genetically, and the proportions of each color type vary among different populations. However, whether melanistic or pale, individuals retain their original color morph after

An immature Red-tailed Hawk (*Buteo jamaicensis*). Photograph by Mark A. Chappell.

each molt. The plumage colors of one population—which for years was considered a distinct species, the "Harlan's Hawk"—range from very light to very dark.

Food: Red-tailed Hawks utilize a wide variety of vertebrate prey, depending on local availability, and individuals are said to develop preferences for particular prey species. Small mammals, including various mice, rats, ground squirrels, and rabbits, predominate in the diet. This hawk regularly eats reptiles, especially snakes, birds, and even large invertebrates.

An adult Ferruginous Hawk (*Buteo regalis*). Photograph by Galen L. Pittman.

Ferruginous Hawk
Buteo regalis (Gray)

Status: The Ferruginous Hawk occurs all year and breeds locally in the west. During migration and in winter, it occurs eastward in progressively reduced numbers. Vagrants are widespread, especially in late summer.

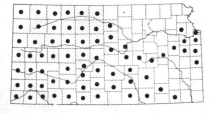

Period of Occurrence: The species is resident all year in the west and is present eastward chiefly from late September to mid-April. Extreme dates outside of the normal breeding area are 5 September and 18 April.

Breeding: The Ferruginous Hawk nests primarily in the steeply eroded canyons along the Smoky Hill River from Gove County westward. In 1979, Stan Roth located 52 active nests; 6 were in cottonwood and locust trees, and the remainder on rock faces, bluffs, and pinnacles. The nest is a large, bulky mass of sticks and weed stalks lined with finer materials. A pair frequently has several nests within a small area and may alternate among them in successive years. The three to four eggs are creamy white to bluish white with variable amounts of light brown to rich brown spotting. Incubation, which lasts 28 days, begins before the laying of the last egg, so that the young hatch at intervals of several days. The young fledge in about two months; individuals from nests near canyons may wander along the slopes for some distance before they fledge.

Habits and Habitat: These hawks spend much of their time sitting on the ground or on low perches, or soaring high overhead. They hunt from the air or a perch, or by waiting near burrows of prairie dogs or ground squirrels. In winter, birds disperse eastward to farmlands, marshes, and other open areas where small rodents are numerous.

Field Marks: The Ferruginous Hawk is our largest *Buteo,* and dark-phase birds are frequently confused with eagles. Both dark- and light-phase birds usually may be identified by the white patch on the wings, which is best seen on the down stroke; the white, or light, unbarred tail; and the tarsi, which are feathered to the toes.

Food: The species eats chiefly small mammals, especially prairie dogs, gophers, and ground squirrels. They also eat snakes, large insects, and occasionally small birds.

An adult Rough-legged Hawk (*Buteo lagopus*). Photograph by David A. Rintoul.

Rough-legged Hawk
Buteo lagopus (Pontoppidan)

Status: The Rough-legged Hawk is a common transient and winter resident, mainly in the western half of the state.

Period of Occurrence: The species
is most common between early
October and late April, with extreme dates for confirmed sightings of 20 September and 11
May. Any sightings outside of
these extremes need verification.

Habits and Habitat: This hawk breeds in central and northern Canada
and visits Kansas in winter. Its arrival time and the number of birds
vary with the southern limit of snow cover. It is an open-country bird
that is most frequently seen sitting on an exposed perch, soaring
overhead, or coursing slowly back and forth over a field in search of
prey. It hovers more, often into a stiff wind or with rapidly beating
wings, than other *Buteo* and tends to be more crepuscular than other
hawks. When prey is abundant, as on irrigated cropland, birds may
flock loosely. Individuals may return to the same general area in
successive years. A wintering bird banded at Stockton, Rooks
County, was killed at Great Bend, Barton County, six years later
(Kennard 1975).

Field Marks: The name "rough-legged" refers to the feathers which
extend down the legs to the toes. There is great variation in plumage
from the typical "light" birds (with a light head and a dark abdominal
band) to others that appear nearly black at a distance; there is also a
bewildering range of intermediates. In any plumage, there is usually a
whitish patch at the base of the tail.

Food: The diet consists almost entirely of small rodents, chiefly mice.

An adult Golden Eagle (*Aquila chrysaetos*). Photograph by Mike Blair, courtesy Kansas Department of Wildlife and Parks.

Golden Eagle
Aquila chrysaetos (Linnaeus)

Status: The Golden Eagle is an uncommon transient and winter visitor, chiefly in the west. There is one early report of breeding and recent nesting in four far-western counties.

Period of Occurrence: The species is most common from early October through early April. Extreme dates for nonbreeding birds are 2 September and 8 May. Midsummer vagrants occur occasionally in the east.

Breeding: Courtship involves spectacular aerial maneuvers, and pairs are said to mate for life. Recent nests in Kansas were built in isolated trees in native grassland or on the steep sides of deeply eroded gullies. Nests may be rebuilt and used in successive years, or a pair may alternate among several nests in the same area. The two or three eggs are white with light brown spotting. Eggs are laid in early March, and the young fledge from early to mid-July. Incubation is largely by the female, but the male shares brooding of the young. When a nest is approached, adults typically depart and observe from a distance.

Habits and Habitat: The Golden Eagle is not closely related to the Bald Eagle, and more nearly resembles a large *Buteo* in its habits. It occurs most regularly over open grasslands in western Kansas but in winter occurs sporadically eastward. Birds are usually shy and difficult to approach, and most nesting sites are fairly isolated. Each pair occupies a large home range of up to 35 square miles. Most hunt either from a perch or by a steep dive from a considerable height; pairs frequently hunt together. Ely once watched a speck high overhead develop into a plunging Golden Eagle, which made an unsuccessful dive at a nearby jackrabbit that Ely had not seen. The jackrabbit escaped by zigzagging through a barbed wire fence as the eagle bounced along the ground in hot pursuit. Although eagles are very powerful birds, the size of their usual prey is greatly exaggerated, as is their ability to carry off large prey—although Thompson found the legs of a young pronghorn beneath a nest site in Montana. An eagle weighs 8 to 12 pounds, and it would be difficult, if not impossible, for a bird to carry prey of equal weight.

Food: Within its extensive range, which covers most of the North Temperate Zone, eagles feed on a great variety of vertebrates, with jackrabbits, cottontails, rodents, and snakes predominating; they also take larger prey occasionally. However, studies show that their predation on healthy domestic livestock has been greatly exaggerated (Wiley and Bolen 1971). A considerable amount of carrion may be eaten in winter.

American Kestrel
Falco sparverius (Linnaeus)

Status: The American Kestrel is present all year but is rare in western Kansas in winter. It breeds throughout the state.

Period of Occurrence: The kestrel is most abundant during migrations from March through April and from September through October.

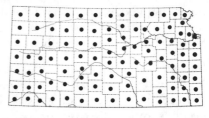

Breeding: Courtship involves much aerial display and calling, and birds are then very conspicuous. The male brings food to the female and continues to feed her during incubation. Kestrels nest in cavities in trees, martin houses, crevices in stone buildings, and nooks and crannies in buildings and bridges. Nest height varies from 10 to 30 feet above ground. Most egg laying is in mid-April, and the three to five eggs are white or light buff with fine brownish spots. Incubation lasts about 30 days, and the young remain in the nest for a month before fledging. The family remains together for an extended time thereafter while the young perfect their flying and hunting skills.

Habits and Habitat: The present name is preferable to the old "Sparrow Hawk," because it indicates their closer relationship to the Old World kestrels than to the sparrowhawks, which are similar to our Sharp-shinned Hawks and Cooper's Hawks. Kestrels prefer open areas with scattered trees and frequently nest in parks, towns, and along rivers. They hunt primarily from an exposed perch such as an overhead line but also hover frequently; while facing into the wind they remain stationary or beat their wings very rapidly, providing the basis for the name "windhover." Most individuals migrate, but a few winter, often near deserted buildings which provide roosting cover and food in the form of sparrows or small mammals. Kestrels migrate during the day and frequently congregate along roadsides or field borders where perches and food are abundant. The call note is the often-repeated, very familiar "killy-killy-killy" or "kle-kle-kle." Some individuals become fairly tame and nest in the cramped quarters of a backyard martin house.

Food: The species eats chiefly large insects such as grasshoppers, but also, especially in winter, small mammals such as mice and small birds.

An immature female American Kestrel (*Falco sparverius*). Photograph by David A. Rintoul.

They also eat lizards and small snakes. Ely once saw a male laboriously carrying a small cottontail which it soon dropped. The retrieved bunny (alert and active) weighed 63.2 grams, probably over half the weight of the kestrel.

An adult Merlin (*Falco columbarius*). Photograph by C. L. Cink.

Merlin
Falco columbarius (Linnaeus)

Status: The Merlin is an uncommon transient and rare winter visitor. It is now less common than formerly but apparently still occurs regularly.

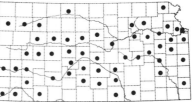

Period of Occurrence: Dates of specimens range from 14 August to 10 June. Recent sightings are chiefly between early October and late March, with extreme dates of 14 August and 15 May. Summer sight records need confirmation.

Habits and Habitat: The Merlin was formerly called the "Pigeon Hawk," either because of a presumed resemblance to a pigeon in flight or because it preyed on pigeons! In appearance and actions, however, it is a typical falcon. It feeds primarily on small birds caught during active pursuit. Goss (1891) reported that it captured birds as large as a Passenger Pigeon. Using old nests of other species or merely nesting on the ground, the species nests primarily in Canadian boreal forests; a few nest as far south as northwestern Nebraska. Most birds winter south of the United States. In Kansas, birds are seen most often perched on exposed tree limbs or on overhead wires, often in parks, cemeteries, or at the edges of towns.

Field Marks: The Merlin lacks the American Kestrel's head markings and reddish brown coloration above. Some immatures passing through western Kansas are very pale and almost sandy brown.

Food: The species eats primarily small birds (up to flicker-size) and also large insects such as dragonflies, which it captures on the wing. One Merlin's stomach held 34 dragonflies. It occasionally feeds on small mammals such as mice.

An adult Peregrine Falcon (*Falco peregrinus*). Photograph by Tom Mosher.

Peregrine Falcon
Falco peregrinus (Tunstall)

Status: The Peregrine Falcon formerly bred in Woodson and Ellis counties and was a regular transient statewide. It is now a rare transient and occasional winter visitor across the state, especially near mudflats and open water.

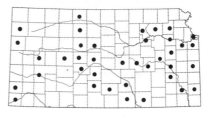

Period of Occurrence: Recent records are from 5 September to 31 May, with one record in Barton County on 25 July. Midsummer sightings and winter records some distance from open water need confirmation.

Breeding: The very small Kansas breeding population disappeared about 1880 as a result of human settlement. A single eyrie had been found on the Saline River in Ellis County, and a few pairs nested along the Neosho River in Woodson County in cavities in huge sycamores. That was unusual, as most Peregrine Falcons nest on tall, steep cliffs, preferably with grassy ledges and overlooking a broad hunting territory. The three to four eggs, creamy white to pinkish and variably marked with brown, are laid in a bare scrape; the Kansas population laid in early March. Peregrine Falcons here are usually silent, but they are very noisy during courtship and often when defending the eyrie. Courtship includes very spectacular dives, swoops, and other aerial maneuvers.

Habits and Habitat: The Peregrine Falcon, or "Duck Hawk," once had a nearly worldwide distribution, but the population of the eastern United States was wiped out. The beautiful eggs were prized by collectors, and the birds themselves were and still are a favorite of falconers. These factors, in addition to hunting and continued disturbance of the eyries, caused a decline in numbers by the early twentieth century. Widespread use of pesticides, which Peregrine Falcons accumulate in their bodies from their prey, was the final blow. The pesticides caused thin eggshells; young in the eggs were crushed or the eggs were infertile, which made extinction inevitable. Favored eyries often had been occupied for many consecutive years—one in Europe for over 350 years! Birds from artificial breeding programs are now being reintroduced successfully throughout the former range. At present, the nearest breeding populations are in Colorado and the Black Hills of North Dakota.

The Peregrine Falcon is a magnificent bird that Sprunt (1955) considered "the ultimate of the avian kingdom" and "supreme" among birds. In Kansas, most individuals are seen during migration, usually in open areas such as mudflats where shorebirds and waterfowl concentrate. It hunts in flight, often while soaring high over the prey. It attacks with a steep power dive, or "stoop," from above, and the prey is either snatched from the air or killed by a blow from the clenched foot. A speed of up to 175 MPH has been reported, but that has not yet been confirmed. Its stoop is an awesome sight, whether it is after prey or defending its eyrie.

Food: The diet is almost entirely birds—chiefly shorebirds, waterfowl, and, in the Arctic, large numbers of ptarmigan and colonial seabirds. Occasionally it takes small mammals and large insects.

Nestling Gyrfalcons (*Falco rusticolus*). Photograph by Max C. Thompson.

Gyrfalcon
Falco rusticolus (Linnaeus)

Status: There is only one Kansas specimen of the vagrant Gyrfalcon. Goss (1886) reported that the specimen was "captured near Manhat-

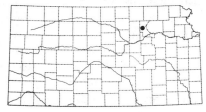

tan, December 1, 1880 by A. L. Runyan" and presented to C. P. Blachley. His statement was repeated by all writers until Johnston (1960) gave the locality as "Ashland, Clark County." The specimen was one of several mounted birds transferred from Kansas State University to the University of Kansas. In 1963, Thompson remade the mount into a study skin and discovered the Ashland, Clark County, label on the bottom of the stand bearing the mount. Riley County is more logical.

This species, our largest true falcon, has been reported during the winter with increasing frequency in nearby states and should be looked for in Kansas. Some individuals are white with dark flecks; others are slaty gray or brownish gray, more uniform in color than the Peregrine Falcon and without the inconspicuous facial pattern.

Prairie Falcon
Falco mexicanus (Schlegel)

Status: The Prairie Falcon is an uncommon winter resident in the west and is rare in the east. It is casual in summer in the west, where local nesting is suspected but not yet documented.

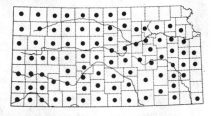

Period of Occurrence: This falcon is a regular resident in the west from early September to late March and occurs casually in summer. It occurs eastward in decreasing numbers, chiefly from mid-November to mid-March.

Breeding: The species may nest, at least occasionally, in the badlands of western Kansas. Most individuals reported during the summer are probably wandering subadults or postbreeding birds, but a pair did summer in Scott County in 1952. A mummified falcon chick found in Gove County may have been one of this species. Elsewhere, nests are on steep bluffs and escarpments. The eggs are laid in a bare scrape, usually in a pocket beneath an overhanging ledge. Old nests of hawks, ravens, or eagles are sometimes used.

Habits and Habitat: This falcon's flight is direct and swift, with short, powerful beats of the pointed wings; it often flies close to the ground. It is usually an open-country species and spends much of its time on exposed perches such as utility poles. It hunts either by direct pursuit or by a rapid dive or stoop from above. Small prey is snatched in flight; larger prey is killed by a blow from the clenched foot. Such behavior is spectacular, and the prey rarely escapes. The falcon has also been seen hopping on the ground after grasshoppers. It is very similar to the Peregrine Falcon in many of its habits, but many falconers consider it irascible and difficult to train. Several observers have commented on its habit of harassing larger birds such as herons, both when they approach the nest and merely in "play." The pair (especially the female) defends the nest by screaming and diving and at such times may attack and kill other birds in the neighborhood.

Food: Prairie Falcons eat primarily birds, as large as Rock Doves, and small mammals, especially young prairie dogs and ground squirrels. They take lizards and large insects infrequently. The percentage of birds in the diet increases in winter.

An adult Prairie Falcon (*Falco mexicanus*). Photograph by Mike Blair.

Ring-necked Pheasant
Phasianus colchicus (Linnaeus)

Status: The Ring-necked Pheasant is an introduced common resident in the center and northwest that becomes progressively less common in the east and south.

Period of Occurrence: The species is an introduced resident.

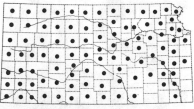

Breeding: The Ring-necked Pheasant nests commonly in the northwest and central part of the state; from the center eastward, breeding becomes sporadic, and in some years, this bird may be absent from the southeastern corner. It has become more common in south-central Kansas since 1980. Nests are located primarily in fence rows adjacent to cropland, ditches, shelterbelts, and hayfields. The number of eggs in the clutch varies but averages from 9 to 10; incubation takes about 23 days. Most breeding starts in April and extends into August. They have only one brood but may renest if the first nest is destroyed early in the season. The cocks establish territories in the spring, and their crowing can be heard up to a mile away. After breeding, the female tends the nest and young, which are precocial and leave the nest within hours to follow the adult. The young grow rapidly and are capable of limited flight within a week of hatching; they are independent within eight weeks.

Habits and Habitat: Ring-necked Pheasants frequent the same general habitat as their breeding habitat. During the nonbreeding season, they occur in small groups or as solitary adults. Wintering birds use milo fields to obtain an adequate food supply. They may leave their feeding areas to rest in pastures. The pheasants prefer the drier areas of the state and are quite rare in the extreme east along the Missouri border. This pheasant, originally introduced from China in the early 1900s for hunting, occupies a niche that seems to be filled by no other game bird, at least in the western portion of the state. It is a popular game bird, and many out-of-state hunters flock to Kansas for the November opening of the season. In 1986, a total of 723,288 cocks were harvested.

Food: The diet is varied but consists mainly of seeds and grains, with a mixture of insects and other vegetable matter.

An adult Ring-necked Pheasant (*Phasianus colchicus*). Photograph by Mike Blair.

An adult Ruffed Grouse (*Bonasa umbellus*). Photograph by Gene Brehm, courtesy Kansas Department of Wildlife and Parks.

GROUSE AND PRAIRIE-CHICKENS
Ruffed Grouse
Bonasa umbellus (Linnaeus)

Status: The Ruffed Grouse was a former resident of eastern Kansas but was extirpated. Since 1983, it has been reintroduced in the following counties: Atchison, Bourbon, Douglas, Jefferson, Johnson, Linn, and Miami. Prior to its reintroduction, it had not been reported since the early 1900s. Goss (1886) stated, "A resident in the eastern portion of the state prior to its settlement; but, being a bird of the woods, its

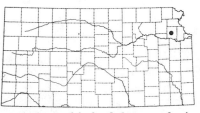

171

range was confined to the timber skirting the streams, and, upon the settlement of the same, they quickly disappeared, as the tramping and browsing of the cattle during the winters destroyed the undergrowth, their favorite resorts, and left them no longer a hiding place or natural home." Since Goss's time, the eastern Kansas habitat has changed radically, and more woodland is probably present now than in his day. We hope that reintroduction will return this fine game bird to the state.

The only early specimen was taken in "Southeastern Kansas" between 1885 and 1910 and was collected and mounted by A. J. C. Roese. It is at the University of Kansas Museum of Natural History.

An adult Sage Grouse (*Centrocercus urophasianus*). Photograph by David A. Rintoul.

Sage Grouse
Centrocercus urophasianus (Bonaparte)

Status: The Sage Grouse, a hypothetical species, is included here on the basis of Goss (1886): "Included as an occasional resident of western Kansas on the authority of Mr. Will. T. Cavanaugh, Assistant Secretary of State, who informs me that while hunting buffalo during 1871, 1872, 1873 and 1874, he occasionally met with and shot the birds in the sage brush near the southwest corner of the State."

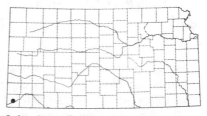

The Sage Grouse probably occurred in limited numbers, since it was recorded in nearby Cimarron County, Oklahoma, as recently as July 1920 (Sutton 1967).

An adult male Greater Prairie-Chicken (*Tympanuchus cupido*). Photograph by David
A. Rintoul.

Greater Prairie-Chicken
Tympanuchus cupido (Linnaeus)

Status: The Greater Prairie-Chicken is a locally common resident in
the eastern third of the state. It is most common in the Flint Hills,
uncommon and local in the
north-central part of the state,
and rare in the northwest. It
seems to be expanding into its
former range in the northwest.

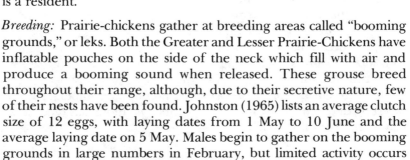

Period of Occurrence: The species
is a resident.

Breeding: Prairie-chickens gather at breeding areas called "booming
grounds," or leks. Both the Greater and Lesser Prairie-Chickens have
inflatable pouches on the side of the neck which fill with air and
produce a booming sound when released. These grouse breed
throughout their range, although, due to their secretive nature, few
of their nests have been found. Johnston (1965) lists an average clutch
size of 12 eggs, with laying dates from 1 May to 10 June and the
average laying date on 5 May. Males begin to gather on the booming
grounds in large numbers in February, but limited activity occurs

there throughout the year. Booming grounds in Kansas may have as many as 100 males, but usually only one male is dominant and copulates with most of the females. Females normally do not return to the booming grounds after copulation unless their nest is destroyed. The nest is usually placed in grassland, and one egg a day is laid. Incubation takes 23 to 26 days, and the young stay with the female from six to eight weeks (Johnsgard 1973).

Habits and Habitat: Thanks to the extensive grasslands in the Flint Hills, Kansas has the largest known populations of this grouse. There are estimates of as many as 750,000. Fairly large areas of grassland are necessary for their survival, although they also feed in nearby grain fields. Hunting them for market in the late 1800s and the early 1900s nearly caused the prairie-chicken to become extinct, but strict protection by the state has brought them back to their former abundance in the east. They are also repopulating northwestern Kansas in suitable habitat. Until recently, Kansas was the only state that allowed hunting of the Greater Prairie-Chicken. There were 64,169 harvested in 1986. During November, hunters from all over the United States come to the Flint Hills for this species, whose rapid, erratic flight makes it a difficult target.

Field Marks: The pouches in the Greater Prairie-Chicken are orange, while the pouches in the Lesser species are a reddish purple. There is a noticeable difference in the "booming" call of the two species.

Food: The Greater Prairie-Chicken subsists primarily on seeds and cultivated grains, but in the warmer parts of the year it also eats insects—primarily grasshoppers and crickets (Bent 1932). If the weather remains warm into November, its diet may keep it out of grain fields during the opening of the hunting season.

An adult Lesser Prairie-Chicken (*Tympanuchus pallidicinctus*). Photograph by Gerald J. Wiens.

Lesser Prairie-Chicken
Tympanuchus pallidicinctus (Ridgway)

Status: The Lesser Prairie-Chicken, a local resident in the southwestern part of the state south of the Arkansas River, now occurs in the sand-sage prairie as far east as Pratt County. It formerly was found east to at least Neosho County in winter (Goss 1891). A specimen taken in Logan County on 1 January 1921 is the northernmost state record.

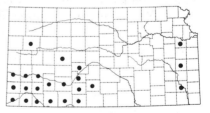

Period of Occurrence: The species is a permanent resident.

Breeding: The Lesser Prairie-Chicken, like the Greater, forms leks where the males meet and try to entice a female to copulate. Little is known about clutch size, but on 28 May 1920, Colvin found a nest near Liberal that contained 12 eggs; a nearby nest also contained 12 eggs on 2 June 1920, and a third contained 13 eggs (Bent 1932). The nest is a scrape in the sand lined with grasses (ibid.). The incubation and details of raising the young are approximately the same as that of the Greater Prairie-Chicken and are described in that account.

Habits and Habitat: Lesser Prairie-Chickens are more restricted in the state due to their limited habitat, which is being further diminished as the sand-sage prairie is plowed and irrigated. They can be observed at the Pratt Wildlife Area and on the Cimarron National Grasslands in Morton County. The U.S. Forest Service in Elkhart erects an observation blind each year, which is open to the public.

Apparently Lesser Prairie-Chickens were abundant at the turn of this century. Colvin states that in 1904, his brother observed 15,000 to 20,000 chickens around one grain field in the sandhills just inside the Kansas line in Seward County (Bent 1932). The dust bowl days of the 1930s helped to decimate these large populations, which have not reached their former abundance since. Today's estimates of the Lesser Prairie-Chicken population in Kansas are from 10,000 to 15,000 birds.

This species is currently hunted in Kansas, but due to their small numbers and the difficulty of hunting them, only 1,494 were harvested in 1986. The biggest threat to the Lesser Prairie-Chicken is the continued conversion of the sand-sage prairie to farmland. Such land is marginally arable and is worthless without irrigation. When future groundwater supplies diminish, will the area revert to sand-sage prairie in a form usable by prairie-chickens?

Food: The species eats seeds and cultivated grains, along with insects, mainly grasshoppers (Colvin 1914).

An adult Sharp-tailed Grouse (*Tympanuchus phasianellus*). Photograph by Randy Rogers, courtesy Kansas Department of Wildlife and Parks.

Sharp-tailed Grouse
Tympanuchus phasianellus (Linnaeus)

Status: The Sharp-Tailed Grouse formerly occurred in western Kansas, with definite records from Ellis County (Allen 1872) and a mounted specimen taken in Cheyenne County on 24 October 1886. Goss (1891) reported it to be a common resident in the western part of the state. There are some recent reports from the northwest of birds that may be 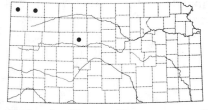 wandering in from Nebraska. Recently, the Kansas Department of Wildlife and Parks reintroduced this grouse into Rawlins County. Randy Rogers of the Kansas Department of Wildlife and Parks found nonbanded birds at a "dancing ground" in Rawlins County, indicating that the species may have reestablished itself.

Breeding: This species presumably bred in the 1800s and probably now breeds in the northwestern part of the state, at least in Rawlins County.

Habits and Habitat: The Sharp-tailed Grouse's requirements are very much like those of the other prairie-chickens primarily grasslands, although it is also found in shortgrass prairie. The males form "booming grounds" and dance and inflate their neck pouches to attract females. Hybridization between the Greater Prairie-Chicken and the Sharp-tailed Grouse occurs.

Food: The major part of the Sharp-tailed Grouse's diet is weed seeds and cultivated grains; insects are taken in smaller amounts (Bent 1932).

An adult male wild Turkey (*Meleagris gallopavo*). Photograph by Mike Blair.

TURKEYS
Turkey
Meleagris gallopavo (Linnaeus)

Status: The Turkey was formerly an abundant resident but was extirpated in the early 1900s. It reappeared about 1958 in Cowley and Barber counties, coming from native and introduced stock in Oklahoma. Recently, the Kansas Department of Wildlife and Parks successfully reintroduced birds into other areas that they once populated.

Period of Occurrence: The Turkey is a permanent resident.

Breeding: Little is known about its breeding prior to the middle of the century, when nesting again occurred in Cowley County in south-central Kansas. Since then, it has become a common breeding bird in the southern tier of counties and has been introduced to many other counties to the north, where its range continues to expand. The gobbler struts and displays to the females. Although several cocks may use the same strutting area, the dominant male generally consum-mates. The female begins egg laying in late April or early May. The clutch size ranges from 8 to 15 eggs and the young hatch in about 28 days (Johnsgard 1979). The young are able to fly within two weeks and roost in trees as soon as they can. Six to seven months after they hatch, young males break away from the family unit and form their own flocks. Numbers of Turkeys in Kansas flocks may exceed 100.

Habits and Habitat: Turkeys occur in areas of riparian woodland where cover is available. During the nonbreeding season, they are silent, and it may be difficult to find them, despite their large size. During the breeding season, males can be heard for a considerable distance as they strut and gobble to attract females. One gobbler came to within 50 feet of Thompson, gobbling and strutting and seemingly oblivious to his presence. Wild turkeys are generally wary and run or take flight when frightened. However, if unmolested, they may become quite tame and come into barnyards to feed. When frightened, Turkeys take to the air without hesitation, providing a memorable sight.

Food: Turkeys feed primarily on seeds and secondarily on insects. In eastern Kansas, they feed on acorns when available, as well as weed seeds and cultivated cereal grains. In western Kansas, cereal grains and weed seeds make up the bulk of the diet.

An adult Northern Bobwhite (*Colinus virginianus*). Photograph by Mike Blair, courtesy Kansas Department of Wildlife and Parks.

QUAIL
Northern Bobwhite
Colinus virginianus (Linnaeus)

Status: The Northern Bobwhite has been recorded in all 105 counties. Apparently the eastern race, *C. v. virginianus,* moved westward with the settlement of Kansas, and the race *taylori* moved eastward from the western part of the state (Goss 1891).

Period of Occurrence: This quail is a permanent resident.

Breeding: The Northern Bobwhite breeds throughout the state but is more abundant in the eastern half than in the western portion. Laying begins in early to mid-April, with an average clutch size of about 12 to 14 eggs. Females that are unsuccessful in the first nesting attempt may renest, but then they have smaller clutches. This renesting results in the apparently "late" broods, which are frequently seen in September. There appears to be no second nesting when the first is successful. Stoddard (1931) found that about 25 percent of the males assist in incubation. A check of hunters' bags indicates that the fall population of young birds may be as high as 85 percent. (Johnsgard 1973). This corresponds closely with the annual mortality rate and indicates that most breed only once during their lifetime.

Habits and Habitat: The Northern Bobwhite is a bird of timber and prairie-forest ecotones. It is most plentiful in the eastern half where it finds an abundance of habitat to its liking. In the western half, the bobwhite is found mainly along streams with sufficient cover. During feeding hours, it may be found in grain fields but it is usually never far from dense cover. This species is the prime bird hunted for sport in Kansas, with a harvest of 1,924,939 in 1986. Kansas ranks second only to Texas in the number bagged each year.

Bobwhite numbers fluctuate from year to year, depending greatly upon the severity of winter. They seem unable to survive when snow depths exceed a few inches for any length of time. Bobwhites may become quite tame when unmolested and then feed around houses. They have been seen feeding, seemingly oblivious to the bustle around them, in the middle of residential areas in fairly large towns.

Food: The Northern Bobwhite feeds primarily on weed seeds, cereal grains, and insects.

An adult Scaled Quail (*Callipepla squamata*). Photograph by Gene Brehm, courtesy Kansas Department of Wildlife and Parks.

Scaled Quail
Callipepla squamata (Vigors)

Status: The Scaled Quail is a locally common resident south of the
Arkansas River and west of Meade County.

Period of Occurrence: The species
is a permanent resident.

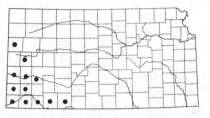

Breeding: This bird should breed
wherever it occurs. However,
there are few breeding records
for the state and confirmed
breeding only in Hamilton,
Kearny, Finney, Stanton, Morton, Stevens, and Clark counties (Tordoff 1956). Its Kansas breeding requirements are not recorded, but
they are assumed to be in sand-sage prairie habitat. It lays 9 to 16 eggs
with an average of 12 to 14 (Bent 1932).

Habits and Habitat: This quail inhabits shortgrass prairie interspersed
with yucca and sagebrush. In Kansas, it is frequently found around
homesteads, particularly those that have woodpiles, old machinery, or
other forms of protection from the rigors of winter. When it is
disturbed, it typically chooses to run rather than fly; this characteristic
makes it difficult for the hunter to spot it. The Scaled Quail is frequently called "blue quail." Like the Northern Bobwhite, it forms
coveys which may contain 75 to 100 birds. These two species are
known to hybridize occasionally in the wild.

Food: The species feeds mainly on weed seeds but also on insects and
cultivated grains. Cultivated grains apparently do not form a major
part of the diet (Johnsgard 1973).

Yellow Rail
Coturnicops noveboracensis (Gmelin)

Status: The Yellow Rail is a rare and possibly overlooked migrant that occurs in the eastern part of the state at least as far west as Barton County. There were only five 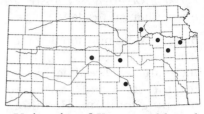 known specimens prior to 1986, all taken in April, September, and October. In the fall of 1986, more than 30 birds struck the WIBW-TV tower near Topeka. These specimens are in the Museum of Natural History at the University of Kansas. Although Goss (1891) considered it a summer resident, there seems to be no evidence of breeding.

Period of Occurrence: Spring records date from 18 April to 28 May, and fall records from 13 September to 21 October.

Breeding: There is no evidence, other than Goss's statement, that the bird breeds in Kansas. The nearest known breeding area is in North Dakota.

Habits and Habitat: Very little is known about the habits of this species in Kansas, because it is so secretive that few birdwatchers have seen it. Two specimens were caught by L. L. Dyche's dog in Douglas County. It probably occurs during migration in marshy areas, such as Cheyenne Bottoms Wildlife Management Area in Barton County and Quivira National Wildlife Refuge in Stafford County. Ivan Boyd observed a Yellow Rail in 1974 at Haskell Bottoms in Douglas County; look for it in this area. This rail feeds in the late evening, and the best ways to try to find it would be to play a tape recording of its call or to use a hunting dog to sniff it out.

Food: The Yellow Rail forages on snails and other small invertebrates in the drier parts of large grass and sedge growing in freshwater marshes (Ripley 1977).

Black Rail
Laterallus jamaicensis (Gmelin)

Status: The Black Rail is a rare local summer resident which, because it is shy and not easily seen, is probably more common than records indicate.

Period of Occurrence: There are few data on when the Black Rail occurs in Kansas. Johnston (1965) records the extreme dates as from March 18 to September 26.

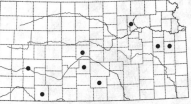

Breeding: The first breeding record was from Manhattan, Riley County, where Dr. C. P. Blachley collected a set of eight eggs in June 1880. Nests or specimens taken during the breeding season have since been recorded from Finney, Barton, Franklin, Kingman, and Meade counties. The Black Rail prefers to nest in marshy areas or in meadows. Its nest is made of grass or sedges, and the clutch size is from 6 to 10 eggs.

Habits and Habitat: The Black Rail is usually found in wet meadows or meadows near marshes, such as Cheyenne Bottoms Wildlife Management Area and Quivira National Wildlife Refuge. It is secretive, but when a tape recording of its call is played late at night in its territory, the Black Rail may approach the recorder. There are reports of this species being picked up by hand as it tried to locate its "adversary." Apparently this bird does not require large areas of marshland or wet meadows, because several Kansas records are from areas with only a few suitable acres.

Food: Black Rails consume insects and some seeds of water plants (Ripley 1977).

An adult King Rail (*Rallus elegans*). Photograph by Roger Boyd.

King Rail
Rallus elegans (Audubon)

Status: The King Rail is an uncommon summer resident in suitable habitat throughout the state.

Period of Occurrence: The King Rail has been recorded 11 months out of the year from 10 February through 28 December; both extreme dates are from Barton County. Although it has not been recorded in January, it may

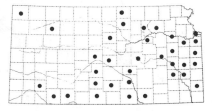

remain throughout the year if there is some open water. Spring migration begins 12 April, and the last date of fall departure is 14 October.

Breeding: The King Rail probably nests regularly only in Barton and Stafford counties and at the Slate Creek Marsh in Sumner County. There are known breeding records for 10 counties. Although regular at the large, central Kansas marshes, the King Rail is able to adapt to small areas as well. A brood was discovered in Cowley County in a wetland area of a little over one acre. A road-kill in Sumner County was near a roadside ditch, where water remained year-round and where cattails were growing. The normal clutch size is 6 to 14 eggs, with an incubation period of about 20 days. The male assists in incubation. When the young hatch, they immediately leave the nest.

Habits and Habitat: Like other rails, the King Rail is a bird of the marshes. It occurs regularly at Cheyenne Bottoms Wildlife Management Area and at Quivira National Wildlife Refuge. It occurs irregularly in other areas, depending on the amount of rainfall; areas that are wet one year after high rainfall will be used but abandoned the next year when the area dries. This bird is secretive but may be seen feeding along the edges of marshes in the early morning or late evening. It is vocal and may be attracted to a tape recording of its call. When disturbed, it usually runs swiftly through the marsh but may fly with its legs dangling and seemingly under poor control. The King Rail is the largest rail in Kansas.

Food: This species subsists mainly on animal matter, with crayfishes making up a large portion of its diet. It also eats small frogs, fishes, snails, and insects. Vegetable matter including seeds and tubers has also been recorded.

Virginia Rail
Rallus limicola (Vieillot)

Status: The Virginia Rail is an uncommon summer resident in marshes throughout Kansas and a casual winter resident in suitable habitat.

Period of Occurrence: The Virginia Rail arrives in migration about mid-April and departs by mid-October. It has been recorded in every month except February.

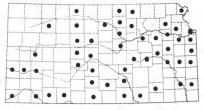

Breeding: The only breeding records are from Barton, Ottawa, and Morton counties, but it undoubtedly breeds regularly also at Quivira National Wildlife Refuge. Clutch size is from 6 to 13 eggs (Ripley 1977), and incubation takes 18 to 20 days with both the male and female incubating. The young leave the nest immediately after they hatch and are quite adept both at scurrying through the marsh grass or at swimming, if necessary. This species may have two broods in one season (ibid.).

Habits and Habitat: This "miniature King Rail" prefers the same type of habitat, namely marshes composed of cattails, sedges, and grasses. It is vocal during the breeding season and can be called readily with a tape recording of its vocalizations. Use of this technique frequently causes Virginia Rails to seem common where previously none had been heard. Often it can be seen in early morning at sunrise or in the late evening just at sunset, when it comes out to feed along the edge of the marsh. When it is frightened into flight, it flies awkwardly with its legs dangling, like other rails. Although it is on the game bird list, it is not regularly hunted in Kansas.

Food: The Virginia Rail eats slugs, snails, small fishes, insect larvae, and earthworms (Ripley 1977).

A juvenile Sora (*Porzana carolina*). Photograph by Marvin D. Schwilling.

Sora
Porzana carolina (Linnaeus)

Status: The Sora is a common transient throughout the state in suitable habitat and a summer resident in marshes and wet grasslands.

Period of Occurrence: Although it is most abundant during spring and fall migration, it may be a winter resident in suitable habitat. The usual date of spring arrival is 6 April, and that of fall departure is 22 October. How-

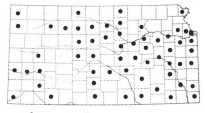

ever, there are records for every month except January.

Breeding: This little rail is an irregular summer resident with nesting records from only Barton, Finney, and Miami counties. It probably nests regularly in Barton and Stafford counties. The nest is placed in cattails, rushes, or sedges, usually near open water above flood level, sometimes on the ground and at other times attached to reeds. The number of eggs varies from 6 to 18, but the usual number is 10 to 12

(Ripley 1977). The incubation period is 18 to 20 days, and the young are precocial.

Habits and Habitat: This bird of the marsh and wet grassy meadows is, like other rails, difficult to observe except in early morning or evening when it comes out to feed along the edges. A tape recording of its call is the easiest way to lure the species or even to determine its abundance in an area. When startled, the Sora takes wing and makes a haphazard flight with its legs dangling. Rails migrate at night and are frequently found dead at the foot of television transmitter towers, which they seem to hit surprisingly often. Thompson found one dead in a field after a violent thunderstorm, the apparent victim of either heavy rain or hail.

Although the Sora is listed as a game bird in Kansas, it probably receives little hunting pressure. It was considered to be a delicacy by the Indians and our forefathers in the East (Ripley 1977).

Food: The principal foods are insects, crustaceans, seeds, and vegetable matter (Ripley 1977).

An adult Purple Gallinule (*Porphyrula martinica*). Photograph by Galen L. Pittman.

GALLINULES
Purple Gallinule
Porphyrula martinica (Linnaeus)

Status: The Purple Gallinule is an occasional summer visitant to the eastern half of Kansas. There are specimen records for Sedgwick, Riley, and Douglas counties; all others are sight records. The first state record was in Douglas County on 26 April 1896.

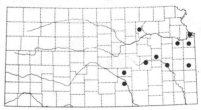

Period of Occurrence: The few dates on record are all from early spring and early summer; the earliest is 4 April, and the latest is 17 June.

Breeding: The Purple Gallinule is not known to breed in Kansas but does breed in southeastern Oklahoma.

Habits and Habitat: There are no data for Kansas, but look for it in marshy or swampy areas with emergent vegetation. It frequently walks on lily pads or lotus.

Food: The Purple Gallinule usually eats aquatic insects, spiders, small frogs, and vegetable matter (Ripley 1977).

An adult Common Moorhen (*Gallinula chloropus*). Photograph by David A. Rintoul.

Common Moorhen
Gallinula chloropus (Linnaeus)

Status: The Common Moorhen is a rare summer resident in the central and eastern part of Kansas and was first recorded in 1878 in Gove County. It is now a regular low-density breeder at Cheyenne Bottoms Wildlife Management Area.

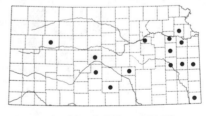

Period of Occurrence: The Common Moorhen (formerly called the "Common Gallinule") has been recorded from 26 March through 27 October (Jefferson County).

Breeding: This rare gallinule may breed throughout the state in suitable habitat. Most breeding records are from Cheyenne Bottoms in Barton County, and there are others (or specimens taken during the breeding season) from Coffey, Stafford, Kingman, Shawnee, and Douglas counties. Look for the nest in marshy areas. It is usually built of dead reeds, cattails, sedges, or other vegetation and may be placed on land, in the water near emergent vegetation, in bushes, or, occasionally, in trees (Ripley 1977). The number of eggs varies, but Johnston (1965) lists the mean for Kansas as 10. The incubation period is about 20 days, and the young are precocial. After three to four weeks, the female abandons the chicks and may start another brood.

Habits and Habitat: Common Moorhens have many habits of the American Coot. They live in marshy areas and are frequently seen with coots, from which they can be distinguished by their bright red bill (the coot's is almost all white). At Cheyenne Bottoms, they are usually seen feeding on vegetation around the dikes. When frightened, they quickly melt away into the vegetation. Although they seem to prefer marshes and marsh edges, they can swim quite well.

Food: This gallinule is primarily a vegetarian but also eats insects and molluscs.

Adult American Coots (*Fulica americana*). Photograph by Frank S. Shipley.

American Coot
Fulica americana (Gmelin)

Status: The American Coot is a common, sometimes abundant, transient throughout the state and is a local summer resident. It has been recorded in every county.

Period of Occurrence: The species has been recorded throughout the year but is most common from 23 February to 28 November. It is rare in winter.

Breeding: Breeding records in Kansas are not numerous, with most from Cheyenne Bottoms Wildlife Management Area in Barton County and from the Quivira National Wildlife Refuge in Stafford County. The coots are numerous in both areas in summer and are assumed to be fairly common breeders. There are also nesting records from Harvey, Finney, Sedgwick, Rooks, and Morton counties, but they probably breed regularly in other counties that have appropriate habitat.

The coot's nest is placed on a mound of old reeds and is usually anchored to new growth. Sometimes the coot makes little effort to conceal the nest and even places it in the open. The number of eggs varies from six to fifteen, but averages about 10. The young leave the nest soon after they hatch; they are distinctive, as they are basically black with scarlet, hairlike down.

Habits and Habitat: This rail is a bird of marshes, rivers, ponds, and lakes. During migration, large rafts of several hundred birds can be seen around large impoundments or marshes, such as Cheyenne Bottoms and the Quivira Refuge. It is not as shy as other rails and may become quite tame when unmolested. It is frequently seen on the dikes of Cheyenne Bottoms, grazing on grasses or just lounging. When startled on water, the American Coot starts running on the water, flapping its wings rapidly until it can gain enough momentum to become airborne. Once aloft, it flies strongly, unlike other rails. It is on the game bird list but is not actively hunted because it is not much of a target and its flesh is said to be less than palatable. This is the "mudhen" described by most hunters.

Food: The American Coot is primarily a vegetarian but may eat some animal matter, such as insects and molluscs.

Adult Sandhill Cranes (*Grus canadensis*). Photograph by Mike Blair, courtesy Kansas Department of Wildlife and Parks.

CRANES
Sandhill Crane
Grus canadensis (Linnaeus)

Status: The Sandhill Crane is a common transient in the western part of the state and is rare in the east. Most records come from west of the Flint Hills, and it gradually becomes more common westward. It occurs casually in summer and in winter.

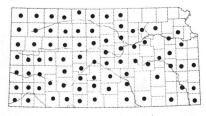

Period of Occurrence: The main migration begins in March, with 10 March the average arrival date; the earliest record is 4 February. Spring migration is usually over by 26 April but may continue until 13 May. The main fall migration begins on 8 October and runs through 23 November; the earliest record is 27 August. Summer occurrences are rare. Winter records should be verified, because the Sandhill Crane is frequently confused with the Great Blue Heron.

Habits and Habitat: The Sandhill Crane, unlike its relative the Whooping Crane, frequently feeds in old grain fields or in new wheat fields in the spring. A flock of over a thousand was observed in a sorghum field near Udall, Sumner County, in 1982; the flock remained for three days. Migratory Sandhill Cranes are regularly observed at Cheyenne

Bottoms Wildlife Management Area and Quivira National Wildlife Refuge. These cranes are wary and take wing when approached; the flock near Udall became nervous when an observer moved closer than half a mile. The calls of the Sandhill Cranes as they fly overhead are an unforgettable sound. The birds are generally heard before they are seen.

Field Marks: These cranes typically fly in groups, making a bugling call as they pass overhead, whereas Great Blue Herons are generally seen singly and are usually quiet during flight. Sandhill Cranes fly with the neck extended; Great Blue Herons fly with the neck pulled back into an S-shaped curve.

Food: These cranes are omnivorous and feed on anything that moves, including frogs, snakes, small rodents, insects, and invertebrates. They also eat vegetable matter such as grain and weed seeds.

Whooping Cranes (*Grus americana*). Photograph by Gene Brehm, courtsey Kansas Department of Wildlife and Parks.

Whooping Crane
Grus americana (Linnaeus)

Status: The Whooping Crane is a rare spring and fall migrant through the state. Central Kansas seems to be the principal flyway, with most records from Cheyenne Bottoms Wildlife Management Area and Quivira National Wildlife Refuge.

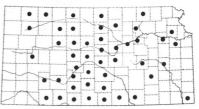

Period of Occurrence: The species has been recorded from 10 February through 28 April in the spring, and in the fall from 5 October through 16 November. The immature bird that appeared with Sandhill Cranes at Quivira Refuge on 10 February 1987 had wintered in Oklahoma. During a cold spell, it retreated back to Oklahoma until 18 March.

Habits and Habitat: The Whooping Crane is primarily a bird of the prairie marshes in Kansas. Most records come from three areas: Cheyenne Bottoms in Barton County, Quivira Refuge in Stafford County, and Kirwin National Wildlife Refuge in Phillips County. These areas are either marshes or large bodies of water with suitable places for the cranes to rest. Whooping Cranes are occasionally seen near farm ponds. Several have been radio-tagged and followed on their migration routes by U.S. Fish and Wildlife Service airplanes. One tagged group spent the night near Eureka in Greenwood County, and another flock overflew the state. Population numbers are on the rise, and the chances of seeing a Whooping Crane are increasing. The population reached a low of 20 birds in 1941 and increased to a high of 177 in the spring of 1987. There are 27 birds in the Gray Lake flock in Idaho, 110 birds in the Wood Buffalo National Park in Canada, and 40 birds in captivity. Many hazards confront migrating cranes. Two of the three young cranes radio-tagged in 1981 died when they hit power lines. One of the Gray Lake flock was killed in a barbed wire fence.

Unfortunately, unless the weather is inclement, Whooping Cranes do not linger in the state. They generally spend one night and are off on their way early the next morning. Unless immediate word gets out when they land and the birdwatcher travels during the night to see them before they depart the next morning, the chances of observing them are slim.

Food: Whooping Cranes consume mostly animal matter, such as frogs, snakes, and, probably, insects. Undoubtedly, they also eat some vegetable matter. On their wintering grounds, they eat many marine animals.

An adult Black-bellied Plover (*Pluvialis squatarola*) in winter plumage. Photograph by David A. Rintoul.

PLOVERS
Black-bellied Plover
Pluvialis squatarola (Linnaeus)

Status: The Black-bellied Plover is an uncommon transient throughout the state and is more common in the spring than in the fall.

Period of Occurrence: This shorebird migrates late, with most records in late April. The earliest spring record is 9 April, and stragglers remain until 19 June. The southward migration begins about 8 August (the earliest

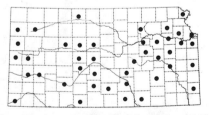

record is 1 July), and migration is generally finished by 21 November. Fall transients have been seen as late as 2 December.

Habits and Habitat: The Black-bellied Plover frequents marshy areas, occasionally sandbars on large rivers, and, less frequently, low-mowed meadows and plowed fields. Although large flocks are reported from

203

outside Kansas, within our state it is most often seen singly. It typically associates with sandpipers.

Field Marks: It is easily identified in flight in all plumages by the black feathers under the wing next to the body.

Food: This plover feeds primarily on invertebrates around marshes. In open fields and grassland, it feeds on insects.

An adult Lesser Golden Plover (*Pluvialis dominica*). Photograph courtesy Kansas Department of Wildlife and Parks.

Lesser Golden Plover
Pluvialis dominica (Müller)

Status: The Lesser Golden Plover is an uncommon transient in the east and in central parts of the state and is rare in the west.

Period of Occurrence: The spring migration begins in late March, with 21 March the earliest date; it usually lasts until late May, but there is an 18 June record. The fall migration starts in early September, with early birds recorded 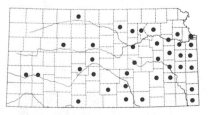 on 20 July. Most have departed by 31 October, but vagrants have been seen in November, January, and February.

Habits and Habitat: The Lesser Golden Plover is a bird of various habitats in its passage through Kansas. While it does not seem to congregate in large flocks in marshes and wet meadows, it is seen in the Flint Hills, often in areas of pasture that have recently been burned. In such areas, flocks of 50 to several hundred birds are often observed during spring migration. They apparently feed on insects that have survived the ravages of the prairie fire. Most of the birds passing through Kansas have not yet attained full breeding plumage. Although they sometimes are abundant in spring in burned areas in the Flint Hills, the fall passage is far less spectacular. Most of the Lesser Golden Plovers that nest in the far north of the North American continent move eastward in the fall and fly over the Atlantic Ocean to South America. Comparatively few use the central flyway in the fall.

This plover was a famous game bird in days gone by. Audubon (1840) writes of a hunt near New Orleans in which parties of 20 to 50 hunters stationed themselves at different places in the vicinity of Lake St. John. He calculated that approximately 48,000 golden plovers were shot that day. Such wholesale slaughter was commonplace.

Food: In Kansas, the principal food is probably insects. It eats berries and other vegetable matter on the breeding grounds.

An adult Snowy Plover (*Charadrius alexandrinus*) with hatchlings. Photograph by Ed and Jean Schulenberg.

Snowy Plover
Charadrius alexandrinus (Linnaeus)

Status: The Snowy Plover, a summer resident of central and southwestern Kansas around salt flats, always occurs in small numbers.

Period of Occurrence: The earliest spring arrival date for the Snowy Plover is 24 March; the average is 8 April. The average departure date is 1 September, and 10 October the latest.

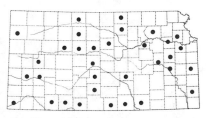

Breeding: This species breeds on white saline flats where its cryptic coloration makes it difficult to spot. There are nesting records from Comanche, Barton, Stafford, Clark,

Russell, Meade, Finney, and Rooks counties, and it may nest around the Slate Creek Marsh in Sumner County where it is present every year. At present, Quivira National Wildlife Refuge seems to be its main breeding area, with Cheyenne Bottoms Wildlife Management Area used in the years when the salt flats are exposed. The nest is a depression on the salt flat where usually three eggs are placed. The average egg-laying date is 10 June. The incubation period is 24 to 28 days. The young are precocial and fledge in 28 days (Boyd 1972).

Habits and Habitat: Snowy Plovers are nearly invisible on the white salt flats, which are their haunts in Kansas. Their light grayish backs and white bellies blend with the white background so well that observers frequently do not see them unless the plovers move. They are usually found singly or in pairs while in Kansas, but they flock on their wintering grounds.

Field Marks: This plover may be confused with two others, the Semipalmated and Piping Plovers, which also occur in Kansas. The Snowy Plover's incomplete neck ring and light coloration readily separate it from the Semipalmated, and its blackish legs, from the Piping Plovers. Neither the Piping nor the Semipalmated Plover nests in Kansas.

Food: This species feeds on insects and aquatic invertebrates along the mudflats which it frequents.

A juvenile Semipalmated Plover (*Charadrius semipalmatus*). Photograph by Marvin D. Schwilling.

Semipalmated Plover
Charadrius semipalmatus (Bonaparte)

Status: The Semipalmated Plover is an uncommon transient throughout the state.

Period of Occurrence: The species has been recorded from 22 March through 8 June and is most common from 7 April to 21 May. Its fall arrival is around 20 July, and it remains until 13 October. Most fall migrants do not arrive until around 12 August.

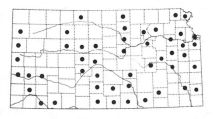

Habits and Habitat: This plover occupies marshes, sandy riverbanks, and temporary water pools. It migrates alone or with only one or two others. The Semipalmated Plover is the commonest of the three small plovers that occur in Kansas and is usually easy to find during migration at Cheyenne Bottoms Wildlife Management Area, Quivira National Wildlife Refuge, and Slate Creek Marsh in Sumner County.

Field Marks: This "miniature Killdeer" has only one collar instead of the Killdeer's two and is the much smaller of the two species.

Food: In Kansas, this species feeds mainly on aquatic invertebrates and some dryland insects.

An adult Piping Plover (*Charadrius melodus*). Photograph by Marvin D. Schwilling, courtesy Kansas Department of Wildlife and Parks.

Piping Plover
Charadrius melodus (Ord)

Status: The Piping Plover is a rare transient throughout the state.

Period of Occurrence: There are spring records for the Piping Plover as early as 21 March and as late as 21 May. Fall migration records begin 7 July and run through 12 September, but it probably occurs later.

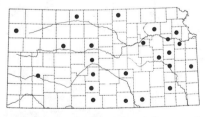

Breeding: There are no records of this bird breeding in Kansas, but search for it in western Kansas, because it breeds directly to the north along the Platte River in Nebraska, and to the west in Washington County, Colorado; Roger Boyd observed it breeding in Oklahoma at Optima Reservoir, about 60 miles south of Liberal. It breeds in areas of salt-encrusted gravel, sand, or pebbly mud around the sparsely vegetated shorelines of shallow lakes and impoundments (Johnsgard 1979).

Habits and Habitat: The Piping Plover occurs mostly in central Kansas at Cheyenne Bottoms Wildlife Management Area and Quivira National Wildlife Refuge. While it is rare in other parts of the state, it might be seen in these marshes, with a little diligence, in April and early May. This plover occupies sandy areas bordering vegetation and open saline flats. Like its close relative the Snowy Plover, the Piping Plover is nearly invisible against the dirty white salt flats. However, its rapid movements and sudden stops expose its presence. The Piping Plover is becoming increasingly rare due to destruction of its breeding habitat. The U.S. Fish and Wildlife Service has recently added it to the Threatened Species list. Several projects are under way to see if its decline can be halted.

Food: The Piping Plover eats aquatic invertebrates and dryland insects.

An adult Killdeer (*Charadrius vociferus*) on nest. Photograph by C. L. Cink.

Killdeer
Charadrius vociferus (Linnaeus)

Status: The Killdeer is a common summer resident throughout the state but occurs rarely in winter around open water.

Period of Occurrence: The Killdeer is a year-round resident in some areas, but most individuals are migratory. The spring migration starts in late February and early March. Killdeers usually depart Kansas by mid-November but 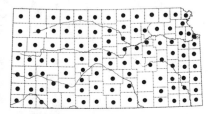 may remain quite common until December. If rivers and other bodies of water freeze early, they leave earlier.

Breeding: This species breeds throughout Kansas. The eggs are laid from 10 March to 10 July, with a usual clutch of four. The nest is placed in a depression, sometimes a great distance from water. Plowed fields, barnyards, roads, and gardens are favorite nesting sites, albeit sometimes hazardous. There are few rural Kansans who have not observed the broken-wing act put on by the distraught parents of young Killdeer, and many a farmer has stopped his tractor to search for the carefully camouflaged nest so as not to crush the eggs. Killdeers may have two broods. Thompson observed a pair fledge young in a field; a few weeks later, apparently the same pair brought off another group on the same acre. Both parents incubate and rear the young. Incubation takes approximately 21 days. The young are precocious; when they leave the nest soon after hatching, they seem to be more legs than body.

Habits and Habitat: The Killdeers' Latin name *vociferus* is aptly applied to these noisy birds, whose habit of flying up at every disturbance and crying "killdeer" has saved many from would-be predators. They can be quite obnoxious to a hunter trying to stalk game or a birdwatcher trying to get a better look at a rare bird. When unmolested, they may be quite tame and locate close to human habitation. Thompson had one breeding pair with young in the yard about 50 feet from the back door; they became tolerant of humans and allowed people to approach to within 30 feet or so before taking wing. Killdeers form large flocks during migration, particularly in the fall, when groups of 30 to 40 birds are not uncommon.

Food: Killdeers eat primarily insects, including grasshoppers, caterpillars, weevils, and many other insect pests. Aquatic invertebrates are also in the diet.

An adult Mountain Plover (*Charadrius montanus*). Photograph by Roger Boyd.

Mountain Plover
Charadrius montanus (Townsend)

Status: The Mountain Plover, a once-common summer resident of the high plains of western Kansas, is now reduced in numbers and is quite rare. Goss (1891) considered it a common bird, but the plowing of the shortgrass prairie has left little breeding habitat.

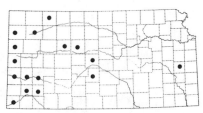

Period of Occurrence: Records are scanty and range from 18 April to 16 September. The species undoubtedly arrives much earlier and probably leaves much later.

Breeding: Although it was once considered abundant in the summer, the Mountain Plover is now probably a rare breeding bird. The most recent breeding record is from Hamilton County (Rising and Kilgore 1964). In 1982, young birds were brought from Colorado and raised in pens north of Sharon Springs in Wallace County. They were released in the fall in the hope that they would return in 1983 or 1984 to breed. As of 1986, there has been no indication that any of the birds returned. The nest is a slight depression which may be lined. The Mountain Plover probably starts nesting in May and usually lays three eggs.

Habits and Habitat: This species occurs only on the dry upland shortgrass prairie during the breeding season; however, during the nonbreeding season, it may be found in wetter areas. There are records for Cheyenne Bottoms Wildlife Management Area. More observations are needed from Greeley, Hamilton, Wallace, and other western counties that still possess large tracts of shortgrass prairie.

Food: This plover feeds mainly on insects; grasshoppers are probably the largest part of the diet.

Black-necked Stilt
Himantopus mexicanus (Müller)

Status: The Black-necked Stilt is a rare summer resident at Cheyenne Bottoms Wildlife Management Area and Quivira National Wildlife Refuge and is more common at the latter. It is a sporadic visitor elsewhere in the state.

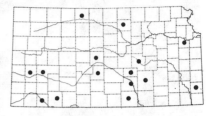

Period of Occurrence: The records for the Black-necked Stilt's arrival and departure are scant. The extremes are a 21 March arrival and a 3 September departure.

Breeding: This shorebird is known to breed only at Cheyenne Bottoms and at Quivira Refuge. Its numbers seem to be increasing at Quivira Refuge and decreasing at Cheyenne Bottoms, where many water problems in the last few years have made the area unsuitable for nesting. The Black-necked Stilt may have been a breeding bird long before its first nest was found in the 1960s; a hundred years ago, Goss (1886) said, "Without doubt the birds occasionally breed in southwestern Kansas." The stilts' nesting sites and nests are highly variable. Sometimes they nest on open ground with no vegetation and with their eggs upon bare earth; at other times the nest is built upon elaborate platforms made of sticks. Bent (1927) quotes a Mr. Dawson who said stilts had elevated their nests and eggs when floodwaters threatened to swamp them. Apparently twigs, earth, or anything movable was forced under the eggs to protect them. The usual clutch is four eggs. The young are precocious and leave the nest as soon as their wobbly legs allow.

Habits and Habitat: The Black-necked Stilt is a true marsh bird which frequents shallow marsh edges and shorelines. Its very long legs make it adept at probing in quite deep water for food. Kansas is on the northern edge of its range in the central plains; to find and observe it is well worth the effort.

Field Marks: This species is one of the more easily identified shorebirds because of its contrasting black-and-white patterns and pink legs.

Food: The food is varied and consists mainly of animal matter, including insects, small crayfishes, snails, and tiny fishes.

An adult Black-necked Stilt (*Himantopus mexicanus*). Photograph by Galen L. Pittman.

An adult male American Avocet (*Recurvirostra americana*). Photograph by Frank S. Shipley.

AVOCETS
American Avocet
Recurvirostra americana (Gmelin)

Status: The American Avocet is a common migrant and summer resident in the central and western parts of the state and is an uncommon-to-rare transient in the east.

Period of Occurrence: The American Avocet arrives in Kansas around 1 April and departs around 21 October. The extreme dates are 13 March and 27 December.

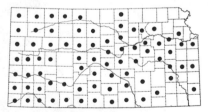

Breeding: Although the American Avocet is now a common breeding bird at Cheyenne Bottoms Wildlife Management Area and Quivira National Wildlife Refuge, apparently it has not always been common. Goss (1886) listed it as a rare breeding bird. Tordoff (1956) considered it an uncommon breeding bird in the west, and it probably rarely nests elsewhere. The increase in breeding density may be a result of a normally stabilized water supply at the refuges—although their status at Cheyenne Bottoms is uncertain due to high-water levels followed by no water over the past few years. Bent (1927) lists the avocet as breeding at Dodge City (Ford County) and Larned (Pawnee County) but gives no specifics. The nest is placed on bare ground, or it may be an elaborate structure of grass and sticks, with possibly some feathers added. Like the Black-necked Stilt (a close relative), the avocet also attempts to elevate its nest when floodwaters threaten. The usual clutch size is four, and the young are precocial.

Habits and Habitat: The large size and coloration of these magnificent shorebirds leaves no doubt in the minds of even amateur birdwatchers as to their identity. Their bright white, buff, and black coloration draws attention, as does their fierce nest defense; anyone who approaches an avocet's nest will soon know that it is forbidden territory by the diving and calling of the parents. As noise-makers, they are second only to Killdeers. Cheyenne Bottoms and Quivira Refuge are excellent areas to observe large numbers of these birds. As they feed, they make sweeping motions through the mud with their up-curved bills to catch small aquatic invertebrates as they are dislodged. American Avocets also swim well, and it is not uncommon to see them swimming in water much deeper than the length of their legs.

Food: The species eats aquatic invertebrates as well as insects along the shoreline and also some vegetable matter, such as grasses and aquatic vegetation.

An adult Greater Yellowlegs (*Tringa melanoleuca*). Photograph by Ed and Jean Schulenberg.

SANDPIPERS
Greater Yellowlegs
Tringa melanoleuca (Gmelin)

Status: The Greater Yellowlegs is a common migrant throughout the state, although a casual summer and winter visitor.

Period of Occurrence: The Greater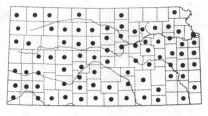
Yellowlegs is one of the earlier
shorebirds to appear in the
spring. The normal arrival time
is around 21 March; the earliest
record is 27 February. It generally leaves by 22 May but has been
recorded on 12 June. The average southward arrival is around 2
August; 12 July is the earliest date. Migration continues until 29
October, with an extreme fall date of 16 December. Birds recorded in
the summer are probably first-year, nonbreeding birds that have only
moved as far north as Kansas. Also, shorebirds thought to be nonbreeding birds sometimes return south soon after reaching the breeding grounds. That may account for the large number of shorebirds
found in Kansas in late July and August.

Habits and Habitat: These yellowlegs are usually found around
marshes, rivers, lakeshores, or temporary pools of water. They, like
the Killdeer, are very vocal and are one of the first marsh birds to cry
an alarm when possible danger approaches.

Field Marks: Distinguishing the Greater from the Lesser Yellowlegs is a
hard task visually unless the two are seen side-by-side. However, the
calls differ; the Greater Yellowlegs usually has a three-note whistle,
while the Lesser Yellowlegs has a one- or two-note whistle, rarely
three-notes.

Food: Greater Yellowlegs eat primarily aquatic invertebrates and small
minnows. In damp grassy meadows, they probably eat insects and
worms.

An adult Lesser Yellowlegs (*Tringa flavipes*). Photograph by Gerald J. Wiens.

Lesser Yellowlegs
Tringa flavipes (Gmelin)

Status: The Lesser Yellowlegs is a common transient throughout the state. It is occasionally seen also in summer and in winter.

Period of Occurrence: The Lesser Yellowlegs is another early migrant that arrives in Kansas around 1 March and remains until 1 June. Its southward fall migration begins around 12 July and continues to around 9 November, although birds have been sighted throughout the winter.

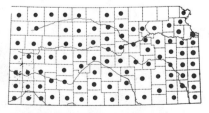

Habits and Habitat: This yellowlegs has a tendency to flock more than does the Greater Yellowlegs. See the species account for the Greater Yellowlegs for more information.

Food: The diet is the same as the Greater Yellowlegs'.

Solitary Sandpiper
Tringa solitaria (Wilson)

Status: The Solitary Sandpiper is an uncommon transient throughout the state and may be recorded in nearly all the summer months.

Period of Occurrence: The Solitary Sandpiper arrives in Kansas on 26 March and stays until 21 May. Although there are records for all the summer months, the main southward migration starts around 12 July and runs until 5 October.

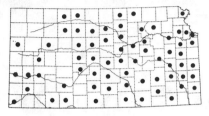

Habits and Habitat: As its name indicates, this sandpiper is largely a solitary species that is rarely found in flocks. It inhabits marshes, lakeshores, vegetated river bars, woodland pools, and temporary pools of water in meadows. While not a shy bird, it frequently goes unnoticed until flushed. It breeds in trees in the muskegs of the north; unusual for a shorebird, it lays its eggs in old nests of songbirds.

Field Marks: In flight, the conspicuous white outer tail feathers with black bars make a good field identification mark. While standing quietly, it nods its head.

Food: The Solitary Sandpiper feeds on aquatic invertebrates, including insects.

An adult Willet (*Catoptrophorus semipalmatus*) in winter plumage. Photograph by David A. Rintoul.

Willet
Catoptrophorus semipalmatus (Gmelin)

Status: The Willet is an uncommon transient throughout the state.

Period of Occurrence: The species has been recorded from 7 April until 11 June and from 1 August through 24 October. There are casual records for all of the summer months.

Breeding: Although the Willet does not breed in Kansas, it breeds nearby in the sandhills of Nebraska. This may account for our summer records.

Habits and Habitat: This large shorebird is found in Kansas around marshes, river bars, lakeshores, ponds, and temporary pools of water. During migration, the Willet is generally seen in small flocks. It is one of the larger shorebirds that passes through Kansas.

Field Marks: The Willet's spring and fall plumages are different, but it can be identified at all seasons by the white and black wing pattern in flight. A noisy bird when disturbed, it makes the distinctive call "wee-willet," the probable origin of its name.

Food: The Willet generally probes in the ground for invertebrates, but it also takes some insects. Most of its food is aquatic larvae, molluscs, and small animals, but it also eats some vegetable matter.

An adult Spotted Sandpiper (*Actititis macularia*). Photograph by Marvin D. Schwilling.

Spotted Sandpiper
Actitis macularia (Linnaeus)

Status: The Spotted Sandpiper is a common transient throughout the state. It is a rare summer resident.

Period of Occurrence: The Spotted Sandpiper arrives as early as 27 March and remains in small numbers throughout the summer. The earliest spring arrival date is 19 March, with most spring migrants passing through 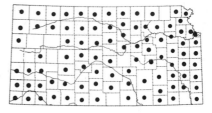 by 28 May. They return on their way south on 15 July and leave by 4 November. There is one midwinter record on 20 December.

Breeding: Breeding records are spotty, possibly due to lack of observations rather than lack of nesting birds. There are nesting records for Barton, Harvey, Meade, Rooks, and Leavenworth counties. The nest may be well away from water and placed in grass or under bushes. The usual clutch size is four. The female establishes the territory, and the male is either rejected or accepted; if the latter, breeding and egg laying get under way rapidly. The female may remain monogamous or, leaving the male to incubate, pair with another male and start another brood. The incubation period is normally 20 to 24 days. The young are precocial. Fledging occurs in 17 to 18 days after hatching.

Habits and Habitat: The Spotted Sandpiper occurs around lakes, ponds, streams, temporary pools, and marshes. It is one of the few sandpipers found along woodland streams. This sandpiper becomes very tame when unmolested and feeds close to fishermen. Johnsgard (1981) considers the Spotted Sandpiper to be one of the most abundant and widespread shorebirds in North America.

Field Marks: Several of its characteristics make it easy to identify. When it feeds along the shoreline, it teeters—a trait exhibited by no other shorebird in Kansas. Another good field identification is its flight pattern when flushed; it then uses only half a wingbeat, exposing the narrow white wing stripe. It does not flock.

Food: The Spotted Sandpiper eats both aquatic and terrestrial invertebrates, including insects. It also catches insects out of the air.

An adult Upland Sandpiper (*Bartramia longicauda*). Photograph by David A. Rintoul.

Upland Sandpiper
Bartramia longicauda (Bechstein)

Status: The Upland Sandpiper is a common migrant in the eastern half of the state and is uncommon in the west. It breeds commonly in the Flint Hills and less commonly elsewhere; it may be absent in the extreme west as a breeding bird.

Period of Occurrence: The earliest recorded arrival date is 6 March, but most birds arrive around 4 April. The latest departure date is 26 September, but most birds have left by late August. The south-ward migration begins very early, and the call of the Upland Sandpiper can be heard commonly at night in early July, as they pass overhead.

Breeding: There are few nesting records, due to the difficulty of discovering the nest. Johnston (1965) has summarized most Kansas nesting records. He stated that eggs were laid from 21 April until 10 June, with the average clutch date of 5 May. The female lays four eggs in a small depression in the prairie, usually under a clump of grass. The nest is lined with grass. The incubation period is 24 days (Johnsgard 1981). The young leave the nest soon after hatching and are attended by one parent, usually the male (ibid.). Buss (1951) suggested that both parents attend the young. The young fledge in 32 to 34 days (ibid.). The adult "sits tight" and will not flush until almost stepped on. Even then, it moves only a few feet away, trying vainly to distract the would-be predator. Thompson found a nest in which the young were just starting to hatch, and he trapped and banded the adult. When it was released, instead of flying out of his hand, it stood up and "scolded" him. After a minute, it jumped to the ground and returned to the nest to finish the hatching process.

Habits and Habitat: The Upland Sandpiper is a bird of the tall- and mixed-grass prairies of the eastern half of Kansas. It sometimes seems as if an Upland Sandpiper is atop each post in the Flint Hills. In the spring, its ascending and then descending song, a part of courtship ritual, is inseparable from the Flint Hills. After each flight song, the bird may dive toward the ground and alight daintily, holding the wings above the back before folding them. During the breeding season, the adults use a shallow wingbeat. After breeding and rearing are over, they drop the flutter wingbeat, become strong fliers, and migrate to Argentina for the winter.

The time has probably come to lay to rest certain myths about the population of Upland Sandpipers. Many recent statements about its scarcity have been based on observations in the eastern United States, where few large tracts of open grassland remain. The Upland Sandpiper is not rare in the central United States in mixed-grass prairie, and most Kansans consider it an abundant bird in the Flint Hills. Upland Sandpipers do not appear to nest in prairies of less than about 40 acres, which may explain its present scarcity in the eastern United States.

This species is tame during the breeding season but becomes quite wary afterwards.

Food: The diet is primarily insects.

A mounted exhibit specimen of the Eskimo Curlew (*Numenius borealis*). Photograph by Marvin D. Schwilling.

Eskimo Curlew
Numenius borealis (Forster)

Status: The Eskimo Curlew, a formerly abundant migrant through Kansas, is now on the verge of extinction. However, enough records from North and South America keep surfacing to make one believe that there must be a small breeding population still extant. In 1982 at Cheyenne Bottoms Wildlife Management Area, Ed Martinez observed a small curlew

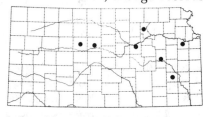

for several minutes. The bird was obviously too small for a Whimbrel and may well have been an Eskimo Curlew. Even as late as 1903, Snow (1903) listed it as an abundant migrant. There are five known Kansas specimens, one each from Russell, Ellis, Lyon, Woodson, and Douglas counties.

Period of Occurrence: In the past, the species occurred from 13 April through 15 June and from 5 to 28 September.

Habits and Habitat: The Eskimo Curlew, which flew in huge flocks, was hunted to the verge of extinction for market. There was a noted decline in numbers in the 1870s, and by the turn of the century it had become an uncommon bird, despite Snow's 1903 listing of it as abundant.

Food: Like all upland curlews, this species feeds on insects and, during the summer, on berries—primarily the Crowberry *(Empetrum nigrum).*

An adult Whimbrel (*Numenius phaeopus*). Photograph by David A. Rintoul.

Whimbrel
Numenius phaeopus (Linnaeus)

Status: The Whimbrel is a rare transient throughout the state. Most recent sightings are from Cheyenne Bottoms Wildlife Management Area. There is one known speci-men, which was collected on 22 May 1963 in Barton County.

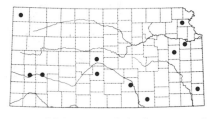

Period of Occurrence: The follow-ing records are all from Barton County: spring arrival, 3 April, and spring departure, 22 May. The first southward migrants appear on 30 June, and the last record is on 24 October.

Habits and Habitat: All records from Kansas have been from marshes or lakeshores.

Food: The Whimbrel probes for its food in marshes. Its food in Kansas probably consists mainly of invertebrates such as insects and worms. On the breeding ground, it also eats berries.

An adult Long-billed Curlew (*Numenius americanus*). Photograph by Marvin D. Schwilling, courtesy Kansas Department of Wildlife and Parks.

Long-billed Curlew
Numenius americanus (Bechstein)

Status: The Long-billed Curlew is an uncommon transient in the western half of the state and rare in the eastern half. It breeds rarely in the southwest and appears casually as a nonbreeder elsewhere in summer.

Period of Occurrence: The earliest record is 23 March; most have departed by 17 May, although a few remain to nest. Dates for the

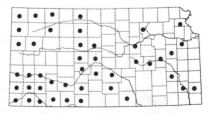

southward migration are hard to determine, but birds have been seen from 21 August to 25 September. There are records for all summer months.

Breeding: The Long-billed Curlew was formerly a breeding bird of the High Plains, where Dr. J. A. Allen found it breeding in the 1870s (1872). The only modern breeding records are from Morton, Finney, and Stanton counties. It builds its nest in arid places in western Kansas, usually remote from water. The nest is a shallow depression, possibly lined, and contains four eggs. The young are precocial and leave the nest as soon as they dry. More up-to-date information on the Kansas breeding of this species is needed.

Habits and Habitat: Unquestionably, Long-billed Curlews are the most spectacular shorebirds occurring in the state. They stand 18 to 20 inches tall, and their beak, which curves downward, may be up to 10 inches long. The easiest place to observe them is at Cheyenne Bottoms Wildlife Management Area or Quivira National Wildlife Refuge. They are also readily observed in the summer on their nesting grounds on dry upland pastures in Morton County. Although they are never abundant, there is a reasonably good chance of seeing them during migration, when they can be found probing soft mud with their long bill. They associate quite readily with their smaller cousins, dwarfing them in the process.

Field Marks: Besides their spectacular body size and long beak, the Long-billed Curlews can be identified when they fly by the cinnamon-colored linings of their underwings.

Food: The species probes in the mud for invertebrates such as worms. In upland areas, it feeds on insects and probably on berries when available.

Hudsonian Godwit
Limosa haemastica (Linnaeus)

Status: The Hudsonian Godwit is an uncommon spring migrant that probably occurs most often in the central portion of the state. It is occasionally common during spring migration at Cheyenne Bottoms Wildlife Management Area, Quivira National Wildlife Refuge, and Slate Creek Marsh (Sumner County). It is a rare fall migrant.

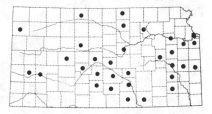

Period of Occurrence: The Hudsonian Godwit arrives on its way north around 8 April and completes its spring migration by 23 May. There is one summer record for 30 June. The return migration begins on 4 August and is over by 26 September.

Habits and Habitat: This is one of the larger shorebirds passing through Kansas, and it is certainly one of the most beautiful. The Hudsonian Godwit feeds in water nearly as deep as the length of its legs, and it frequently plunges its head underwater to probe the bottom of the marsh. It is usually found in flocks. Its northward spring migration is largely through the interior of the United States. In the fall, however, they congregate around James Bay in Canada, then swing eastward out over the Atlantic Ocean en route to their wintering grounds in southern South America.

Feeding in water three to four inches deep sometimes causes problems for this bird. Near Emporia, Wimmer (Andrews 1954) found a Hudsonian Godwit unable to fly. It had stepped into an open mussel which had promptly closed; the extra weight was too great for the godwit to carry. The mussel was broken loose and the bird released.

Field Marks: The Hudsonian Godwit is quickly identified by its dark chestnut color and its slightly upturned bill.

Food: The species probes in soft mud for invertebrates.

An adult Marbled Godwit (*Limosa fedoa*). Photograph by Mark A. Chappell.

Marbled Godwit
Limosa fedoa (Linnaeus)

Status: The Marbled Godwit is an uncommon migrant throughout the state and is probably most common in the central third.

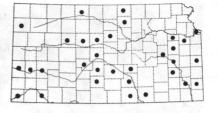

Period of Occurrence: It arrives around 3 April and remains to June 19. The southward migration begins 9 September and finishes by 13 October, with a late date of 23 November.

Habits and Habitat: In Kansas, the Marbled Godwit is generally seen with other shorebirds, frequently with Hudsonian Godwits. It is a regular visitor to Cheyenne Bottoms Wildlife Management Area and Quivira National Wildlife Refuge, although not nearly as common as the Hudsonian Godwit in the spring.

Field Marks: Among shorebirds, this species is second in size only to the Long-billed Curlew, a bird with which a careless observer might confuse it. Its coloration is similar to the Long-billed Curlew's, but the godwit's bill turns up and the curlew's turns down. Both have cinnamon-colored underwings.

Food: The godwit probes in the mud with its long bill for invertebrates.

An adult Ruddy Turnstone (*Arenaria interpres*). Photograph by Mark A. Chappell.

Ruddy Turnstone
Arenaria interpres (Linnaeus)

Status: The Ruddy Turnstone is a rare migrant throughout the state. Most observations come from Barton and Stafford counties.

Period of Occurrence: The species occurs in spring from 18 April to 12 June but is most common in Barton County from 18 May to 1 June. The fall passage is from 9 August to 8 October, but most pass through Cheyenne Bottoms 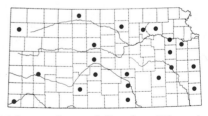 Wildlife Management Area from 20 September to 8 October. There is one late date of 11 December.

Habits and Habitat: The Ruddy Turnstone is found here along shorelines of marshes, lakes, and rivers, away from vegetation. On its regular migration routes, flocks sometimes contain thousands, but in Kansas, it occurs either singly or in very small flocks.

Food: In Kansas, the Ruddy Turnstone probably feeds mainly along muddy shorelines. Along coastal beaches elsewhere, it flips over stones and other objects to reach the insects underneath.

Red Knot
Calidris canutus (Linnaeus)

Status: The Red Knot is a rare spring and fall transient, mainly in central Kansas. Most records come from Cheyenne Bottoms Wildlife Management Area in Barton County.

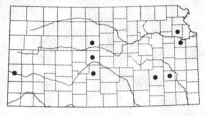

Period of Occurrence: The Red Knot has been recorded from 17 April through 1 June in the spring, and 2 August through 26 September in the fall, with an extreme date of 10 October. Most records are in September.

Habits and Habitat: Red Knots are usually found around mudflats in marshes. Although they are rare here and usually found singly, flocks on the wintering grounds in South America may contain 10,000 or more. This species is one of the more attractive shorebirds in breeding plumage. Because of its rarity in the state, very little is known about it locally. Ed Martinez has banded several at Cheyenne Bottoms, but few other ornithologists have seen it in Kansas.

Food: The species probably feeds on aquatic invertebrates which it probes for in the mud.

An adult Sanderling (*Calidris alba*). Photograph by Galen L. Pittman.

Sanderling
Calidris alba (Pallas)

Status: The Sanderling is an uncommon transient at Cheyenne Bottoms Wildlife Management Area and Quivira National Wildlife Refuge. Its status elsewhere in the state is not well known, but it is probably a rare transient.

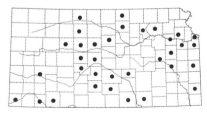

Period of Occurrence: This shorebird has been recorded from 14 March but is more common from 20 April through 8 June. There are a few summer records in July and August. The southward migration begins around 8 August, and most have passed through by 16 October. There is an extreme date of 9 November.

Habits and Habitat: Like so many of the shorebird transients in Kansas, the Sanderling is a long-range migrant. It breeds in the high Arctic tundra and winters on the coasts of North America and south to Argentina and Chile. It prefers sandy shorelines to mud and tends to occur in areas of the marshes that have a sandy substrate. It occurs here either on mudflats or along river sandbars.

Field Marks: The Sanderling is one of the easier sandpipers to recognize, as it has a conspicuous white wing stripe in flight and in the spring has a very pale gray appearance, even with the rusty-brown back and head.

Food: The Sanderling feeds on invertebrates obtained from probing the sand and is adept at stealing fishermen's bait along the Gulf Coast. Johnsgard (1981) also lists vegetable matter.

An adult Semipalmated Sandpiper (*Calidris pusilla*). Photograph by Frank S. Shipley.

Semipalmated Sandpiper
Calidris pusilla (Linnaeus)

Status: The Semipalmated Sandpiper is a common transient through-out the state and is casual in winter and summer.

Period of Occurrence: The Semipalmated Sandpiper has been recorded in the spring from 4 April through 3 June, with an extreme date of 11 March. The fall migration begins in July and runs through 24 October, but 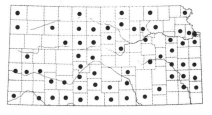 some remain until 25 November. There is a 28 December record.

Habits and Habitat: This species is one of the most common sandpipers migrating through Kansas; like most sandpipers that pass through our area, it breeds in the northern tundra. It feeds in marshes, temporary ponds, and on sandbars and frequently mixes with other "peeps" (the nickname for small sandpipers) in enormous flocks.

Field Marks: Although this sandpiper and the Western Sandpiper have partially webbed feet, this feature is useful only in the hand. The grayer coloration of the Semipalmated Sandpiper and its black feet and bill may be useful in helping to separate it from the Western and the Least Sandpipers.

Food: Bent (1927) lists the diet as insects, small molluscs, worms, and crustaceans.

An adult Western Sandpiper (*Calidris mauri*). Photograph by Marvin D. Schwilling.

Western Sandpiper
Calidris mauri (Cabanis)

Status: The Western Sandpiper is a common transient through the central part of the state but uncommon elsewhere. It has been recorded in early winter.

Period of Occurrence: This sandpiper arrives around 10 April and departs 6 June, with the earliest spring arrival on 12 March. The fall migration is from 18 July through 24 Sep- 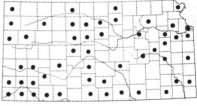 tember; the latest fall record is 25 October. It is casual in early winter, with recorded dates of 17–27 December.

Habits and Habitat: The Western Sandpiper is commonly found associating with other "peeps" in the central Kansas marshes. It feeds in large mixed flocks on the mudflats, where it uses its drooped bill to probe for invertebrates. It breeds in the tundra of Alaska and commonly winters along the far southern coasts of North America and south into South America.

Field Marks: This species closely resembles both the Least and Semipalmated Sandpipers. It can be separated from the Least

Sandpiper by the all-black legs, drooping bill, and light breast. The Western Sandpiper is more rufous on the back than the Semipalmated Sandpiper and is somewhat larger.

Food: This sandpiper feeds mainly on invertebrates that it probes for in the mud or catches on the surface.

An adult Least Sandpiper (*Calidris minutilla*). Photograph by Frank S. Shipley.

Least Sandpiper
Calidris minutilla (Vieillot)

Status: The Least Sandpiper is a common transient throughout the state. It is casual in summer and winter.

Period of Occurrence: This little shorebird has been recorded in the spring as early as 5 March but is more common from 4 April through 28 May, with a late record of 10 June. There are summer records for July, but the 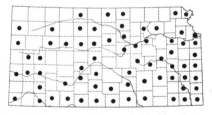 main fall migration starts around 6 August and runs through 24 October. There is an extreme date of 25 November, and early winter records run from 11 December through 27 December.

Habits and Habitat: The Least Sandpiper is yet another breeding shorebird of northern North America that passes through Kansas in migration. It is probably one of the most common of the small "peeps," and flocks of several hundred birds at the central Kansas marshes are not uncommon. This bird's bill is short, and most of the feeding is done at or near the surface of the mud.

Field Marks: This smallest of Kansas shorebirds is readily distinguished from other "peeps" by its rusty coloration and yellowish legs.

Food: The species eats small crustaceans, insects, and other invertebrates.

An adult White-rumped Sandpiper (*Calidris fuscicollis*). Photograph by Galen L. Pittman.

White-rumped Sandpiper
Calidris fuscicollis (Vieillot)

Status: The White-rumped Sandpiper is a common, sometimes abundant, migrant through central Kansas. It is uncommon elsewhere. It occasionally occurs in the summer.

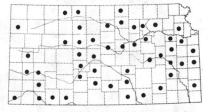

Period of Occurrence: The White-rumped Sandpiper is the latest spring migrant of all the shorebirds. The earliest ever recorded was on 27 March, but the majority of the migrants do not arrive until mid-May, then passing through until around mid-June. Birds have been seen in July. The southward migration begins in late August and runs to 26 September, with an extreme date of 2 October.

Habits and Habitat: This shorebird passes through the state before and after breeding in northern North America. It is particularly abundant in the marshes of Cheyenne Bottoms Wildlife Management Area and Quivira National Wildlife Refuge, where flocks of many thousands have been observed. It prefers the open mudflats.

Field Marks: The white rump for which this sandpiper is named is visible only in flight. It is similar to the Baird's Sandpiper but is streaked on the back instead of scaled. The late migration helps to separate it from some of the other "peeps." The white rump is a good field mark late in the spring, when this is the most common shorebird in the central Kansas marshes.

Food: There is little known about the diet, but it is assumed to be insects and other invertebrates.

An adult Baird's Sandpiper (*Calidris bairdii*). Photograph by Mike Blair, courtesy Kansas Department of Wildlife and Parks.

Baird's Sandpiper
Calidris bairdii (Coues)

Status: The Baird's Sandpiper is a common transient and casual summer visitor throughout the state.

Period of Occurrence: This species is one of the earliest shorebirds in the spring; the earliest record is on 25 February. Most of the birds return in late March and depart by 23 May. There is a summer record for 14 July. For the fall,

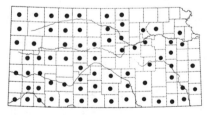

Baird's Sandpipers arrive in August and depart by 21 October; the extreme departure date is 6 December.

Habits and Habitat: The Baird's Sandpiper is another tundra breeder that passes through Kansas. It is a long-distance migrant that winters as far south as Tierra del Fuego. It tends to stay around grassy marshes but also feeds on mudflats with other "peeps." It inhabits temporary pools in fields after heavy rains.

Field Marks: The scaled back and the breast's dark markings on a buffy background help to identify this species. When folded, the wings extend beyond the end of the tail.

Food: Most sandpipers are mud probers, but the Baird's Sandpiper feeds primarily on surface insects (Bent 1927).

An adult Pectoral Sandpiper (*Calidris melanotos*). Photograph by C. L. Cink.

Pectoral Sandpiper
Calidris melanotos (Vieillot)

Status: The Pectoral Sandpiper is a common transient throughout the state in spring and fall. The few birds recorded during the summer are probably birds who have dis-
continued their northward movement.

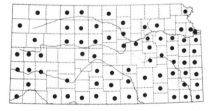

Period of Occurrence: There are spring records from 14 March until 5 June. They occur sporadi-
cally in the summer, with a 7 July record. The main influx in the fall starts around 10 August; the last fall record is on 26 November.

Habits and Habitat: The Pectoral Sandpiper is a breeding bird of the tundra, passing through Kansas on its way both north and south. It is one of the larger sandpipers and frequents the grassy edges of marshes, flooded fields, and river bars.

Field Marks: The sharp line of demarcation on the breast and the large size will help to separate this sandpiper from the other "peeps." It may be confused with the Sharp-tailed Sandpiper *(Calidris acuminata),* but the latter has a more rufous crown and its breast is suffused with a buffy-orange coloration. (There are no records of the Sharp-tailed Sandpiper from the state, but look for it in the fall.)

Food: Bent (1927) lists the food as amphipods, vegetable matter, insects, and spiders.

An adult Dunlin (*Calidris alpina*). Photograph by Frank S. Shipley.

Dunlin
Calidris alpina (Linnaeus)

Status: The Dunlin is a rare transient in the east and central part of the state and is casual in early winter. Most records are from Cheyenne Bottoms Wildlife Management Area and Quivira National Wildlife Refuge.

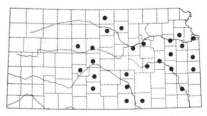

Period of Occurrence: There is a sight record on 11 March, but most spring observations fall between 4 April and 26 May, with a late date of 6 June. The fall passage is usually between 17 August and 27 October, and extreme dates are 15 July and 28 November. There is a winter record of a bird observed in Sedgwick County in January.

Habits and Habitat: This "red-backed" sandpiper is most often seen on mudflats or sandy beaches. Thompson has observed it numerous times on the north end of Quivira Refuge, where it fed with other small sandpipers on the barren flats. Outside of the central Kansas region, one might observe this species with some frequency at the Slate Creek Marsh in Sumner County. It uses its down-curved beak to probe in the mud for food.

Field Marks: The combination of a rufous back and black belly makes the Dunlin unmistakable in Kansas during spring migration. In the fall, the drooping bill, gray plumage, and white wing stripe will assist in identification.

Food: The Dunlin probes the mud or sand bottoms in shallow water or mudflats. It feeds primarily on invertebrates.

Curlew Sandpiper
Calidris ferruginea (Pontoppidan)

Status: The Curlew Sandpiper is a casual visitor. There is one specimen from Cheyenne Bottoms Wildlife Management Area, collected on 4 August 1972; it is in the Fort Hays State University collection. There are three additional sightings: 8 August 1969, 15 May 1971, and 18 July through 3 August 1975. All were seen at Cheyenne Bottoms by Ed Martinez.

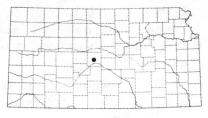

An adult Stilt Sandpiper (*Calidris himantopus*). Photograph by Frank S. Shipley.

Stilt Sandpiper
Calidris himantopus (Bonaparte)

Status: The Stilt Sandpiper is a common transient in central Kansas but uncommon elsewhere.

Period of Occurrence: The species may arrive as early as 12 March but generally arrives on 6 April and departs by 1 June, with a late spring record of 7 June. The autumnal passage begins in mid-summer on 18 July. Most birds

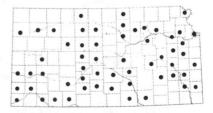

have passed through by 25 September; there is a late record of 19 November.

Habits and Habitat: This sandpiper feeds frequently with other small sandpipers along the edges of ponds and mudflats, sometimes belly-deep in water. It frequently submerges its head while feeding. This species breeds in areas above the timberline in the Arctic and sub-Arctic and winters as far south as northern Argentina.

Field Marks: The rufous lores, ear coverts, barred underparts, U-shaped white upper tail coverts, and long legs make this species unmistakable in the summer plumage. The fall plumage is gray, but the white upper tail coverts and long bill help to identify it.

Food: This species feeds primarily on aquatic invertebrates.

Buff-breasted Sandpiper
Tryngites subruficollis (Vieillot)

Status: The Buff-breasted Sandpiper is an uncommon transient in the eastern and central part of the state.

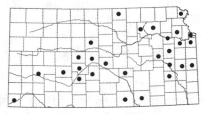

Period of Occurrence: In the spring, the Buff-breasted Sandpiper is either rare or just is unobserved as it passes through. One spring specimen was taken 12 May, and spring sightings date from 16 April to 12 May. Most sight records are for August, with an early fall record on 21 July. Most birds do not arrive until 4 August, and the last birds travel through about 8 October. There is an 11 November sight record.

Habits and Habitat: Unlike many shorebirds, this species tends to feed in dry areas. It has been observed in plowed fields near Cheyenne Bottoms. In the east, it seems partial to alfalfa fields in fall migration. Thompson saw one bird feeding with Lesser Golden Plovers in a burned-over pasture in the Flint Hills on 16 April. In August, Thompson observed another individual feeding on mudflats with other small shorebirds and a Black-bellied Plover at the Winfield Gun Club, Sumner County. Ed Martinez occasionally nets them on mudflats at Cheyenne Bottoms. However, the species generally favors dry uplands in migration and on the wintering grounds in southern South America (Johnsgard 1981).

Field Marks: The buffy plumage and yellow legs are distinctive in all seasons.

Food: The Buff-breasted Sandpiper feeds primarily on terrestrial insects and other invertebrates.

Ruff
Philomachus pugnax (Linnaeus)

Status: The Ruff is a vagrant. There is one specimen, collected on 22 June 1982 at Cheyenne Bottoms Wildlife Management Area. There are three sight records: one near Manhattan, in Pottawatomie County, on 23 May 1964 by L. Edmunds; one at Marais des Cygnes, Linn County, 20 May 1985 by David Seibel; one at Cheyenne Bottoms, Barton County, 12–17 May 1986 by Wayne Hoffman and others.

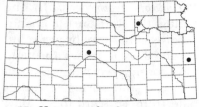

This species is primarily an Old World bird that occasionally occurs in the contiguous United States. It is a regular but rare fall migrant in the Pribilof Islands, Alaska, and a few birds wander from time to time into the eastern United States, where it has been recorded in most states east of the Rocky Mountains.

Adult Short-billed Dowitchers (*Limnodromus griseus*). Photograph by David A. Rintoul.

Short-billed Dowitcher
Limnodromus griseus (Gmelin)

Status: The Short-billed Dowitcher is a rare transient through central Kansas. It has also been recorded in the east, but most records are from Barton and Stafford counties.

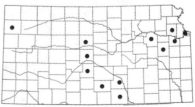

Period of Occurrence: The specimen records are from 14 to 31 May. Sight records seem to indicate that this species arrives after the Long-billed Dowitcher in the spring and before it in the fall. Spring sight records are from 21 April to 8 June, and fall records from 9 July to 10 October. Ed Martinez netted a bird at Cheyenne Bottoms on 24 September.

Habits and Habitat: This dowitcher winters primarily along seacoasts. Although there are subspecies nesting inland, most birds tend to migrate to the coastal areas and not through Kansas. Undoubtedly, most of those migrating through Kansas are confused with the Long-billed Dowitcher and overlooked, especially when they are in winter plumage.

Field Marks: See the account of the Long-billed Dowitcher.

Food: The species eats invertebrates obtained by probing in the mud.

An adult Long-billed Dowitcher (*Limnodromus scolopaceus*). Photograph by Frank S. Shipley.

Long-billed Dowitcher
Limnodromus scolopaceus (Say)

Status: The Long-billed Dowitcher is a common transient around wetlands, especially Cheyenne Bottoms Wildlife Management Area and Quivira National Wildlife Refuge. It is a casual summer visitant and has been recorded in early winter.

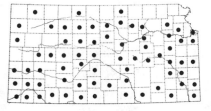

Period of Occurrence: The earliest recorded date in spring migration is 27 February, but most birds start to arrive 26 March and depart northward by 28 May. Some birds are seen in summer, with a 19 June record and other records from 10 July. The main fall migration starts around 24 July and lasts through 10 October, with a late date of 23 November.

Habits and Habitat: This long-billed shorebird is one of the more common and attractive shorebirds. The Long-billed Dowitcher can be found in the central Kansas marshes, feeding in the mudflats and along the muddy shoreline. They sometimes congregate in flocks of several hundred birds, probing the mud for invertebrates. It is not uncommon to see them up to their bellies in water as they feed. This shorebird winters farther north than most shorebirds that pass through our area; some birds move no farther south than the Gulf

Coast. It is somewhat surprising that more have not been recorded here in winter.

Field Marks: This species and the Short-billed Dowitcher are extremely difficult to distinguish in the field. The one Short-billed Dowitcher that Thompson saw in Kansas was not associating with the Long-billed Dowitcher. The plumage of the Long-billed Dowitcher is somewhat darker than that of the Short-billed, and the belly is marked with bars instead of spots. In the hand, the different tail pattern is visible; the Long-billed Dowitcher has narrow white bars and wide dark bars, while the Short-billed Dowitcher has wide white bars and narrow dark bars. Both species have long bills and, in flight, a conspicuous white rump. The two species are easily confused, and only in the hand can a bird be absolutely identified.

Food: The primary food is invertebrates obtained while probing in the mud.

An adult Common Snipe (*Gallinago gallinago*). Photograph by Galen L. Pittman.

Common Snipe
Gallinago gallinago (Linnaeus)

Status: The Common Snipe is a common spring and fall transient in wetlands throughout the state. It is casual in summer and rare in winter.

Period of Occurrence: This snipe arrives in the fall as early as 26 August, but most transients wait until 15 September to make an appearance. Most birds probably pull out in early November, but

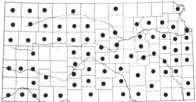

some birds stay all winter. The last ones depart for the breeding grounds about 11 May, with some leaving as late as 3 June. The bird has been sighted in all months.

Habits and Habitat: A question put to many of us when we were young was, "Would anyone like to go snipe hunting?" Imagine finding out that there really is a snipe and that it is indeed hunted. This species is the only shorebird other than the woodcock that can be hunted in Kansas. Its sudden rise from underfoot and its rapid flight make it an elusive target. Although it is a game bird here, not many hunters seek it out. It is usually found in wet boggy areas such as Cheyenne Bottoms or Quivira Refuge, where it may be very common. In wintertime, its haunts are any marshy areas which remain ice-free and provide enough cover.

Although the Common Snipe does not breed in Kansas, it breeds as far south as Nebraska and Iowa.

Food: Snipes eat primarily invertebrates, which they obtain by probing in the ground with their long bills.

An adult American Woodcock (*Scolopax minor*) on nest. Photograph by Marvin D. Schwilling.

American Woodcock
Scolopax minor (Gmelin)

Status: The American Woodcock is an uncommon transient in the eastern and central part of the state and rare in the west. It breeds locally in the east. There are several winter records for the state.

Period of Occurrence: Although the American Woodcock has been recorded nearly every month of the year, most records are from April through November. Most

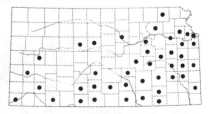

migrants from the south arrive around 4 April, with the last birds crossing the area by late May. Fall passage begins in late August and continues into November.

Breeding: The woodcock breeds locally in the eastern third of the state. The nest is placed on the ground in an area with short trees interspersed with grassland or boggy areas. The four eggs are laid in March or April in a depression, with little effort made to construct a formal nest. It is well camouflaged, and the incubating bird will leave the eggs only when nearly stepped on. The eggs are light brown to buff with numerous small spots. The young hatch in about 21 days and, like most shorebirds, are capable of leaving the nest within a few hours. Bent (1927) and others have reported that the woodcock has been seen carrying a young bird between its legs and flying with it to safety. The young are nearly full grown in four weeks.

Habits and Habitat: The American Woodcock is primarily a bird of eastern forestland and is recorded in the western part of the state only in those areas that have woodland. It is usually not seen until it erupts from underfoot and flies a zigzag pattern through the trees in an effort to escape. That makes it an exceedingly difficult target for hunters. Because of its low numbers, it is not hunted much in Kansas.

Food: The species eats mostly earthworms, hence the need for the birds to be around wet, boggy ground.

An adult female Wilson's Phalarope (*Phalaropus tricolor*). Photograph by Frank S. Shipley.

PHALAROPES
Wilson's Phalarope
Phalaropus tricolor (Vieillot)

Status: Wilson's Phalarope is a common transient statewide and a local summer resident in the central and west, primarily at Cheyenne Bottoms and Quivira Refuge. It has bred at least once in Lincoln County.

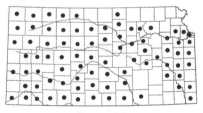

Period of Occurrence: This phalarope has been recorded as early as 2 February and as late as 5 December. The normal time span is from 4 April to 20 October. Kansas has a small breeding population, and most birds travel north of the state to breed. The northward migration finishes about 31 May, and the southward migration commences in late July and runs through 20 October.

Breeding: There are few nests known here, although breeding is not uncommon in the Cheyenne Bottoms and Quivira Refuge areas in the summer. Nesting records are available from Barton, Lincoln, Stafford, and possibly Meade counties. The nest, usually located in a wet, marshy area, is a slight depression in the ground lined with plant material. The female apparently makes the nest with the male adding the lining (Johnsgard 1979). The female lays the eggs, then the male incubates and cares for the young. The normal clutch is four eggs, and the incubation period is anywhere from 16 to 22 days. Most eggs are laid in May and June in Kansas (Johnston 1964). The young are precocious and leave the nest soon after hatching.

Habits and Habitat: This bird is an inhabitant of wet, marshy areas and in migration occurs near lakes and ponds. Its peculiar habit of spinning as it feeds makes it immediately identifiable as a phalarope. While it rotates, the phalarope apparently kicks up food with its feet and, with quick jabs of its bill, plucks the food out of the water. These antics, combined with its beautiful colors, make the bird an instant hit with birdwatchers. The three species of phalaropes are among the few species in the avian world in which the females are more brightly colored than the males. Another oddity is that as soon as the female lays the eggs, she leaves the area, and the male takes over all responsibility for incubation and caring for the young.

Food: Wilson's Phalarope feeds mostly on invertebrates, primarily insects.

An adult female Red-necked Phalarope (*Phalaropus lobatus*). Photograph by David A. Rintoul.

Red-necked Phalarope
Phalaropus lobatus (Linnaeus)

Status: The Red-necked Phalarope is a rare transient throughout the state, with most records from Barton and Stafford counties.

Period of Occurrence: There are sight records from 19 April to 28 May and from 18 August to 28 October.

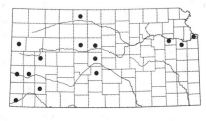

Habits and Habitat: In its migration through Kansas, the Red-necked Phalarope is found primarily around marshes, lakes, and ponds. It can sometimes be found with the Wilson's Phalarope. Like the other phalaropes, it spins in circles while feeding. Its northward migration carries it to its sub-Arctic breeding grounds. Its wintering grounds are worth mentioning, since phalaropes as a group are the only "shorebirds" that winter at sea in the Pacific and Atlantic oceans. Great rafts of thousands of birds far from land have been described by naturalists.

Field Marks: In winter plumage this species may be difficult to separate from the Wilson's Phalarope. The Red-necked Phalarope usually has a darker dorsal pattern, shorter bill, and a dark stripe through the eye. There is a definite white wing stripe visible during flight.

Food: Aquatic insects make up the bulk of the diet.

An adult Red Phalarope (*Phalaropus fulicaria*). Photograph by Galen L. Pittman.

Red Phalarope
Phalaropus fulicaria (Linnaeus)

Status: The Red Phalarope is a casual transient, with most records from Cheyenne Bottoms. Parmelee et al. (1969b) listed four specimens in 1959 and 1963 from Cheyenne Bottoms and six records, including a group of five birds, on 22 September 1968. A bird seen on 10 May 1967 had fairly bright plumage. There are now several more records since  Parmelee's publication, and the dates of occurrence have been extended to 5 November with an extreme date of 5 December. There are additional specimens from Douglas, Franklin, and Barton counties and recent sight records for Linn and Morton counties.

Habits and Habitat: The Red Phalarope should be looked for in wet, marshy habitat. LIke the other phalaropes, it spins for its food.

Field Marks: The rusty reddish spring plumage is unmistakable, but the winter plumage resembles the other two phalaropes'. The Red Phalarope differs in having a more uniformly gray appearance and a dark gray stripe through the eye. Of the three species, its bill is stouter and more flattened.

An adult Pomarine Jaeger (*Stercorarius pomarinus*). Photograph by Galen L. Pittman.

JAEGERS
Pomarine Jaeger
Stercorarius pomarinus (Temminck)

Status: The Pomarine Jaeger, usually a marine species, is a vagrant in Kansas. There is one specimen which was taken on 10 October 1898 on the Kansas River near Lawrence in Douglas County. There are unconfirmed sight records from Cheyenne Bottoms from 18 September to 8 November. Since this species is primarily marine except when it breeds, any sight records are questionable.

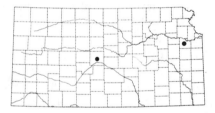

Adult Parasitic Jaegers (*Stercorarius parasiticus*). Photograph by Galen L. Pittman.

Parasitic Jaeger
Stercorarius parasiticus (Linnaeus)

Status: The Parasitic Jaeger is a casual fall transient primarily at Cheyenne Bottoms Wildlife Management Area and Quivira National Wildlife Refuge. There are eight sight records between 1965 and 1985 from Barton, Coffey (a good photograph), Finney, Jefferson, Russell, Stafford, and Woodson counties. There is one specimen record from Cheyenne

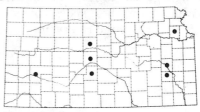

Bottoms taken on 16 October 1965. This species is the most commonly occurring jaeger in Kansas, but jaegers are hard to identify, especially in immature plumage, and sight records are open to question. Even specimens have been incorrectly identified; the only Pomarine Jaeger for the state was considered to be a Parasitic Jaeger until Tordoff (1956) reexamined the skin and discovered the misidentification, 58 years after it was collected.

An adult Long-tailed Jaeger (*Stercorarius longicaudus*). Photograph by Galen L. Pittman.

Long-tailed Jaeger
Stercorarius longicaudus (Vieillot)

Status: The Long-tailed Jaeger is a vagrant in Kansas. There is one specimen from Cheyenne Bottoms, taken on 23 June 1955. There are also sight records, three from Cheyenne Bottoms and one from Lovewell Reservoir, Jewell County. This species is the smallest of the jaegers and in breeding plumage the easiest to identify. Watch for all these species of jaegers on our large reservoirs.

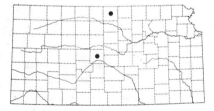

An adult Laughing Gull (*Larus atricilla*) in winter plumage. Photograph by David A. Rintoul.

GULLS
Laughing Gull
Larus atricilla (Linnaeus)

Status: The Laughing Gull is a casual visitor. There is one specimen taken in Marion County on 15 May 1933 and additional sight records from Barton, Sumner, and Shawnee counties. Sight records span from 4 April to 15 June in the spring, 7 to 28 July in the summer, and 19 August to 8 October in the fall. Look for it flying with the large number of Franklin's Gulls that migrate through the state.

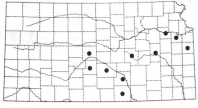

Adult Franklin's Gulls (*Larus pipixcan*). Photograph by David A. Rintoul.

Franklin's Gull
Larus pipixcan (Wagler)

Status: The Franklin's Gull is a common transient throughout but is particularly abundant in the central part.

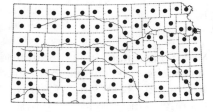

Period of Occurrence: The first birds arrive usually around 10 April and remain until 21 June or so. The return fall migration commences 22 September and lasts until 28 November. They have been reported in all months of the year, but winter records should be verified.

Habits and Habitat: This "seagull," as it is known by most Kansans, is a familiar sight, particularly in the spring, when thousands cross our state heading for their breeding grounds in the northern plains states and Canada. They can be seen following tractors that are working fields, as the gulls swoop down to grab the insects, worms, and probably small rodents that are uncovered. These gulls—their body feathers suffused with pink and their black head and black-and-white wing tips—are a thrill to see as they hover over the tractor. At Cheyenne Bottoms and Quivira Refuge, it is not uncommon to see 10,000 to 20,000 gulls in one day.

Field Marks: The black head and white wing tips with black markings are unmistakable, but watch for the occasional Laughing Gull that has black wing tips with no white patches.

Food: In Kansas, the Franklin's Gull feeds primarily on insects and other invertebrates it obtains along marshes or in open pastures and plowed fields. It frequently forages in burned-over pastures during the spring migration.

Little Gull
Larus minutus (Pallas)

Status: The Little Gull is a vagrant in Kansas. Although there are no specimens, excellent photographs exist of the first record from John Redmond Reservoir, Coffey County. This species was first seen on 3 November 1974 by Jacob H. Miller (1975) and others. It was photographed by Jean Schulenberg on 4 November and remained until 11  November. There have been other records from Kansas since then, from 13 March to May. This species is an Old World bird that has taken up residence in North America around the Great Lakes. Its populations are increasing, and it should be looked for on large impoundments in Kansas.

An adult Common Black-headed Gull (*Larus ridibundus*). Photograph by Galen L. Pittman.

Common Black-headed Gull
Larus ridibundus (Linnaeus)

Status: Although the Common Black-headed Gull is a vagrant in Kansas, look for it among other gulls in migration. There are sight records from Cheyenne Bottoms from 4 April to 25 May and on 5 September. This bird is another Old World gull that is regular in Alaska and occasionally wanders into the interior of North America. The Common Black-headed Gull is placed on the hypothetical list until adequate documentation is obtained.

An adult Bonaparte's Gull (*Larus philadelphia*) in winter plumage. Photograph by David A. Rintoul.

Bonaparte's Gull
Larus philadelphia (Ord)

Status: The Bonaparte's Gull is an uncommon transient, occurring chiefly in the eastern half of Kansas.

Period of Occurrence: The species has been recorded every month from March through December, except for July. The earliest sightings are on 6 March; the latest, on 27 June. The fall records start as early as 7 August,

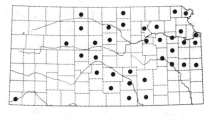

with the last birds leaving on 27 December. However, most sightings are in the late fall from around 12 October to 22 November. When warm weather extends into December, they may remain on the larger reservoirs.

Habits and Habitat: This small gull is usually found with other species of gulls around large water impoundments. Although typically not a common migrant, a flock of 150 was observed in Cowley County for several days on the Winfield City Lake, where it occurs yearly in smaller numbers during fall migration. It nests primarily in trees, from Alaska to central Ontario; as most birds move eastward in migration to the Mississippi Valley, this species misses a large part of Kansas. It captures small prey from the water by flying close to the surface and daintily plucking them from the waves without alighting. Its light, buoyant flight is more reminiscent of a tern than a gull.

Field Marks: The Bonaparte's Gull is one of the two black-headed gulls that occur regularly in the state. It differs from the Franklin's Gull by being smaller and by having a white triangular patch in the forward part of the wing.

Food: The species feeds on invertebrates, primarily insects.

An adult Ring-billed Gull (*Larus delawarensis*). Photograph by Roger Boyd.

Ring-billed Gull
Larus delawarensis (Ord)

Status: The Ring-billed Gull is a common transient and an uncommon winter resident throughout the state. Considerable numbers remain on larger reservoirs and rivers in winter when there is open water.

Period of Occurrence: This medium-sized gull has been recorded in every month of the year. However, most occurrences are during spring and fall migration. Because some birds have spent the winter, it is hard to judge when the spring influx begins. However, numbers increase around 3 March, and many birds remain until 24 May. The fall southward movements start on 27 August; many birds then move farther south, but many spend the winter. During hard winters with no open water, they move out.

Habits and Habitat: The Ring-billed Gull is found around lakes, rivers, and marshes. In the winter, it can frequently be seen feeding around garbage dumps in Sedgwick County. During migration, it feeds in open fields but not as commonly as the Franklin's Gull. Like the latter, it nests primarily in interior North America. It winters along both seacoasts as well as in the interior United States to central Mexico.

Food: This gull is an opportunist which eats anything from garbage to insects. It has been known to eat rodents and other small vertebrates.

California Gull
Larus californicus (Lawrence)

Status: The California Gull is a vagrant to Kansas. There is one specimen (whereabouts unknown) taken by N. S. Goss in Reno County on 20 October 1880. There are additional sight records, all from Cheyenne Bottoms, where Marvin Schwilling observed a bird from 18 to 20 January 1973. Wayne Hoffman made an additional observation  on 15 April 1986. It probably occurs in western Kansas with some regularity, but there are few observers in the area, and thus far it has not been recorded.

Field Marks: This species, with the Herring, Thayer's, Glaucous, and Great Black-backed Gulls, represents a most difficult group to identify. The complex plumages and interrelationships between species cause frequent misidentifications. Many have been misidentified even in museums with the specimen in hand; frequently a gull has been collected, only to find that it was not the species it was thought to have been in the field. It is beyond the scope of this book to provide comprehensive field marks. The reader is referred to Peter Grant's *Gulls: A Guide To Identification* (2d rev. ed., Buteo, Vermillion, South Dakota, 1986).

A subadult California Gull (*Larus californicus*). Photograph by David A. Rintoul.

An adult Herring Gull (*Larus argentatus*). Photograph by John Wachholz.

Herring Gull
Larus argentatus (Pontoppidan)

Status: The Herring Gull is an uncommon transient and an uncommon winter resident on larger impoundments and large rivers.

Period of Occurrence: There are sight records for all months of the year, but it is most common from 1 March to 4 June and from 13 August to 6 November.

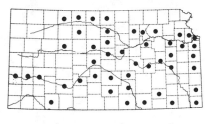

Habits and Habitat: This gull is most common around large reservoirs and large rivers. It frequently mixes with the Ring-billed Gull in wintering flocks. Most of these birds that pass through Kansas seem to be immatures which adds to identification problems. The Herring Gull is one of the most successful breeding gulls in North America; its numbers have increased tremendously, particularly around coastal areas where food at garbage dumps is plentiful. Its numbers are probably higher now than 200 years ago.

Field Marks: See the account for the California Gull.

Food: The Herring Gull, like all gulls, is an opportunist that eats almost anything, from garbage and dead animals to any other material it can scavenge.

Thayer's Gull
Larus thayeri (Brooks)

Status: The status of the Thayer's Gull in Kansas is unknown. It is on the list on the basis of a photograph taken by David A. Rintoul and published in the *Kansas Or-* 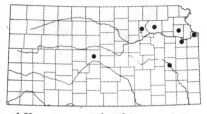 *nithological Society Bulletin* (Cable and Rintoul 1985). This bird was observed on 15 January 1985 on the Big Blue River below Tuttle Creek Reservoir Dam, Riley County. There have been sub-sequent observations in six additional Kansas counties, but no photographs or specimens were taken. All observations were made between 2 September and 17 March. There seems to be a question on the validity of the species (Weber 1981).

Field Marks: See the account for the California Gull.

An adult Glaucous Gull (*Larus hyperboreus*). Photograph by David A. Rintoul.

Glaucous Gull
Larus hyperboreus (Gunnerus)

Status: The Glaucous Gull is a rare winter visitor. It is casual at other seasons. There is one specimen, taken at Cheyenne Bottoms, Barton County. While most records have been from Barton County. there are records from 11 additional counties.

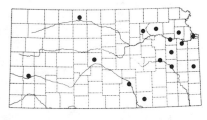

Period of Occurrence: Although most sight records are from November through March, it has been seen at other times of the year. It has also been recorded from 9 September to 10 April and on 3 May.

Habits and Habitat: This gull is normally a bird of the seacoast but occasionally wanders inland. It is found primarily around larger reservoirs or below dams with running water. The bird observed in Cowley County was near a lake only 10 acres in size.

Field Marks: Most large gulls in Kansas that are white, or nearly so, are probably Glaucous Gulls. See the account for the California Gull.

Food: This scavenger eats almost any dead animal around water or any live animal that is small enough to swallow.

An adult Great Black-backed Gull (*Larus marinus*). Photograph by David A. Rintoul.

Great Black-backed Gull
Larus marinus (Linnaeus)

Status: There are two sight records for the Great Black-backed Gull: one for 13 April 1973 and one for 13 April 1974. There are no other records, and until a specimen or satisfactory photograph is taken, it will remain on the hypothetical list.

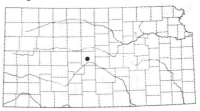

An adult Black-legged Kittiwake (*Rissa tridactyla*). Photograph by Galen L. Pittman.

Black-legged Kittiwake
Rissa tridactyla (Linnaeus)

Status: The Black-legged Kittiwake is a rare transient, with most records from Cheyenne Bottoms, Barton County, where a specimen was taken on 27 October 1969. There are additional records from Coffey, Shawnee, and Sumner counties.

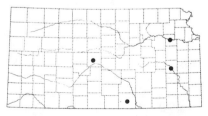

Period of Occurrence: There are records from 26 September to 24 November, 20 March to 28 April, and 27 June to 16 July; the majority of records are in April and October.

Habits and Habitat: This gull is a marine bird that breeds along northern coastal areas and winters primarily at sea. It is a rare treat for it to appear in Kansas. Look for the kittiwake around large bodies of water. Only one of the records was not from a reservoir, and that observation was along the Arkansas River in Sumner County.

Field Marks: This species is a small gull with black wing tips and a light green bill. In winter plumage, the black nape is conspicuous. The immature has a black nape, black bill, black-tipped tail, and a dark band across the top of the wing.

Food: Black-legged Kittiwakes scavenge less than the larger gulls. They feed primarily on the water, gleaning small insects and other invertebrates from the surface. They only occasionally feed along the shoreline.

Sabine's Gull
Xema sabini (Sabine)

Status: The Sabine's Gull is a rare transient, with several specimens and sight records from Cheyenne Bottoms but few records elsewhere. The first specimen is worthy of mention. It was taken by Peter Long at Humboldt, Allen County, and reported by Goss (1891). Goss stated, "A young male, on the 19th of September, 1876, flew into a billiard saloon in Humboldt, Kansas, at midnight, no doubt attracted there by the light of the burning lamps that brightly reflected out into the darkness."

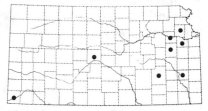

Period of Occurrence: Most records for this species are for September and October, and all specimens were taken between 21 September to 10 October. Sight records are from 21 September to 28 October in the fall, and 13 March to 26 May in the spring.

Habits and Habitat: Like the Black-legged Kittiwake, the Sabine's Gull is primarily a marine gull. After breeding on land, it becomes pelagic. It is one of the most beautiful of the North American gulls when in breeding plumage, and unlike that of most gulls, its immature plumage is also attractive. It is probably the smallest of the gulls that visit Kansas.

Field Marks: In any plumage, the black triangular pattern in the wing tips and bright white secondaries are distinctive. On the immature, the V-shaped tail has a black tip.

Food: This gull feeds mainly on insects and other invertebrates plucked from the water. It is known to feed on mudflats at low tide.

TERNS
Caspian Tern
Sterna caspia (Pallas)

Status: The Caspian Tern is an uncommon transient, chiefly in the eastern and central areas.

Period of Occurrence: This large tern occurs here as early as 11 April, but most records are between 9 May and 19 July, and 26 August and 3 October, with a late record of 25 October.

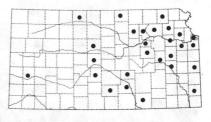

Habits and Habitat: This species is one of the largest terns in the world and the largest tern that visits Kansas. It is seen most frequently around the bigger impoundments, where it sweeps back and forth looking for fishes to eat. Terns dive for food, frequently submerging but generally just hitting the surface to pluck the unfortunate fishes from the water. The terns are the most graceful of all the water birds in Kansas. Their effortless flight, hovering ability, and sudden dives into the water provide much pleasure to the observant birdwatcher.

Field Marks: The sheer size of the Caspian Tern, combined with its large orange bill, makes it easy to identify.

Food: Like most terns, this bird feeds primarily on small fishes obtained by diving into the water.

Adult Common Terns (*Sterna hirundo*). Photograph by Galen L. Pittman.

Common Tern
Sterna hirundo (Linnaeus)

Status: The status of the Common Tern is uncertain, but it probably is a rare migrant. Three specimens were taken prior to 1965, one in Anderson County in 1878 and the other two in Greenwood County in 1912. Other specimens were taken at Cheyenne Bottoms, Barton County, in 1965 and 1968. The close similarity to the Forster's Tern makes sight

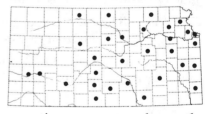

records questionable, unless the two species are seen together or the observer is familiar with both species.

Period of Occurrence: There are records from 22 April to 30 June and 2 September to 3 October. There are two midsummer records on 13 July and 25 July.

Habits and Habitat: Like all other Kansas terns, this bird is found around water. Not unexpectedly, most of the records come from Cheyenne Bottoms and Quivira Refuge. The habits resemble those of the Forster's Tern, with which it occasionally mixes. Kansas is on the fringe of the migration route, as most Common Terns migrate through the Mississippi and Ohio River valleys.

Field Marks: The Common Tern can be distinguished from the Forster's Tern by its darker wing tips and darker mantle. In winter plumage, the Common Tern's black eye patch extends to a black nape, but the Forster's Tern has only the dark eye patch.

Food: This tern eats mainly small fishes, which it obtains by diving from aloft into the water.

An adult Forster's Tern (*Sterna forsteri*). Photograph by David A. Rintoul.

Forster's Tern
Sterna forsteri (Nuttall)

Status: The Forster's Tern is an uncommon transient throughout and local breeder in central Kansas. It is casual in other areas during the summer.

Period of Occurrence: The earliest spring arrival date is 6 April, but most birds arrive about 15 April and remain until 25 June. The fall migration begins as early as 21 August, but the majority of birds arrives from the north around 7 September to 22 October, with a late date of 28 November. Most summer records are from Cheyenne Bottoms and Quivira Refuge, where it nests sporadically.

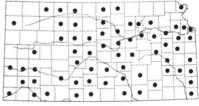

Breeding: The first known nesting was reported in 1962 by Zuvanich (1963) at Cheyenne Bottoms. He found several nests; clutch size averaged 3 eggs at 17 nests and 2 eggs at 3 nests. The eggs were laid in free-floating masses of vegetation, which could rise and fall with the level of water. Eggs have been recorded from 1 June to 12 August, but downy young have been noted as early as 10 June. An incubation period of 23 days has been recorded. The eggs have a light brown base color with darker spotting. The young are active soon after hatching; within a few days, they leave the nest and are quite capable of swimming and running.

Habits and Habitat: The Forster's Tern is a bird of large marshes, rivers, and impoundments. It is the second most abundant tern in Kansas and is particularly easy to observe at Cheyenne Bottoms and Quivira National Wildlife Refuge, where it can be seen moving back and forth looking for small fishes and insect larvae. Upon spying its prey, it dives from high up straight into the water, grasping the prey with its bill. Its grace and beauty make it a favorite of birdwatchers. When at rest, this tern and other terns sit upon exposed mud or sand flats, all facing in the same direction; even then their appearance is graceful.

Food: This tern feeds upon small fishes and insect larvae and has been observed catching flying insects.

An adult male Least Tern (*Sterna antillarum*) on nest. Photograph by Ed and Jean Schulenberg.

Least Tern
Sterna antillarum (Lesson)

Status: The Least Tern is an uncommon transient throughout Kansas and a local summer resident in the central and western parts of the state. It migrates as a family group to wintering grounds in Central and South America.

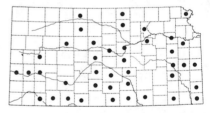

Period of Occurrence: Most records fall within 30 April and 7 September, with extreme dates of 23 March and 27 September.

Breeding: This tern breeds on salt flats and sandbars in central and western Kansas. The number of breeding birds has been greatly reduced in the past few years. They lay their eggs in a depression on the flats at Cheyenne Bottoms and Quivira Refuge or on sandbars on the Cimarron River. Clutch size varies from two to four; at Quivira Refuge and along the Cimarron River, the number of eggs is normally three during June and early July, dropping off to two eggs later in the season. The eggs, creamy to olive buff with black, brown, or bluish gray spots, are incubated from 20 to 22 days. The young remain in the nest for a few days, then become quite mobile and fledge at 28 days. Adult Least Terns feed small fishes to their young. Breeding has been recorded in Barton, Clark, Hamilton, Meade, Rooks, Stafford, and Trego counties. Any breeding locations should be reported to the University of Kansas Museum of Natural History.

Habits and Habitat: These diminutive terns are the smallest found in Kansas. Apparently never really common, they have been designated an endangered species, both in Kansas and nationally, and receive full protection under the law. The best place to observe them is at Quivira National Wildlife Refuge on the salt flats on the north end of the refuge. Small colonies are located along the Cimarron River, but they are difficult to find unless an exact location is known. Roger Boyd, working in cooperation with the Kansas Department of Wildlife and Parks, has been modifying some habitat on the Cimarron River in the hopes of improving nesting success, but insufficient time has elapsed to evaluate the outcome.

Field Marks: The Least Tern is easily identified by its white body, black cap with a white forehead, yellow bill, and small size.

Food: The diet consists almost entirely of small fishes, with an occasional insect.

An adult Black Tern (*Chlidonias niger*). Photograph by Roger Boyd.

Black Tern
Chlidonias niger (Linnaeus)

Status: The Black Tern is a common transient and local summer resident. It is found only casually in the summer, away from the few breeding sites.

Period of Occurrence: It is usually a late-April migrant but has been seen as early as 20 March. The normal arrival time is 22 April, with a 24 September departure; stragglers occur until 23 October.

Breeding: Parmelee (1961) recorded the first nest of the species from Kansas when he discovered a colony at Cheyenne Bottoms in Barton County. Outside of Barton and Stafford counties, there are no substantiated nesting records here. Johnston (1964) listed Douglas County as a possible breeding site, and it may have nested in Sedgwick

County (Holmes 1958). The nest is built of vegetation floating on water. Eggs are laid from 11 June to 12 July; there are usually three, buff-colored with dark spotting. Incubation lasts about 21 days. The young terns remain in the nest for a few days and then can swim freely nearby.

Habits and Habitat: A true "prairie-type" tern, these birds can be seen in the spring flying northward over the grassland. They frequently forage over small ponds and open streams. Although Black Terns nest in Kansas, the main nesting areas are to the north. Large numbers can be seen at the central Kansas marshes, where apparently many nonbreeding birds remain during the summer, but few nest.

Field Marks: During the spring and summer months, the black bodies of these terns identify them immediately. In fall and winter, the body plumage is white, with a blackish cap on the head.

Food: This tern feeds almost exclusively on insects.

An adult Black Skimmer (*Rynchops niger*). Photograph by Ed and Jean Schulenberg.

SKIMMERS
Black Skimmer
Rynchops niger (Linnaeus)

Status: The Black Skimmer is a vagrant. One specimen was collected in Douglas County on 24 May 1968. There are sight records from Cheyenne Bottoms in Barton County, where Ed Martinez saw a skimmer on 27 and 30 July and again on 1 and 2 August 1977. Tom Cannon and others saw a Black Skimmer in Russell County on 28 to 30 June, 1 to 3 July, and

again on 13 July 1977. All sightings may have been of the same bird.

PIGEONS
Rock Dove (Feral Pigeon)
Columba livia (Gmelin)

Status: The Rock Dove was introduced into Kansas by the early settlers. Feral and semiferal populations now occur statewide in towns and near human habitations; smaller numbers nest locally in holes in steep cliffs or banks, under bridges, and in other "wild" situations.

Period of Occurrence: The species is a permanent, non-native resident.

Breeding: Courtship involves an aggressive approach and contact by the male, with much deep cooing, fanning of the tail, and a slow circular turning or "dance." The pair also spends considerable time nibbling around each other's beaks (the source of the phrase "billing-and-cooing"). Flight displays with a marked clapping of the wings are also a part of courtship. The Rock Dove nests in crannies, on ledges inside or on buildings, under bridges, and, rarely, in crannies of cliffs. The nest may be a flimsy structure or a substantial mass of twigs, weed stems, and grasses; it is often built up by the excrement of the young as they develop. The two eggs are glossy white, and incubation is about 18 days. Both sexes care for the young, which fledge in about five weeks. Eggs have been found during all months (especially in or on buildings), but peak nesting is probably April through June. It normally has several broods. The young are first fed "pigeon milk," a fatty secretion of the crop, and later regurgitated food from the parent's crop.

Habits and Habitat: According to Terres (1980) the Rock Dove was the first bird to be domesticated (about 5000 B.C.), and numerous "breeds" or varieties, including the famous "homing pigeon," have been developed. In most flocks individuals show a great variation in plumage, but the wild pattern is largely gray with a white lower back, two black wing bars, and a black band on the tail. When they are fed and protected, birds become very tame, but feral populations may be very shy and difficult to approach. On occasion, populations build up to such numbers that they create a nuisance or even a potential health problem. Rock Doves are colonial and typically feed and rest in flocks.

They usually feed on the ground and often rest on broad elevated structures such as roofs, but rarely perch in trees or on overhead wires.

Food: The species eats various kinds of seeds, cultivated grains, and berries. In cities and towns, they also eat a wide variety of table scraps.

Band-tailed Pigeon
Columba fasciata (Say)

Status: The Band-tailed Pigeon is a vagrant reported only twice in Kansas. C. W. Hibbard saw one near Kingsdown, Clark County, on 19 July 1963, and Marvin Schwilling collected one in Meade, Meade county, on 9 October 1969. The latter specimen had fed in a hawthorn tree in the yard of Edwin Gibbard for the three previous days. During April 1985, 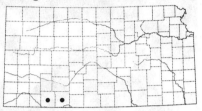 one bird spent a week in western Kansas City, Missouri, only a block from the Kansas line.

An adult White-winged Dove (*Zenaida asiatica*). Photograph by Galen L. Pittman.

DOVES
White-winged Dove
Zenaida asiatica (Linnaeus)

Status: The White-winged Dove is probably a vagrant. There are four sight records from Kansas. The most convincing is a report of one shot from a flock of six or seven by an unidentified hunter about 5 September in 1968 or 1969 in Hodgeman County. A wing was saved by Game Protector Jim Kellenberger and shown to his supervisor but then lost (Schwilling, pers. comm.). Other unconfirmed sight records are from Russell, Linn, and Sedgwick counties during June, September, and October.

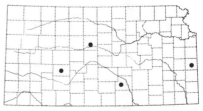

An adult Mourning Dove (*Zenaidura macroura*). Photograph by David A. Rintoul.

Mourning Dove
Zenaida macroura (Linnaeus)

Status: The Mourning Dove is a common to abundant transient and summer resident statewide; it is a local, low-density winter resident, chiefly in the south and east.

Period of Occurrence: The species is present all year, but most summering individuals are replaced in the fall and winter by birds from farther north. It is most abundant from March to November.

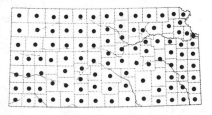

Breeding: Nesting (including attempts at renesting) is almost continuous from early spring through early fall; two or three broods are reared. There are one to three, usually two, glossy white eggs. Clutches have been reported from 28 February to 1 October, with most between April and August. Nesting is often terminated when the hunting season starts on 1 September. Mourning Doves nest almost anywhere—lawns, at the edge of streams or rivers, windbreaks, as well as in cultivated fields, prairies, and open woods. The nest is a platform of plant stems or twigs lined with grass, usually on a horizontal crotch less than 15 feet above ground. Doves are famous for their scanty nests, but nests built in early spring are often bulky, elaborate, and substantial. In some areas, nesting on the ground is common, even when woody vegetation is available. The incubation period is 14 days, with both sexes incubating—the male by day, the female at night. Fledging occurs two weeks later. Birds occasionally nest in loose colonies.

Habits and Habitat: The "turtle dove" is undoubtedly one of our best-known and ubiquitous birds. Its mournful call is heard even in suburban areas, where it nests in shrubbery and often visits feeding stations. Its courtship flight is an ascent with rapidly beating wings, followed by a glide with set wings, back in a half circle to near the point of departure. Pairs are said to mate for life. Although usually considered peaceable, they may fight during the courtship period and at feeders. Doves typically make regular daily flights to water and food sources. In early fall, young birds gather in premigratory flocks and are often conspicuous on overhead wires and fence lines. The flight is strong, direct, and rapid, so this species is a popular game bird. The parents feed the young a regurgitated mixture of predigested food and "pigeon milk," a high-fat, high-protein cheesy substance secreted by the lining of the crop. Doves are among the few birds that drink by sucking rather than by lifting the head for each swallow. Kansas doves are migratory; extensive banding has shown, for example, that Ellis County birds winter in west-central Mexico.

Food: The Mourning Dove eats almost entirely weed seeds and waste grain, with occasional berries, insects, and snails.

Passenger Pigeon
Ectopistes migratorius (Linnaeus)

Status: EXTINCT. The Passenger Pigeon was formerly an uncommon or irregular transient and an occasional or local breeder.

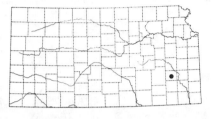

Period of Occurrence: The species was reported from the middle of March through "summer."

Breeding: The only nesting report for Kansas was made by Goss (1886), who stated that "a few to my knowledge breed occasionally in the Neosho Valley . . . about the middle of April." As Kansas was at the periphery of the bird's range, nesting probably was by small groups. The nest was a loose platform of twigs, and a single glossy white egg was laid. Incubation and fledging each took about two weeks, with both parents incubating and rearing the young.

Habits and Habitat: There are few firsthand accounts of the Passenger Pigeon in Kansas, and only three specimens remain (taken by Goss near Neosho Falls, Woodson County, 14 April 1876). Birds were extremely gregarious, and they migrated, fed, roosted, and nested in huge flocks numbering as many as one to three billion birds, according to estimates by early ornithologists. Movements were irregular, and nesting areas changed frequently, probably in response to a shifting food supply. The largest nesting colonies, which contained millions of birds, were in the vast forests of beech, oak, and maple of the Great Lakes states. A nesting in Wisconsin in 1871 covered hundreds of square miles and may have included most of the pigeons nesting in North America that year (Schorger 1955). In less extensive habitat (as presumably in Kansas), birds nested as isolated pairs or in small groups.

Destruction of the Passenger Pigeon, especially in the breeding colonies, was relentless and on a scale difficult to imagine today. During a great nesting in Michigan in 1878, an estimated 1,500,000 carcasses and 80,000 live birds were shipped out by rail alone! The gradual decline, noted by 1851, accelerated rapidly between 1871 and 1880, and the last wild birds were killed in 1899 or 1900. Without the enormous colonial nestings, the species was apparently unable to nest and to reproduce in numbers sufficient for survival. Descriptions of early sightings and the events leading to extinction are presented in several books, including Schorger (1955) and Bent (1940).

Food: Food varied with the season but was chiefly mast (beech nuts, acorns, and chestnuts), various berries, insects, and cultivated grains.

An adult Inca Dove (*Columbina Inca*). Photograph by David A. Rintoul

Inca Dove
Columbina inca (Lesson)

Status: The Inca Dove is a little dove and a casual visitor, usually in late fall or early winter. The one specimen and at least 10 sight records are from 25 August to late June; most are from early October to late December. Except for a group of three individuals in Meade County in 1956–57, all records are of single birds. At least three of the sightings are of 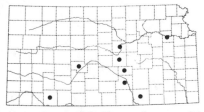 wintering birds (usually at feeding stations): 11 November to 31 March (Sedgwick County); 10 November to 21 January (Harvey County); early winter to 26 March (Meade County). Reports are from eight counties, from Shawnee and Cowley counties west to Meade.

Common Ground-Dove
Columbina passerina (Linnaeus)

Status: A diminutive dove, the Common Ground-Dove is a casual visitor during late fall and early winter. Five specimens and five additional sight records are from 6 October to 20 December. One caught on 28 November died in captivity on 7 December. Reports come from 10 counties west to Edwards and Barton counties; the westernmost sightings were near the Arkansas River. All records are of single birds.

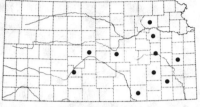

Parakeets
Carolina Parakeet
Conuropsis carolinensis (Linnaeus)

Status: EXTINCT. The Carolina Parakeet was formerly either a resident or a hardy, erratic visitor to eastern Kansas.

Period of Occurrence: The species was reported from late February through August and in October.

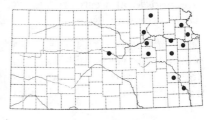

Breeding: The only report of nesting was by Goss (1886), who stated, "In the spring of 1858 a small flock reared their young in a large hollow limb of a giant sycamore tree, on the banks of the Neosho River, near Neosho Falls" (Woodson County). Elsewhere, the few reliable accounts related that birds nested colonially in high tree cavities and laid two to five pure white eggs. Both sexes were said to feed the young.

Habits and Habitat: Carolina Parakeets occurred locally in heavy riparian timber along the Missouri, Kansas, and Neosho rivers and their major tributaries, westward to Riley, Morris, and Ellsworth counties. McKinley (1964) summarized the Kansas records. There are two specimens, one each from Leavenworth and Atchison counties, and at least 17 other distinct sightings. In 1886, Goss stated, "Formerly a common resident in eastern and southern Kansas; but as settlements increased along the streams, rapidly diminished, and I think have not been met with in the state for several years." There are only two sightings after 1860, one of a flock on the Smoky Hill River near Fort Ellsworth in 1865 and one that was shot (but not preserved) near Potter, Atchison County, in 1904. Like most parrots, they travelled in noisy, conspicuous flocks. At night they roosted in hollow trees, with the birds gripping the interior with their beaks. Extinction is believed to have been caused by man. Many were trapped for use as caged birds, and large numbers were killed by hunters or to protect orchards and cultivated crops. When one of a flock was killed, the survivors often hovered overhead, with the result that most or all were also killed.

Food: These parrots ate seeds of various species, especially of thistles and cockleburs and beech, pine, maple, cypress, and elm. They destroyed cultivated fruits, such as apples, oranges, and peaches, but apparently ate only the seeds.

319

CUCKOOS
Black-billed Cuckoo
Coccyzus erythropthalmus (Wilson)

Status: The Black-billed Cuckoo is an uncommon transient and summer resident, principally in east and north-central areas, becoming rare and local westward, especially in the southwest.

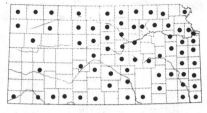

Period of Occurrence: The species normally arrives in mid-May and departs in mid-September; extreme dates are 3 May and 7 October.

Breeding: The nest, composed of twigs and lined with finer vegetation and dead leaves, is often more substantial than that of the Yellow-billed Cuckoo. It is usually placed in a dense thicket 2 to 10 feet above ground. The two to four (usually three) eggs are blue-green, slightly darker and smaller than those of a Yellow-billed Cuckoo. Incubation begins before the clutch is completed and results in a brood with young of different ages. When they hatch, the young have naked black skins but grow rapidly, develop a coat of ensheathed feathers within a week, and leave the nest in 8 to 10 days. Rarely, a Black-billed Cuckoo will lay an egg in the nest of a Yellow-billed Cuckoo or a songbird.

Habits and Habitat: The Black-billed Cuckoo is much less common and more locally distributed than the Yellow-billed, which often occurs in the same areas. It seems to prefer denser, better-developed woodland. Its habits closely resemble those of the Yellow-billed Cuckoo, but its call differs. The concluding notes are grouped into series of three ("kow-kow-kow, kow-kow-kow") which do not get slower. Both species are called "rain crow," but the Black-billed Cuckoo is less familiar, perhaps because it occurs less often in towns. Its sluggishness, slender build, and skulking habits—particularly of the young, which clamber about in vegetation for one to two weeks before flying—give it a reptilian appearance. Ely has caught flightless young that climbed or jumped into a mist net from nearby vegetation.

Food: The major food of both the Black-billed and Yellow-billed Cuckoo is caterpillars, including hairy ones. It also consumes other insects, various anthropods, and occasionally molluscs, small vertebrates, berries, and fruit.

An adult Yellow-billed Cuckoo (*Coccyzus americanus*). Photograph by Gerald J. Wiens.

Yellow-billed Cuckoo
Coccyzus americanus (Linnaeus)

Status: The Yellow-billed Cuckoo is a common transient and summer resident statewide.

Period of Occurrence: The species usually arrives around 4 May and departs about 6 October. Extreme dates are 13 April and 22 November.

Breeding: Nesting takes place from mid-May to September, with a peak of egg laying in June. The nest is a shallow platform of twigs, usually lined with dead leaves and placed on a horizontal branch or crotch within 4 to 20 feet (usually about 6 feet) from the ground. Nests are placed in a variety of trees and shrubs, typically in heavy cover, and are rarely so exposed that the incubating female is readily visible. The two to five (usually three) eggs are bluish green and are often laid several days apart. Incubation begins before the clutch is completed, so the young hatch at different times. They leave the nest up to 10 days before they can fly, clambering about in vegetation where they are attended by their parents. On rare occasions, this species lays an egg in the nest of a Black-billed Cuckoo or some other songbird.

Habits and Habitat: Few common Kansas birds are as seldom seen and as little known to the average citizen as the Yellow-billed Cuckoo. Its skulking habits, lethargic manner, and solitary nature make it difficult to observe. It is better known by its call—a long string of notes terminated by a series of "koup, koup" calls, the pace of which retards near the end. It frequently calls at night and on cloudy days, hence (probably) the common name "rain crow." Although many people recognize its call, few recognize the bird. It is frequently found dead on highways or near picture windows and less often seen alive by the casual observer.

A study near Lawrence found that the young grew at a phenomenal rate and reached over half of their adult weight in just four days (Fitch and von Achen 1973). The developing feathers remain sheathed for an extended period, during which the young look like tiny porcupines. Later, the sheaths burst relatively fast, and a well-feathered chick appears. This cuckoo migrates great distances. A bird banded by Thompson in Cowley County was later found dead in Brazil.

Food: Cuckoos are well known for their diet of caterpillars, including such unlikely types as tent caterpillars; one bird's stomach held 325 hairy individuals. They also eat other insects, various arthropods, small vertebrates (small frogs and lizards), and fruit.

An adult Greater Roadrunner (*Geococcyx californianus*). Photograph by Marvin D. Schwilling, courtesy Kansas Department of Wildlife and Parks.

Greater Roadrunner
Geococcyx californianus (Lesson)

Status: The Greater Roadrunner's status is uncertain, but it is probably a resident in small numbers in counties bordering and south of the Arkansas River and in southeastern Kansas, northeast to Anderson and Linn counties. Its distribution is not well documented, but the northernmost specimen is from Anderson County. Some sight records proved to be of female or immature Ring-necked Pheasants. Goss, in 1886, considered

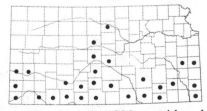

the roadrunner an "occasional visitor in the west." Tordoff (1956) considered it a "resident but with abundance and distribution subject to ide variation; current status unknown." His comments are still appropriate; few recognizable Kansas birds are as little known as this one.

Period of Occurrence: The roadrunner has been reported in all months but chiefly in the late fall and winter; few dates have been recorded. Sight records from northern and central counties need confirmation.

Breeding: The only documented nests in Kansas are from Cowley County (four nests, 19 April to 8 July 1934) and Sumner County (one nest with downy young, 8 August 1957). The nest is a compact structure of sticks lined with grass, feathers, and debris, usually in a tree within 10 feet of the ground. The four to five white eggs are incubated for 18 to 20 days. Both sexes incubate—the male at night, the female during the day—beginning when the first egg is laid. The young fledge in about 30 days. During courtship, the male presents food to the female while tapping his feet and calling softly.

Habits and Habitat: In its usual range (Oklahoma and the southwestern United States to central Mexico), the Greater Roadrunner occurs in semi-arid to arid areas with scattered vegetation. It is essentially a ground-dwelling species able to run up to 15 MPH and is a capable flier when it so chooses. The bird captures food after making a stealthy approach followed by a rapid dash. Roadrunners often perch on fence posts or low perches, especially in early morning when they may spread their wings to the sun. In spring, their "song" (a dovelike cooing) may be heard at sunrise, delivered from a mesa top or elevated perch. It is normally a permanent resident wherever found. In January 1973 one was captured alive, floundering in a snowdrift near Brazilton in southeastern Kansas.

Food: The species eats chiefly small vertebrates (especially lizards and small snakes), large insects and other large anthropods, and occasionally birds' eggs, and fruit.

An adult Groove-billed Ani (*Crotophaga culcirostris*). Photograph by C. L. Cink.

Groove-billed Ani
Crotophaga sulcirostris (Swainson)

Status: The Groove-billed Ani is a casual visitor west to Saline, Stafford, and Ellis counties and has been reported between 15 July and 8 December. Most sightings are in October and November. The 12 records, including 5 specimens and at least 4 well-photographed individuals, are of single birds. Several of the birds remained in an area as long as one month and

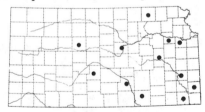

were seen repeatedly by numerous observers. Four sightings were made during November 1977.

Habits and Habitat: The Groove-billed Ani is primarily a tropical species occurring regularly northward to southern Texas. Some individuals, however, wander after the nesting season, and there are sightings in Minnesota and Ontario. In their usual habitat, they travel in small flocks. They prefer brushy pastures and semi-open areas, where they forage on the ground, often accompanying cattle, for grasshoppers and similar insects. The Kansas sightings have been in a variety of locations, including a pecan grove, brushy fields, suburban yards, and farmyards.

Field Marks: A Groove-billed Ani resembles a Common Grackle, with a parrotlike beak and floppy, loose-jointed tail. The grooves on the bill cannot always be seen, so confusion with the Smooth-billed Ani can occur.

OWLS
Common Barn-Owl
Tyto alba (Scopoli)

Status: Small numbers of Common Barn-Owls are permanent, statewide residents.

Period of Occurrence: The species occurs all year.

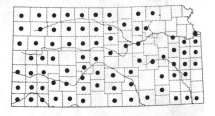

Breeding: Barn-Owls nest most often in an abandoned building, natural cavity of a tree or river-bank, or on flood debris beneath a bridge. The nesting season is extended, with nest records from April through October; probably most eggs are laid from mid-May to mid-June. The eggs are laid on the bare substrate or on debris from previous nestings. The four to seven pure white eggs are laid at intervals of several days, and incubation (about 33 days) begins when the first egg is laid. The young therefore hatch several days apart, and when the food supply is inadequate, smaller, younger chicks may perish. The female incubates, and the male brings food to her and, later, to the nestlings. Although few specific data are available, it is considered a low-density breeder statewide. Birds are said to mate for life.

Habits and Habitat: Although common Barn-Owls are often very closely associated with man, they are so secretive by day that they are seldom seen. The birds are strictly nocturnal, with excellent hearing; experiments have shown that they can catch prey in complete darkness. They hunt primarily over open country and near farm buildings, where they course back and forth with a silent, mothlike flight, pausing to pounce on their rodent prey. In western Kansas, they are most often seen among rock outcrops bordering ravines or rivers. They are commonly called the "monkey-faced owl" because of their heart-shaped facial disk and their habit of lowering the head while swaying from side to side. Although they are usually silent (except for bill clacking and hissing when disturbed) they also make a loud shrill shriek (or screech), which is believed to be a territorial call.

Food: Numerous studies, most of which analyze the remains of regurgitated "pellets," indicate that barn-owls feed predominantly on small rodents, with an occasional larger mammal, such as a small cottontail, as well as a few small birds.

An adult Common Barn-Owl (*Tyto alba*). Photograph by Bob Gress.

An adult Eastern Screech-Owl (*Otus asio*). Photograph by Bob Gress.

Eastern Screech-Owl
Otus asio (Linnaeus)

Status: The Eastern Screech-Owl is a common permanent resident in the east. It is uncommon and local in the west along streams and in towns.

Period of Occurrence: This little owl occurs all year.

Breeding: The species usually nests in a natural cavity such as a woodpecker hole, or in a bird

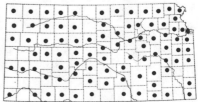

box, and rarely in a crevice in an embankment or in an abandoned hawk or crow nest. The nest is usually 5 to 30 feet above the ground. The four to five glossy white eggs hatch in about 26 days. In Kansas, egg laying is from mid-March to mid-May. The female incubates, and incubation may begin before the clutch is complete.

Habits and Habitat: Screech-Owls occur frequently in suburban areas, parks, and cemeteries but are more often heard than seen. Their most characteristic call is a descending series of whistled, trilling notes (or "whinny"), uttered most frequently just after dark from late fall to early spring. During the day, birds roost quietly in evergreens, dense shrubbery, or in tree cavities. The owl's head often fills the hole and blends in so well with the tree trunk that the bird is nearly invisible. Other birds roost right next to the tree trunks with their plumage compressed; with their ear tufts erect and their eyes slitted, they are usually overlooked, except by small birds which mob them noisily. Roosting birds are often very tame and can sometimes be captured by hand. Handled birds may "play possum" and remain limp with their eyes closed for a considerable period of time.

Sometimes Eastern Screech-Owls are first noticed by a home owner when a brood suddenly appears at a birdbath in midsummer. The adults are very bold when protecting their young, especially after they fledge, and may dive at, or even strike, an intruder. Three different color phases, independent of age, sex, or season, occur in Kansas populations—gray, brown, and reddish brown. It is our only small "horned" owl, and despite its name, it does not screech.

Food: The diet is varied, depending on season and availability. Large insects and other arthropods predominate in summer; small mammals, chiefly mice, and small birds are eaten in winter. At times they eat even crayfishes and earthworms.

Western Screech-Owl
Otus kennicottii (Elliot)

Status: The status of the Western Screech-Owl is not well known. The only sightings have been on the Colorado border where the Cimarron River runs into Morton County. 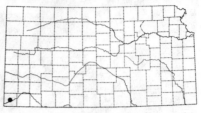 On 11 May 1985, one bird was heard calling there by Scott and Dianne Seltman and L. Smith. On 20 September 1987, five birds were heard calling at the same spot. The Screech-Owls were attracted to a tape recording of their call. More observations from the Colorado rivers entering Kansas are needed.

An adult Great Horned Owl (*Bubo virginianus*). Photograph by David A. Rintoul.

Great Horned Owl
Bubo virginianus (Gmelin)

Status: The Great Horned Owl is a common permanent resident statewide.

Period of Occurrence: The species occurs all year.

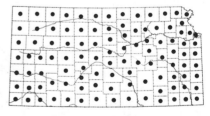

Breeding: The usual nest site is the abandoned stick nest of a large bird or squirrel, a tree cavity, an abandoned building, or a natural cavity in a cliff or riverbank. In some areas, they use artificial platforms. The one to three white eggs are laid directly on the nest substrate at intervals of several days. Incubation, which lasts about 30 days, is chiefly by the female. This bird is our earliest native nester. Courtship calling begins in December, and most females are incubating by mid-February; young fledge by late May.

Habits and Habitat: The "hoot owl" is undoubtedly our most widespread and best-known owl. Although it is not migratory, individuals move about during winter. The Great Horned Owl occurs in a variety of habitats, from deep woods to ravines in open prairie and even in urban parks. It makes a variety of sounds, including a wild, catlike scream believed to be a hunger call. Although it usually spends the daylight hours resting quietly in a secluded spot, it is fully capable of normal activity and occasionally hunts during the day. Roosting Great Horned Owls can often be located through the mobbing activity of crows or other birds. Ely once flushed an owl that was immediately and repeatedly attacked by a screaming Prairie Falcon. Some favorite roosting sites become littered with regurgitated pellets, which can be used by researchers to determine the owl's choice of food. It is a very large, powerful bird, with a wingspan up to 5 feet, and has been reported to kill prey as large as foxes and domestic turkeys.

Another common name, "cat owl," refers to the appearance of the incubating bird as it peers over the top of a stick nest with raised ear tufts and bright yellow eyes. The young owl has an interesting defense display, in which it fully spreads the wings and tail, then hisses and snaps its beak while swaying from side to side.

Food: Food varies according to its availability but is chiefly large rodents, cottontails, and medium-sized birds. Almost any small mammal may be eaten, as well as snakes, fishes, frogs, and large arthropods.

An adult Snowy Owl (*Nyctea scandiaca*). Photograph by Mark A. Chappell.

Snowy Owl
Nyctea scandiaca (Linnaeus)

Status: The Snowy Owl, a rare and irregular winter visitor statewide, is most frequent in eastern and central Kansas.

Period of Occurrence: Extreme
dates are 1 November and 15
April, with most sightings between mid-November and early
February. Notable flights were
reported during 1945–46,
1949–50, 1954–55, 1957–58,
1961–62, 1963–64, and 1974–75.

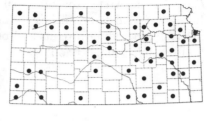

Habits and Habitat: Snowy Owls invade the United States at approximately four-year intervals, in response to fluctuations in the lemming
population at their Arctic breeding grounds. Relatively few birds
reach Kansas during most immigrations, but 81 were reported during
the winter of 1974–75 (Spomer 1981). The birds are so conspicuous,
and often so tame, that until recently a large proportion were killed
before spring. Presently the best places to see Snowy Owls are at
Cheyenne Bottoms and at open areas near the various large reservoirs. The chiefly white plumage and yellow eyes ensure positive
identification under most conditions, but some reports have proved
to be of the much smaller Common Barn-Owl. There is considerable
variation in the amount of black markings; usually the young are most
heavily marked, the females are "intermediate," and the males are
nearly white.

In the Arctic, Snowy Owls inhabit tundra and rest on the ground,
usually on a hummock or low ridge. The clutch size varies, apparently
in response to the size of the local lemming population. It has an
elaborate courtship, which includes aerial displays and a variety of
croaks, whistles, and the more conventional hoots. Adults are very
active in defense of their nest and use distractions, such as the
broken-wing displays, and direct attacks on intruders.

In Kansas, the owls are usually observed sitting on low perches in
open country or coursing low over open fields and marshes in search
of prey. As expected for an Arctic species, birds are active during
daylight hours. The flight is low, steady, and direct, with a jerky
upstroke and short periods of gliding. In Minnesota, Snowy Owls
establish winter territories; this may be true in Kansas as well, because
individuals tend to remain in a local area for an extended period.

Food: In the Arctic, the principal foods are lemmings, ptarmigan, hares, water birds, and fishes; in Kansas, the species takes whatever is available, including rodents and other small mammals, some birds, and possibly some carrion.

Adult Burrowing Owls (*Athene cunicularia*). Photograph by C. L. Cink.

Burrowing Owl
Athene cunicularia (Molina)

Status: The Burrowing Owl is an uncommon transient statewide. It is an uncommon summer resident in the west but may be common locally, and it nests casually eastward to Barton and Sumner counties. It is casual in winter, chiefly in the southwest.

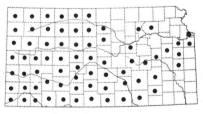

Period of Occurrence: The species is usually present from early March to late October in the west and from mid-April to early August in the east; extreme dates are 6 March and 14 November. Johnston (1965) gives median arrival and departure dates of 9 April and 26 September.

Breeding: Birds nest in burrows, usually those of prairie dogs, badgers, or foxes, but they may occasionally dig their own. The burrow is often 6 to 10 feet long, and the nest chamber may be 2 feet or more below ground. The nest chamber and the burrow entrance may be strewn with bits of manure, food remains, and other debris. The 3 to 10 pure white eggs are incubated almost entirely by the female for 28 days. When they are about three weeks old, the young appear above ground; they fledge about a week later. Most egg laying is about the middle of May.

Habits and Habitat: Although single pairs may occur almost anywhere in the western half of the state, Burrowing Owls are most numerous in prairie dog "towns." The disappearance of breeding birds from several eastern localities (Harvey County in the 1960s and Sumner County about 1930) is probably related to the destruction of prairie dog habitats. During the day, owls are usually seen on low perches or on the ground near a burrow. They are most active at dawn and dusk, when they may be observed hovering high overhead in a most unowlish fashion. They are often very noisy near the nest burrow, which may be used for successive years. After the owlets emerge, the nest site is a very active place, with birds bobbing up and down, running and flying about, or perching serially on fence posts or low mounds. Young are said to have a distress call that closely mimics the rattle of a prairie rattlesnake (Martin 1973). Most birds are migratory, but in some years, a few may remain into at least midwinter, even when the ground is completely covered with snow. It hunts primarily at night and may snatch its food from the ground or out of the air.

Food: The Burrowing Owl feeds largely on insects and various other arthropods but also on small rodents, birds, small snakes, and frogs. Up to 60 locusts have been found in owl stomachs.

An adult Barred Owl (*Strix varia*). Photograph by Mike Blair, courtesy Kansas Department of Wildlife and Parks.

Barred Owl
Strix varia (Barton)

Status: The Barred Owl, a common permanent resident in the eastern third of the state, becomes rare and local westward. It has been reported west to Comanche, Ford, Rush, and Phillips counties. Western sight records need confirmation.

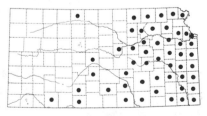

Period of Occurrence: The Barred Owl is a permanent resident in the east, but its status in the west is uncertain. It may be expanding its range or simply wandering.

Breeding: Barred Owls usually nest in densely wooded areas, often along river bottoms. The eggs are normally laid in an unlined tree cavity 25 or more feet above ground, but abandoned hawk and crow nests are occasionally used. Some nest sites have been used repeatedly for up to 35 years. Two to three dull white eggs are laid at intervals of several days, and when the first egg is laid, incubation begins. It lasts about 30 days and is undertaken chiefly, perhaps entirely, by the female. Our very few nest records suggest an egg-laying peak in early March. Young may leave the nest to clamber around nearby when they are about four weeks old, but they do not fly for at least another month.

Habits and Habitat: The species is best known for its unique call "who-cooks-for-you, who-cooks-for-you-all." It is especially vocal during late winter and early spring, when it makes a variety of hoots, whistles, cackles, and whoops. Where they are common, several birds frequently call simultaneously and provide an exciting nighttime chorus. Individuals frequently respond to imitations of their calls and may come close to the caller. Barred Owls are usually more restricted to deeper woods than are Great Horned Owls, and they tend to remain in the same areas throughout the year. Their flight is slow, very buoyant, and highly maneuverable. They hunt sometimes in moderately open country and sometimes during daylight.

Field Marks: Although the calls are distinct, the Barred Owl is often confused visually with the Great Horned Owl when the latter's ear tufts are flattened. However, the Barred Owl's round head, brown eyes, and barred head, throat, and upper breast are distinctive.

Food: This owl's food, highly variable according to its availability, includes small rodents (chiefly mice), birds up to flicker size, large insects, fishes, frogs, and crayfishes.

Long-eared Owl
Asio otus (Linnaeus)

Status: The Long-eared Owl's status is uncertain, but small numbers probably reside permanently over much of the state. It is most often recorded during winter and spring, probably due to an influx of birds from farther north. There are no nesting records from the southeast.

Period of Occurrence: The species has been reported at all seasons

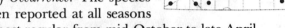

but is most regular from mid-October to late April.

Breeding: This owl breeds locally and normally nests 10 to 20 feet above ground, using the abandoned nest of a crow, magpie, or other large bird. Some birds may rebuild old nests, and others are said to build their own. Courtship includes acrobatic aerial displays, wing clapping, and dovelike cooing. Four to five glossy white eggs are laid at intervals of up to 5 days between mid-March and mid-April; they are incubated for about 26 days. Incubation begins when the first egg is laid, so the owlets often vary considerably in age. Like most owls, the female incubates, the male brings her food, and the young leave the nest long before they are able to fly. Adults are very active in defense of their nest and often employ a broken wing act in an attempt to lure away intruders.

Habits and Habitat: The Long-eared Owl is one of our most nocturnal and secretive owls and, as a result, is little known. It needs wooded areas for nesting, but in western Kansas, a dense windbreak, timber claim, or stretch of riparian woodland suffices. It prefers dense evergreen stands for winter roosting sites, and five to more than a dozen birds may congregate in a single favored area. Even there it may go unseen until discovered by a crow or until its pellets become noticeable. When disturbed at a roost, the owl may compress its thin body even more, lift its "ears" and lean against a tree trunk, using its protective coloration most effectively. The flight is buoyant and wavering, and the species' slim shape, with its relatively long wing and tail, are distinctive. Although it roosts in thick growth, it feeds over more open areas, usually only after dark.

Food: This owl's diet is almost entirely mice and similar small mammals, with occasional small to medium-sized birds, large insects, frogs, and small snakes.

An adult Long-eared Owl (*Asio otus*). Photograph by Ken M. Highfill.

An adult Short-eared Owl (*Asio flammeus*). Photograph by Bob Gress.

Short-eared Owl
Asio flammeus (Pontoppidan)

Status: The present status of the Short-eared Owl is uncertain. It was formerly a widespread and uncommon summer resident but is now very local or absent from much of the west and greatly reduced in numbers in the east. It is a transient and an irregular or local winter resident statewide.

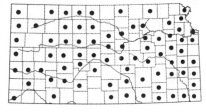

Period of Occurrence: Most records are between 16 October and 15 April, but a few individuals may occur at any time in proper habitat.

Breeding: The Short-eared Owl nests in prairies, marshes, fallow fields, and grain fields. Courtship includes a display performed several hundred feet in the air, in which the male swoops, dives, and somersaults while making chattering, quavering calls and toots, accompanied by wing clapping. The nest, a shallow scrape lined with vegetation and feathers, is often placed at the base of a tall weed. Five to seven dull white eggs are laid at intervals of several days, and incubation, lasting about 23 days, is by the female alone; the male brings her food. Young may wander from the nest in two or three weeks but cannot fly until they are six weeks old; they are dependent on their parents for two months or more.

Habits and Habitat: According to Goss, it was a common resident during the mid-1800s, but since the 1930s, it has been a rare, irregular, or very local summer resident. Its actual breeding status in much of Kansas is still uncertain. Its presence may first be noticed when a bird is seen flying over a roadside field. Nests, which are often in wheat or alfalfa fields, are often destroyed either by farming operations or by predators attracted to the strip of uncut vegetation left by a well-meaning farmer. When defending their nest, birds dive at the intruder and may suddenly tumble from the air to perform a wounded-bird display on the ground.

This species is probably our most diurnal owl, and it is often seen, especially in winter, as it courses low over fields, marshes, or fence rows in search of prey. The hunting flight is characterized by a slow, jerky wingbeat. It may also hover while facing into a strong wind. During winter, these owls may congregate in loose flocks in grasslands where there is good feeding. Thompson has observed flocks of 50 or more at Udall, Cowley County.

Food: Up to 90 percent of its food is small mammals, chiefly mice, with a few small birds and large insects also eaten.

An adult Northern Saw-whet Owl (*Aegolius acadicus*). Photograph by Ed and Jean Schulenberg.

Northern Saw-whet Owl
Aegolius acadicus (Gmelin)

Status: The Northern Saw-whet Owl is a rare local transient and winter resident statewide. It nested in Wyandotte County in 1951.

Period of Occurrence: The extreme
dates for transient and wintering
birds are 14 October and 30 April. Most recent records are between mid-November and
mid-March.

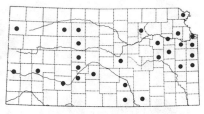

Breeding: A pair found in Kansas
City, Wyandotte County, during the winter of 1950 remained to nest.
Young seen by John Bishop were present until at least September
1951. Birds responded to a taped call at Hillsdale Reservoir, Miami
County, on 27 July 1985. Five to six pure white eggs are laid in a cavity
(usually a woodpecker hole), and the female incubates about 27 days.
The male brings her food and helps feed the young, which remain in
the nest about a month.

Habits and Habitat: Saw-whet Owls normally breed in dense woods
and swamps of the northern United States, southern Canada, and in
mountainous areas farther south. They probably reach Kansas when
they disperse for the winter, rather than as regular migrants. While
here, Saw-whet Owls are completely nocturnal, spend the day roosting in dense conifers or grapevine tangles, and are rarely seen. This
species is very tame. It can usually be approached very closely and can
sometimes be captured by hand. One bird that had been captured in a
mist net was taken to a classroom, where it sat quietly on the back of a
chair for the duration of a 50-minute class period. The courtship call,
which sounds like a saw being sharpened and gives the bird its name,
is rarely heard in Kansas.

Field Marks: Our smallest owl, this species is easily recognized by its
striped face and lack of ear tufts.

Food: In summer, insects are a major source of food. In winter, it feeds
primarily on mice and other small rodents and occasionally on birds.

An adult Common Nighthawk (*Chordeiles minor*). Photograph by Bob Gress.

GOATSUCKERS
Common Nighthawk
Chordeiles minor (Forster)

Status: The Common Nighthawk is a common transient and summer resident throughout the state.

Period of Occurrence: There are sight records for the Common Nighthawk from 29 April to 29 October. There is also an early spring date of 23 March from Sedgwick County.

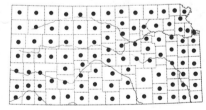

Breeding: This goatsucker is a common breeding bird in most areas. There is no formal nest building; the female simply lays the eggs on the ground in gravelly areas, in burned-over pastureland, and even on flat roof tops. The normal clutch size is two. The eggs, which hatch in about 19 days, have a gray base with darker spotting. The young remain in the nest for approximately three weeks before fledging and continue to be fed for a short period after leaving the nest.

Habits and Habitat: The nighthawk is a common sight in the evening as it forages for insects high overhead. The male's courtship display is responsible for a nickname: the male dives toward the ground, and as he pulls up, air rushes by the wings and gives a characteristic "roar," hence the name "bull bat." The common call is a "peent" call as the bird flies overhead. A careful look around open pastureland in the country often reveals these birds perched upon fence posts during the day. They usually "hold" fairly tightly, then fly off if approached too closely. Although not often cited as a perching place, Ely and Thompson have seen these birds perched on wire fences numerous times. During migration and on cloudy days, nighthawks may feed in the daytime, but generally, they wait until dusk to begin feeding, perch when they can no longer see their prey, and resume feeding at first light. Birds heard calling while flying at night are generally assumed to be courting and not feeding. These birds do not detect their prey by ultrasonic waves, as do swifts and bats, but use their vision to find prey.

Food: The Common Nighthawk feeds entirely on insects, which it captures on the wing.

Common Poorwill
Phalaenoptilus nuttallii (Audubon)

Status: The Common Poorwill is a locally common transient and summer resident. Its present breeding range is unknown, but records show it as breeding sporadically from the eastern to the western borders of the state.

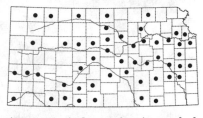

Period of Occurrence: There are records for this goatsucker from 12 April to 2 November and one from a Christmas bird count in Barber County on 23 December 1976. More information is needed.

Breeding: This mainly western species has been recorded nesting as far east as Anderson, Franklin, and Doniphan counties and in fact may be a more common breeding bird of the Flint Hills region than the western part of Kansas. In the east, it seems to prefer upland areas with exposed outcrops of gravel and rock. In the west, it frequents scrubby woodland. Seibel (1975) describes a nest site in Cowley County as "located on top of the highest hill in the area, a rocky, grassy plate about 200 yards above the woods bordering the creek." Thompson has noted the species at the Winfield City Lake, Cowley County, almost always where grass intermingled with rocky areas. Their clutch size is two eggs, which are white with no spotting. The incubation period is about 18 days. The adults are well camouflaged and will wait until almost stepped on before taking wing. The young birds may leave the actual nest but remain nearby.

Habits and Habitat: The Common Poorwill apparently occurs primarily in central and western Kansas, but adequate information is lacking on its range in the east. It commonly sits in the middle of the road late at night, and when car lights shine upon it, its eyes seem to be disembodied red patches. Their name comes from the characteristic call "poorwill" heard at dusk and well into the night. In fact, these birds are heard more often than seen. In the east, grassland seems to be the favorite habitat, and in the west, scrubby woodland and grassland. This species can become torpid with a reduction in body temperature and breathing rate, which could presumably explain the Barber County record in late December.

Food: Goatsuckers feed late in the evening, flying overhead and catching insects in their enormous mouths. Their large mouths may have initiated the myth that they suck the milk from goats.

An adult Chuck-will's-widow (*Caprimulgus carolinensis*). Photograph by Roger Boyd.

Chuck-will's-widow
Caprimulgus carolinensis (Gmelin)

Status: The Chuck-will's-widow is a locally common summer resident in the east. Its western limits are unknown, but the species seems to be moving westward, with recent re- cords from Clark and Edwards counties.

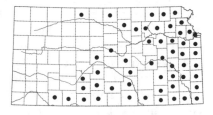

Period of Occurrence: The dates, which run from 9 April to 16 Sep- tember, seem to be recurring dates and so do not represent ex- tremes.

Breeding: The area in which the Chuck-will's-widow breeds is uncer- tain. It is locally common in the east, but most of the western records may be only of migrating birds and not breeding birds. That it does sporadically breed in the west is indicated by a specimen collected by

Rising (1974) on 10 May 1968 in Edwards County. The female had an egg in the oviduct. The species is primarily a southern and southeastern bird in the United States but seems to be extending its breeding range to the north and to the west. Goss (1886) did not record the bird on his list. Snow (1903) considered it to be accidental. By 1956 (Tordoff), it was considered to be a locally common summer resident. Like most caprimulgids, it lays its eggs on the ground, usually on leaf litter in the forest or on the forest edge. The two eggs are white with dark splotches. The incubation period is about 20 days. After the young hatch, they remain in the vicinity of the nest but can scramble around fairly well.

Habits and Habitat: The Chuck-will's-widow is a woodland bird that occurs along stream courses and hillsides covered with trees. It is another of the "birds of the night" whose call can be heard throughout the eastern part of the state in the evening just before dark. Its call is often mistaken for that of the Whip-poor-will. Unless one is close to the bird, only the "will-widow" is heard and not the first "chuck." Also, most people are not aware that there are two caprimulgids with similar calls. This bird can readily be attracted to a tape-recorded call in its territory. In the summer, this species is the most likely of the caprimulgids to be flushed from under foot in the woods. Its mothlike flight takes it a short distance before it alights. It also rests on branches of trees, sitting lengthwise along the limb so that it is nearly invisible.

Food: Its diet consists entirely of insects taken on the wing in the late evening or early morning.

Whip-poor-will
Caprimulgus vociferus (Wilson)

Status: The Whip-poor-will is a locally common transient and summer resident in the east. It breeds west to at least Riley County, but its breeding status and western distribution are poorly known.

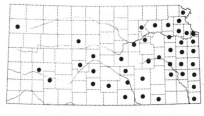

Period of Occurrence: The Whip-
poor-will has been recorded
from 3 April to 14 October.

Habits and Habitat: The range of
the Whip-poor-will in eastern
Kansas seems to be shrinking as the Chuck-will's-widow continues to encroach upon its traditional territory. Both species occupy wood-lands, apparently of the same composition; the Whip-poor-will does not seem to compete and disappears from the area. Most of the records date from the late 1880s to the middle of the 1900s. There is still ample opportunity to observe this species or, more often, to hear it in the extreme eastern part of Kansas. At a Kansas Ornithological Society meeting near the Marais des Cygnes Refuge, the campground resounded all night with the calls of this species and the Chuck-will's-widow, making sleep difficult.

Food: The species feeds at dusk and dawn upon insects taken on the wing.

SWIFTS
Chimney Swift
Chaetura pelagica (Linnaeus)

Status: The Chimney Swift is a common transient and breeding bird in the central and eastern part of the state. It becomes progressively less common heading westward, where its breeding status is uncertain.

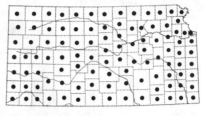

Period of Occurrence: The Chimney Swift has been recorded as early as 31 March, but the normal migration begins around 16 April; the normal fall departure begins 10 October, with an extreme date of 22 October.

Breeding: As its name implies, this swift now nests primarily in chimneys. Prior to man-made structures, it nested in hollow trees and caves. The nest is constructed of small twigs, which the swift takes on the wing from the tops of trees. The nests are placed inside the chimney and held in place by saliva used as a glue. (In fact, Chinese bird's nest soup uses the saliva of Asiatic Swifts, which make a nest of hardened saliva and very few sticks.) The nest is unlined, and the four white eggs are laid on the twigs. The eggs hatch in about 18 days. The young remain in the nest, where they are fed by their parents for an additional four weeks before departure.

Habits and Habitat: These superb flyers are most at home flying above the rooftops looking for insects or performing courtship displays. They are sometimes referred to as "flying cigars." As the name Chimney Swift implies, they are indeed swift, and other members of the family have been clocked at speeds over 100 MPH. They are particularly adept at flying in close formation with wings held high. When approaching the nest site, they circle and then suddenly flutter into the chimney. In the fall, certain areas are used as staging sites for enormous numbers of birds prior to their southward departure. Southwestern College in Winfield has such a staging area, where an estimated 10,000 birds gather in early October prior to their migration. Just at dusk, the birds swirl around the chimneys of the staging area, and as darkness approaches, they swarm down into the large chimneys like miniature tornadoes.

Many people have capped off their chimneys to keep these birds from nesting, in the mistaken belief that the nests harbor insects which

An adult Chimney Swift (*Chaetura pelagica*) clinging to a rock wall. Photograph by Bob Gress.

will get into the house and subsequently on people. Others enjoy the chattering in the chimney and welcome these birds to their home. However, young birds are often killed when a fire is started in the fireplace, so it is a good idea to cap a chimney and discourage such nesting if the fireplace will be used.

Food: Chimney Swifts feed exclusively on insects taken on the wing.

White-throated Swift
Aeronautes saxatalis (Woodhouse)

Status: The White-throated Swift is a vagrant. Sebastian Patti saw two swifts thought to be this species at Point of Rocks, Morton County, from 9 to 11 June 1972. Another bird was observed at Kansas State University, Manhattan, Riley County, on 2 November 1978, by Steve Fretwell (1978) and others. This bird was attempting to roost under the eave of a building. All  of the field marks of the latter were clearly seen. In the absence of a specimen or photograph, the bird is included here as hypothetical.

Magnificent Hummingbird
Eugenes fulgens (Swainson)

Status: The Magnificent Hummingbird, formerly called Rivoli's, is a vagrant, with one record from Boicourt, Linn County (Boyd 1978). This bird, a female, was seen from 18 April to 10 June 1977. Excellent photographs were taken by Martin Pressgrove on 29 May 1977. Allan R. Phillips verified the identification from the photographs. Orville Rice re-ported a "larger hummer" in the Topeka area in 1965, which may have been this species.

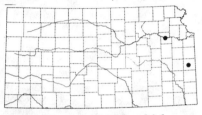

An adult Magnificent Hummingbird (*Eugenes fulgens*). Photograph by David A. Rintoul.

Ruby-throated Hummingbird
Archilochus colubris (Linneaus)

Status: The Ruby-throated Hummingbird is an uncommon transient and summer resident in the east. It gradually becomes less common westerly, where it is a rare transient and casual summer resident.

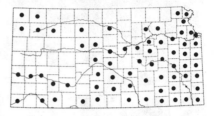

Period of Occurrence: The extreme dates for this "hummer" are 2 April and 24 October. Normally, they arrive about 1 May and remain until 15 October.

Breeding: This minute bird breeds in riparian woodland, cities with trees, parks, and other types of woody situations. The nest is placed on a twig or branch from 5 feet to 50 or 60 feet above ground. The nest is composed of lichens stuck together with spider webs and is lined. The two white eggs are about the size of green peas. The incubation period is 16 days, and the young may fledge from two to four weeks after hatching.

Habits and Habitat: The Ruby-throated Hummingbird is the only truly eastern hummingbird in the United States, and it reaches its westerly limit in Kansas. Although it is occasionally found in western Kansas, it is always rare. This hummingbird comes readily to feeders and is a big hit when it takes up residence. Males are extremely pugnacious and will try to drive away other hummingbirds that want to feed. Trumpet vines are a perennial favorite of hummingbirds and will draw them to a location.

Some birdwatchers have put up several feeders in areas frequented by hummingbirds and have numerous pairs around all summer. One such feeding area in Sumner County has drawn not only this hummingbird but the Broad-tailed and Rufous species as well. Sugar solutions for feeders can be made from table sugar at the rate of 1/4 cup of sugar dissolved in one cup of boiling water. Solutions that are too strong can be harmful to the bird's health. Red coloring may initially attract the birds, but once they find it, the coloring should be omitted from the solution. If red feeders are used, no coloring is needed. In Kansas, the feeders also may attract the Northern Oriole. Hummingbirds have an extremely rapid metabolism which requires that they eat every 10 minutes or so. In the evening, their body temperature is lowered to reduce the rapid metabolism.

An adult Ruby-throated Hummingbird (*Archilochus colubris*). Photograph by David A. Rintoul.

Food: The primary diet of this species is nectar from flowers. Insects are also taken.

An adult Black-chinned Hummingbird (*Archilochus alexandri*). Photograph by Marvin D. Schwilling.

Black-chinned Hummingbird
Archilochus alexandri (Bourcier and Mulsant)

Status: The Black-chinned Hummingbird is best considered a vagrant to Kansas. There is one record, from Elkhart, Morton County, where a male in breeding plumage was seen 8 May 1987 by Sebastian Patti and Marc Radell. Photographs were taken of the bird. The white line on the breast, which clearly showed in the photograph, helps in identifying the 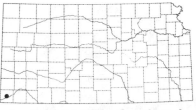 male. The female is inseparable in the field from the female Ruby-throated Hummingbird. The species supposedly has nested in the Oklahoma panhandle near Kenton (Sutton 1967). It is most remarkable that this western species had not been seen prior to 1987, as it has occurred in states farther east than Kansas several times.

Calliope Hummingbird
Stellula calliope (Gould)

Status: The Calliope Hummingbird is a vagrant. The only record is of an immature female collected on the Cimarron River 8 miles south of

Richfield, Morton County, on 3
September 1952. This species is
another of the hummingbirds
from the western states that may
actually be more common here
than a single record would indicate. Any hummingbird seen in

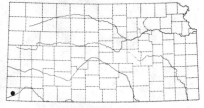

western Kansas is apt to be an unusual species, since none is a regular migrant in the region. However, if additional feeders were available in the western part of the state, more individual sightings might be recorded.

An adult male Broad-tailed Hummingbird (*Selasphorus platycercus*). Photograph by David A. Rintoul.

Broad-tailed Hummingbird
Selasphorus platycercus (Swainson)

Status: The Broad-tailed Hummingbird is a casual visitor. There are two records from Sumner County. An adult male was seen from 13 to 14 August 1979 by several obser-vers. The other was seen at the same locality from 20 to 22 August 1985. The only specimen is that of a adult male taken 15 miles north and 6 miles west of Elkhart, Morton County, on 18 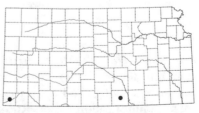 May 1978. It was feeding on black-locust blossoms. There are other, unsubstantiated records for the state.

The male attracts attention in flight by the trilling whistle of air passing over the tail; it is an unforgettable sound.

An adult Rufous Hummingbird (*Selasphorus rufus*). Photograph by David A. Rintoul.

Rufous Hummingbird
Selasphorus rufus (Gmelin)

Status: The Rufous Hummingbird is a rare fall transient, with most records from south-central Kansas. There is one specimen from Barton County on 23 August 1973.

Period of Occurrence: This hummingbird appears in Kansas as early as 21 July and has been seen as late as 4 October. However, most records seem to fall in mid- to late August.

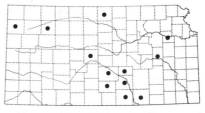

Habits and Habitat: Most records have come from around hummingbird feeders, where Rufous and Ruby-throated Hummingbirds intermix. Having the Ruby-throated Hummingbird for comparison makes identification easier. Rufous Hummingbirds are attracted to red flowers, such as cannas, salvia, and petunias. Like all hummingbirds, this species flies backwards or hovers in one spot with great agility. It is exceptionally pugnacious and will keep all other "hummers" away from its own feeder.

Field Marks: Most of the records for Kansas are of females or immatures. Rufous Hummingbirds are larger than most Ruby-throated Hummingbirds, and the immatures and females have green backs with dull rufous sides. The occasional adult male will have a rufous back and orange-red throat.

Food: This hummingbird's food, like that of most other hummingbirds, is primarily nectar and insects.

An adult Belted Kingfisher (*Ceryle alcyon*). Photograph by Mike Blair, courtesy Kansas Department of Wildlife and Parks.

KINGFISHERS
Belted Kingfisher
Ceryle alcyon (Linnaeus)

Status: The Belted Kingfisher, our only kingfisher, is a common transient and summer resident throughout the state. It is uncommon to rare in winter, occurring chiefly in the east and south.

Period of Occurrence: Although it is a year-round resident, most birds migrate farther south in winter. The bulk of the Kansas records are between March and November.

366

Breeding: This species is a hole-nesting bird that burrows into banks along streams, rivers, and lakes. The tunnel is usually from 2 to 6 feet long but may be up to 15 feet (Johnsgard 1979). The white eggs are laid in the expanded end of the tunnel. The clutch size in Kansas is around six eggs. The incubation period is approximately 23 days. The young remain in the nest for about one month before leaving.

Habits and Habitat: This kingfisher is an inhabitant of streams, rivers, and lakes. Its rattling call is common whenever it is disturbed. It usually perches on a high branch watching the water below for small fishes, its primary food. When it spots potential prey, it dives off the branch headfirst into the water, hoping to catch the prey in its bill. Sometimes it may hover briefly before making the plunge, but most hunting is from perches. The catch is usually taken back to the perch, beaten until stunned, and then eaten headfirst.

Food: Although the primary food of the Belted Kingfisher is small fishes, it takes other vertebrates and insects also.

An adult Lewis' Woodpecker (*Melanerpes lewis*). Photograph by David A. Rintoul.

WOODPECKERS
Lewis' Woodpecker
Melanerpes lewis (Gray)

Status: The Lewis' Woodpecker is a casual migrant in western Kansas and a vagrant in the east. It has been recorded from five counties: Ellis, Morton, Finney, Kearny, and Douglas. Despite speculation that it might breed in southwestern Kansas, there is no evidence to substantiate this; with the increased number of birdwatchers frequenting the area, it surely would have been found were it breeding.

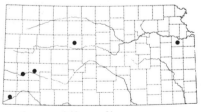

Period of Occurrence: The records are from May, June, July, September, and November.

Habits and Habitat: The Lewis' Woodpecker usually is found along streams with cottonwoods or other types of trees. Like its cousin, the Red-headed Woodpecker, this bird frequently catches insects out of the air like a flycatcher. It has a more crowlike flight and not the bounding flight of other woodpeckers.

Food: This species' main food is insects, which it obtains either by "flycatching" (catching flies by pursuit from a perch) or by excavation of dead wood.

Red-headed Woodpecker
Melanerpes erythrocephalus (Linnaeus)

Status: The Red-headed Woodpecker is a common transient and summer resident statewide. It is a local and irregular winter resident in the eastern one-third of the state.

Period of Occurrence: The Red-headed Woodpecker has been recorded every month of the year. However, it is most common from about 25 April to 26 September. In winter, it is irregular and in most cases, uncommon to rare.

Breeding: This woodpecker probably nests in all counties. It nests in tree cavities, which it excavates, or it may utilize a nest from a previous year, which some other species excavated. The cavities are usually dug out of dead limbs and are from 9 to 14 inches deep. The eggs are laid on chips taken from the inner walls of the cavity. If trees are not available in the western part of the state, they may use utility poles, or man-made cavities. E. A. Stoner even found one using a Blue Jay nest in Iowa (Bent 1939). The eggs are white, and the usual clutch size is three to four eggs. The incubation period is approximately 12 days, and the young fledge in about 18 days.

Habits and Habitat: This magnificent woodpecker is often the only woodpecker seen out in the prairie, far from trees. It tends to nest in trees with softer wood than oak, but prefers oaks and pecan groves as its favorite winter haunts. Like its close kin the Acorn Woodpecker, it stores acorns and pecans for winter food. Whether or not it remains for the winter depends on the local food supply. Like all woodpeckers, it possesses strong claws with which it clings to the bark as it excavates for insects. The tail is very stiff and is used for a prop. Woodpeckers can be quite vocal, and experienced birdwatchers can easily distinguish their different call notes. They are particularly noisy in the spring during mating and in winter tend to be much quieter. This woodpecker's habit of digging into utility poles has not endeared it to utility companies.

Field Marks: The completely red head, contrasted with the blue-black and white of the rest of the body and wings, is spectacular and immediately draws attention. This color combination is found in no other species in Kansas. The Red-bellied Woodpecker is sometimes

Adult Red-headed Woodpeckers (*Melanerpes erythrocephalus*) at nest. Photograph by Gerald J. Wiens.

confused with the Red-headed, but in the latter species, the red covers the top of the head, nape of the neck, and also the throat. The Red-bellied Woodpecker has no red on the throat.

Food: The Red-headed Woodpecker eats a variety of food, including fruit, and may cause considerable damage to crops. They also eat acorns, pecans, corn, and other types of seeds. They eat eggs and nestling birds of other species, and insects, some of which have been found alive wedged in cracks, presumably stored for a future banquet. Thus they are apparently omnivorous and utilize anything they can swallow.

An adult Red-bellied Woodpecker (*Melanerpes carolinus*). Photograph by Gerald J. Wiens.

Red-bellied Woodpecker
Melanerpes carolinus (Linnaeus)

Status: The Red-bellied Woodpecker is a common resident in the east and is irregular in the central area of the state. Its western status is uncertain, although it seems to be expanding its range westward along the wooded streams and rivers.

Period of Occurrence: This woodpecker is a resident.

Breeding: Like all of our woodpeckers, this species nests primarily in trees. The entrance to the nesting cavity is usually on the underside of a leaning limb. The birds prefer dead limbs for the nest site but occasionally use soft, deciduous trees. The nesting cavity is about 12 inches deep and has wood chips located in the bottom. Usually five white eggs are laid, most in late April. During the incubation period of 12 days, the eggs are attended by both parents, as is incubation by most woodpeckers. The young remain in the nest around 20 days before fledging. They may remain with the parents for a time, but family groups usually break up in the fall.

Habits and Habitat: The Red-bellied Woodpecker is mainly a forest woodpecker that lives in riparian woodland, but it has readily adapted to cities with mature trees. As the trees along the stream courses in the western part of the state have matured, this species has moved in. In winter, it readily comes to feeders, where it takes both suet and sunflower seeds. At feeders, it is often mistaken for the Red-headed Woodpecker (see Field Marks under that species). It has the undulating flight of most woodpeckers that seems to be timed just right for landing on a limb on the upward swing.

Field Marks: The zebralike stripes on the back and red forehead and nape distinguish this species from our other woodpeckers. The female has a gray forehead, with the red beginning just above the eyes and extending backward down the nape.

Food: The species eats fruits and seeds and is known to store food for future use. In winter, it frequents pecan groves and also eats other types of nuts and seeds found in the forest.

Yellow-bellied Sapsucker
Sphyrapicus varius (Linnaeus)

Status: The Yellow-belled Sapsucker is an uncommon transient and winter resident throughout.

Period of Occurrence: This sap-sucker has been recorded from 3 October to 28 April. There is an early fall arrival record of 4 September and a late departure of 14 May.

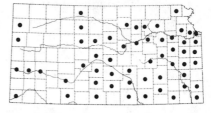

Habits and Habitat: In winter here, this species is found associated primarily with conifers. More often than not, their borings on pine trees are more evident than the birds themselves. They peck out small holes, sometimes making an almost perfect girdle around a tree. If the holes are too close together, they can kill it, but most often, the damage is superficial and the tree survives quite nicely. The holes collect sap, which the birds then feed upon. According to McAtee (1911), these birds use 246 species of native trees and 6 vines, as well as 31 species of introduced trees. However, in Kansas one rarely sees the results of their work except on conifers. This bird might go unnoticed were it not for its peculiar call. When approached, it moves very quickly to the other side of the tree and remains inconspicuous.

Field Marks: Most of these birds in Kansas lack the colorful plumage depicted in field guides. They are rather drab, but the white slash in the wing and their habitat are identification aids.

Food: Their primary food appears to be sap from trees, but they also consume insects and fruit.

Red-naped Sapsucker
Sphyrapicus nuchalis (Baird)

Status: The Red-naped Sapsucker is a recently resurrected species that is probably a casual migrant through western Kansas. Tordoff (1956) lists three specimens from Wallace and Morton counties. The adult male differs from the Yellow-bellied Sapsucker in having a red, instead of a black, nape. More information and specimens are needed to delineate its range and density in Kansas.

An adult Williamson's Sapsucker (*Sphyrapicus thyroideus*) at nest. Photograph by Marvin D. Schwilling.

Williamson's Sapsucker
Sphyrapicus thyroideus (Cassin)

Status: There is only one record of the Williamson's Sapsucker, that of an adult male seen at Concordia, Cloud County, on 4 April 1935, by

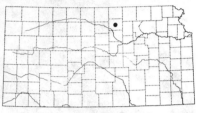

Dr. J. M. Porter. Thompson read Dr. Porter's journals at the Museum of Natural History at the University of Kansas, but Porter had described no plumages in his notes on that day. Although this species has been seen as far east as Chicago, it is rarely seen out of the Rocky Mountain region. This sight record is open to question, and the species remains on the hypothetical list.

An adult Ladder-backed Woodpecker (*Picoides scalaris*). Photograph by David A. Rintoul.

Ladder-backed Woodpecker
Picoides scalaris (Wagler)

Status: The Ladder-backed Woodpecker is an uncommon resident of southwestern Kansas, where it has been recorded from Hamilton, Morton, and Clark counties. It has been recorded nesting only in Morton County. Tordoff (1956) considered this to be a common bird and listed six specimens, all from Morton County. This bird seems to be increasing in numbers along the Cimarron River.

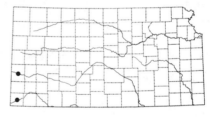

Period of Occurrence: The species is a resident.

Breeding: There are recent breeding records for Morton County along the Cimarron River. Johnston (1964) did not report it as a breeding bird for Kansas. Ely saw a male leaving a nesting cavity along the Cimarron River in Morton County on 3 June 1968. Adult birds were seen going in and out of a presumed nesting cavity in a Black Willow *(Salix niger)* near the same area in May 1984. The woodpecker lays from two to six white eggs, and the incubation period is about 13 days (Johnsgard 1979). They probably remain in the nest from 18 to 25 days, but little is known about the fledging period. Additional observations are needed from southwestern Kansas to determine breeding numbers.

Habits and Habitat: The Ladder-backed Woodpecker is primarily a bird of the southwestern United States. It reaches its northeastern limits in southwestern Kansas, where it is found frequenting the cottonwoods and willows along the Cimarron River.

Field Marks: The Ladder-backed Woodpecker is readily distinguished from the Downy Woodpecker by the barring on the back that resembles a ladder.

Food: The species feeds upon wood-borer larvae and other insects gleaned from trees. They have also been observed feeding upon the cactus fruit.

An adult male Downy Woodpecker (*Picoides pubescens*). Photograph by David A. Rintoul.

Downy Woodpecker
Picoides pubescens (Linnaeus)

Status: The Downy Woodpecker is a common resident in the central and east of the state but local and irregular in the far west.

Period of Occurrence: This wood-pecker is a resident.

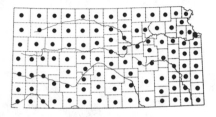

Breeding: The species is a breed-ing bird wherever there are woods, and it commonly breeds in cities with mature trees. The nest is usually placed in a dead limb, with the entrance hole on the underneath side. The eggs are laid in the cavity on wood chips. Most nests are about 20 feet above ground in Kansas. The clutch size is about four white eggs, which are laid from 11 April to 10 June; most eggs are laid approximately 5 May. The incubation period is 12 days, and the young fledge in about 30 days.

Habits and Habitat: The Downy Woodpecker is usually associated with woodland or scrub, but it is not unusual to see it feeding in the fall on sunflowers as the seeds mature. They also open the sunflower stems to get at the insects. This species is the common woodpecker seen in towns and the one most likely to frequent feeders in winter. It becomes quite tame at feeders and is easily approached. The Downy Woodpecker, like other woodpeckers, drums on hollow objects, utility poles, or any other object that echoes the drum beat. This drumming is thought to be part of the courtship ritual, as it is more common in the spring than at any other time of year and is not used for hunting for food. When searching for food, the Downy Woodpecker pecks quietly to dislodge wood chips and, of course, any grubs that may be buried. Each species of woodpecker has its own distinctive drumming pattern, and experienced observers can distinguish between them. When the bird is chipping away at logs in a quiet area, follow the pecking sounds to locate it.

Field Marks: This species is the smallest woodpecker in Kansas except for the Ladder-backed, and that bird occurs only in a very restricted area of the state. The black-and-white coloration and small size of the Downy Woodpecker help to separate it from the Hairy Woodpecker, which, although the same color, is noticeably larger. In the hand, the Downy Woodpecker's white outer tail feathers have black bars and the Hairy Woodpecker's are plain white.

Food: Its primary food appears to be insects, especially grubs from the wood, and ants. It extracts grubs from a hole by its long tongue which is barbed on the end. After the grub has been speared, it is very difficult for it to escape. The species feeds on suet and sunflower seeds in the winter and also comes to feeders in the summer to eat sunflower seeds.

An adult Hairy Woodpecker (*Picoides villosus*). Photograph by Marvin D. Schwilling.

Hairy Woodpecker
Picoides villosus (Linnaeus)

Status: The Hairy Woodpecker is a common bird statewide, but it is not as abundant as the Downy Woodpecker.

Period of Occurrence: The Hairy Woodpecker is a permanent resident of Kansas.

Breeding: The Hairy Woodpecker breeds throughout the state. Courtship begins in early spring with mate selection, then

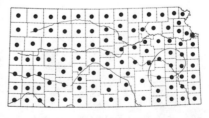

nest building starts. The process is a fairly long excavation that takes from one to three weeks. The nest holes seem on the average to be higher in a tree than those of Downy Woodpeckers. Eggs are laid from late March to late May. They are placed in the nesting cavity on wood chips. There are usually four white eggs which hatch in about 12 days. Both parents care for and feed the young, which remain in the nest for about 28 days.

Habits and Habitat: The Hairy Woodpecker occurs in riparian woodland, cities, and large woodlots. It is much shyer than the Downy Woodpecker and is much more reluctant to come to feeders. (Thompson has only seen one at a feeder in 20 years.) When confronted by a person, it normally goes around to the other side of the tree or simply flies away. This woodpecker also drums during courtship.

Food: The main food is insects, particularly grubs of long-horn beetles. A woodpecker stomach examined by one scientist contained over 100 larvae. Ants rank second to grubs, and much smaller amounts of vegetable matter are also taken.

An adult Northern Flicker (*Colaptes auratus*). Photograph by David A. Rintoul.

Northern Flicker
Colaptes auratus (Linnaeus)

Status: The Northern Flicker is a common transient and summer resident throughout the state and a locally common winter resident. Although the red-shafted race (*C. a. cafer*) is present in winter, there is no evidence that it breeds here.

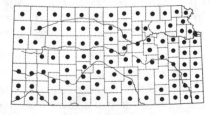

Period of Occurrence: The species has been recorded all months of the year. The Red-shafted Flicker is a winter resident only, and many of the wintering birds appear to be hybrids between the yellow-shafted race (*C. a. auratus*) and the red-shafted. Most of our breeding birds probably move southward in the winter; our wintering populations are northern and western individuals. The largest influxes during migration seem to be in April and again in September and October. It is difficult to pinpoint dates, since wintering birds and transients may overlap.

Breeding: This woodpecker is much less confined to woodland than the others in the state. Although it usually nests in tree cavities, it may utilize a stump in the middle of a field, far away from trees. The male typically picks and constructs the nest, which may be commonly reused year after year. There are usually six white eggs which are laid on wood chips. Both parents take turns at incubation, with the male usually taking the nighttime shift like most woodpecker males. The young hatch in about 12 days and fledge in 25 to 30 days. The young can be quite noisy in the nest and, as they grow older and stronger, climb to the entrance and clamor loudly for food as the parents approach.

Habits and Habitat: The Northern Flicker is the second largest of our woodpeckers and the most terrestrial. It frequently feeds on lawns and in pasture land, eating ants and other animal and vegetable matter. Interesting experiments have been carried out with flickers and their moustaches (only males have them), which are black on the yellow-shafted race and red on the red-shafted race. When a black moustache was painted on a female, the male drove her from the nest, even though he had been mated to her for several weeks. To the Northern Flicker, as with all other hole-nesting birds, the European Starling has been devastating, because it frequently takes over the nest and drives the flickers away. In fall migration, flickers sometimes group in large flocks as they move southward.

Field Marks: Identification of flicker subspecies in Kansas is difficult, especially in winter. From below, the yellow-shafted race shows golden wing and tail feathers, and the red-shafted race shows orange underwings and tail. Usually hybrids can be identified only in the hand. The red-shafted male has no red on the nape, while the yellow-shafted male has a red nape.

Food: The main diet is of ants and other insects. Ants are frequently taken, even in winter, when the flicker tears into their nests in old, rotten trees. They feed at anthills and even tear the hill apart to get to the larvae. They also take some vegetable matter when ants are not available.

An adult Pileated Woodpecker (*Dryocopus pileatus*). Photograph by Marvin D. Schwilling.

Pileated Woodpecker
Dryocopus pileatus (Linnaeus)

Status: The Pileated Woodpecker is a very large woodpecker that occurs only east and northeast from Sumner County. It is expanding into its former range in the eastern one-third of the state and is now considered to be an uncommon resident. Goss (1886) considered it to be not an uncommon resident along heavily wooded streams. Snow (1903) considered 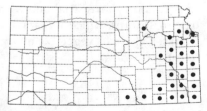 it to be a rare resident. Tordoff (1956) mentions several counties and that it was again expanding into its former range.

Period of Occurrence: There are records for all months of the year, and it is probably a year-round resident wherever it occurs.

Breeding: There are nesting records for Cowley, Linn, Elk, Cherokee, and possibly Stafford counties. It is a year-round resident in Sumner County, but no nest has been found. The nest is usually in a dead tree anywhere from quite close to the ground to 60 feet up. The large hole itself is usually oblong and very distinctive. Because the birds are so wary, it is difficult to see the adults coming to the nest site unless the observer is absolutely motionless. Pairs tend to return to the same nest site year after year. The hole is excavated to a depth of 15 to 26 inches, where three to four white eggs are laid on wood chips. Incubation lasts for about 18 days. The young are naked when they hatch and within a couple of weeks have attained half of their adult size. Thompson observed young being fed in Cowley County; the adult remained outside the nest while the young clamored with their heads out of the hole. The parents continue to feed the young for some time after they leave the nest.

Habits and Habitat: The Pileated Woodpecker occurs primarily in large mature forests. In Cowley and Sumner counties, it is particularly common along the Arkansas River. It wariness makes it difficult to spot, unless the birdwatcher is familiar with its drumming sound or call notes. The bird steals away in silent flight when people approach. The drumming is very distinctive and is the loudest sound in the forest in spring. It is very loud at first, then gradually trails off into silence. The bird frequently attracts attention with its loud calls, which are louder than most woodpeckers. Although not much of a nuisance here, it has destroyed utility poles in other states.

Field Marks: This crow-sized bird with its black-and-white wing pattern is almost unmistakable in flight. Both sexes have a bright red head pattern, but the female's is less extensive than the male's. The flight is crowlike, without the typical undulations of other woodpeckers.

Food: The chief food appears to be carpenter ants. This bird, like the flicker, is very terrestrial and feeds on ant mounds and around the base of stumps, which it tears apart looking for ants and grubs. In winter, it also eats vegetable matter. It infrequently comes to feeders to eat suet.

BIBLIOGRAPHY

Albert, J. W.
 1848. Notes on a military reconnaissance from Fort Leavenworth, in Missouri, to San Diego, in California. Wendell and Benthuysen, Washington, D.C. Pp. 386–405.

Allen, J. A.
 1872. Notes of an ornithological reconnaissance in portions of Kansas, Colorado, Wyoming, and Utah. Bull. Mus. Comp. Zool. 3(6):113–183.

Alvarez del Toro, Miguel.
 1971. Las aves de Chiapas. Gob. del Estado de Chiapas. Tuxtla Gutierrez, Chiapas. 270 pp. + color plates.

American Ornithologists' Union.
 1983. Check-list of North American birds, 6th ed. Allen Press, Lawrence, Kans. 877 pp.

Andrews, Ted.
 1954. Hudsonian godwit snagged by clam. Kansas Orni. Soc. Bull. 5(2):19.

Audubon, John James.
 1840. The Birds of America, 1840–1844. J. J. Audubon, New York.

Baird, S. F., J. Cassin, and G. N. Lawrence.
 1858. Reports of explorations and surveys to ascertain the most practicable and economic route for a railroad from the Mississippi river to the Pacific ocean, made under the direction of the secretary of war in 1853–6, according to acts of congress of March 3, 1853, May 31, 1854, and August 5, 1854. Vol. IX. A. O. P. Nicholson, Washington, D.C. 1005 pp. '

Bent, Arthur Cleveland.
 1919. Life histories of North American diving birds. Government Printing Office, Washington, D.C. xiii + 245 pp.

 1921. Life histories of North American Gulls and Terns. Government Printing Office, Washington, D.C. x + 345 pp.

 1922. Life histories of North American petrels and pelicans and their allies. Government Printing Office, Washington, D.C. xii + 343 pp.

 1923. Life histories of North American wild fowl. Part 1. Government Printing Office, Washington, D.C. ix + 244 pp.

 1925. Life histories of North American wild fowl. Part 2. Government Printing Office, Washington, D.C. x + 314 pp.

 1926. Life histories of North American marsh birds. Government Printing Office, Washington, D.C. xii + 490 pp.

 1927. Life histories of North American shore birds. Part 1. Government Printing Office, Washington, D.C. ix + 420 pp.

 1929. Life histories of North American shore birds. Part 2. Government Printing Office, Washington, D.C. ix + 412 pp.

 1932. Life histories of North American gallinaceous birds. Government Printing Office, Washington, D.C. xi + 490 pp.

 1937. Life histories of North American birds of prey. Part 1. Government Printing Office, Washington, D.C. viii + 398 pp.

 1938. Life histories of North American birds of prey. Part 2. Government Printing Office, Washington, D.C. viii + 482 pp.

1939.   Life histories of North American woodpeckers. Government Printing Office, Washington, D.C. viii + 334 pp.

1940.   Life histories of North American cuckoos, goatsuckers, hummingbirds and their allies. Government Printing Office, Washington, D.C. viii + 506 pp.

Boyd, Roger L.

1972.   Breeding biology of the snowy plover at Cheyenne Bottoms Waterfowl Management Area, Barton County, Kansas. Master's thesis, Kansas State Teachers College, Emporia.

1978.   Rivoli's hummingbird in Linn County, Kansas. Kansas Orni. Soc. Bull. 29(1):10–11.

Brecheisen, William R., and Eva M. Brecheisen.

1986.   Trumpeter swans wintering in Kansas. Kansas Orni. Soc. Bull. 37(2):29–30.

Bryant, Ralph L.

1983.   Eared Grebes make first recorded nesting attempt in Kansas. Kansas Orni. Soc. Bull. 34(3):27.

Buss, I. O.

1951.   The upland plover in southwestern Yukon Territory. Arctic 4:204–213.

Cable, Ted T., and David A. Rintoul.

1985.   Thayer's Gull in Riley County: First documented occurrence in Kansas. Kansas Orni. Soc. Bull. 36(2):21–22.

Collins, Joseph T., Ed.

1985.   Natural Kansas. University Press of Kansas, Lawrence. xii + 226 pp.

Colvin, Walter.

1914.   The lesser prairie hen. Outlook 63:608–614.

Coues, Elliott.

1965.   Ornithology of a prairie journey, and notes on the Birds of Arizona. Ibis 1:157–165.

1871.   The Yellow-headed Blackbird. Amer. Naturalist 5:91.

Fitch, Henry S., and Pennie von Achen.

1973.   Yellow-billed cuckoo nesting at the University of Kansas Natural History Reservation. Kansas Orni. Soc. Bull. 24(2):12–15.

Fremont, John C.

1845.   Report of the exploring expedition to the Rocky Mountains in the year 1842 and to Oregon and north California in the years 1843–4. Blair and Rives, Washington, D.C.

Fretwell, Stephen.

1978.   White-throated swift at Manhattan, Kansas. Kansas Orni. Soc. Bull. 29(4):31–32.

Goodrich, Arthur L.

1946.   Birds in Kansas. Report of the Kansas State Board of Agric., June 1945. 340 pp.

Goss, Nathaniel S.

1878.   Breeding of the duck hawk in trees. Bull. Nuttall Orni. Club 3:32.

1883.   A catalogue of the birds of Kansas. Kansas Publ. House, Topeka.

1886.   A revised catalogue of the birds of Kansas. Kansas Publ. House, Topeka. iv + 76 pp.

1891.   History of the birds of Kansas. Crane and Co., Topeka. 692 pp.

Graber, Richard, and Jean Graber.
  1951.   Notes on the birds of southwestern Kansas. Trans. Kansas Acad. Sci.
            54(2):145–174.
Grant, Peter.
  1986.   Gulls: a guide to identification, 2d ed. Buteo, Vermillion, S.D.
Gregg, Josiah.
  1844.   Commerce of the prairies, or the journal of a Santa Fe trader during
            eight expeditions across the great western prairies, and a residence of
            nearly nine years in northern Mexico. 2 vols. J. and H. G. Langley, New
            York.
Gress, Bob, and Joe Schaefer.
  1984.   Great egrets nesting in Sedgwick County. Kansas Orni. Soc. Bull.
            35(2):21–22.
Holmes, Carl S.
  1958.   Checklist of summer birds of Cadillac Lake, Wichita, Sedgwick
            County, Kansas. Kansas Orni. Soc. Bull. 9(2):12–13.
Horak, Jerry.
  1985.   Bringing back the geese. Kansas Wildlife 42(1):18–21.
Johnsgard, Paul A.
  1973.   Grouse and quails of north America. Univ. Nebraska Press, Lincoln.
            xviii + 553 pp.
  1979.   Birds of the Great Plains. Univ. Nebraska Press, Lincoln. xiv + 539 pp.
  1981.   The plovers, sandpipers, and snipes of the world. Univ. Nebraska
            Press, Lincoln. xvi + 493 pp.
Johnston, Richard F.
  1960.   Directory to the bird-life of Kansas. Univ. Kansas Mus. Nat. Hist. Misc.
            Publ. 23:1–69.
  1964.   The breeding birds of Kansas. Univ. Kansas Publ. Mus. Nat. Hist.
            12:575–655.
  1965.   A directory to the birds of Kansas. Univ. Kansas Mus. Nat. Hist. Misc.
            Publ. 41:1–67.
Kennard, John H.
  1975.   Longevity records of North American birds. Bird-Banding 46:55–73.
Kortright, Francis H.
  1942.   The ducks, geese and swans of north America. Stackpole, Harrisburg,
            Pa., and Wildlife Management Institute, Washington, D.C. 476 pp. +
            36 color plates.
Kuchler, A. W.
  1974.   A new vegetation map of Kansas. Ecology 55:586–604.
Lantz, D. E.
  1899.   A Review of Kansas Ornithology. Part 1: The Bibliography of Kansas
            Birds. Kansas Acad. Sci. 16:224–244.
Lewis, M., and W. Clarke.
  1814.   History of the expedition under command of Captains Lewis and
            Clarke to the sources of the Missouri, thence across the Rocky Moun-
            tains and down the river Columbia to the Pacific Ocean. 2 vols. Brad-
            ford and Inskeep, New York.
Long, W. S.
  1934.   The Birds of Kansas. Univ. Kansas, Lawrence. Unpub. Manuscript.
            292 pp.

1935.   Observations on the November birds of western Kansas. Univ. Kansas
          Sci. Bull. 22(12):225–248.
1940.   Check-list of Kansas birds. Trans. Kansas Acad. Sci. 43:433–456.
Maximilian Prinz zu Wied.
1839.   Reise in das innere Nord-America in den jahren 1832 bis 1834. 2 vols.
          J. Hoelscher, Coblenz, West Germany.
McAtee, Waldo Lee.
1911.   Woodpeckers in relation to trees and wood products. U.S. Dept. Agric.
          Biol. Surv. Bull. 39.
McAtee, Waldo Lee, and F. E. L. Beal.
1912.   Some common game, aquatic and rapacious birds in relation to man.
          U.S. Dept. Agric. Farmers Bull. 497.
McKinley, Daniel.
1964.   History of the Carolina Parakeet in its southwestern range. Wilson
          Bull. 76:68–93.
Martin, Dennis J.
1973.   A spectrographic analysis of burrowing owl vocalizations. Auk
          90:564–578.
Miller, Jacob H.
1975.   Little gull at John Redmond Reservoir, Coffey County, Kansas. Kansas
          Orni. Soc. Bull. 26(2):9–10.
Palmer, Ralph S., Ed.
1962.   Handbook of North American birds. Vol. 1. Yale Univ. Press, New
          Haven, Conn. vii + 567 pp.
1976a.   Handbook of North American birds. Vol. 2. Yale Univ. Press, New
          Haven, Conn. xi + 421 pp.
1976b.   Handbook of North American birds. Vol. 3. Yale Univ. Press, New
          Haven, Conn. 560 pp.
Parker, James.
1979.   The Mississippi kite. Kansas Fish and Game 36(3):4–8.
Parker, James, Elizabeth Bennett, and Richard Chipman.
1983.   Second record of the magnificent frigatebird for Kansas. Kansas Orni.
          Soc. Bull. 34(1):18–19.
Parmelee, David F.
1961.   A nesting colony of black terns in Kansas. Kansas Orni. Soc. Bull.
          12(4):25–27.
Parmelee, David F., and H. A. Stephens.
1964.   Status of the harris hawk in Kansas. Condor 66:443–445.
Parmelee, David F., Marvin D. Schwilling, and H. A. Stephens.
1969a.   Charadriiform birds of Cheyenne Bottoms. Part 1. Kansas Orni. Soc.
          Bull. 20(2):9–13.
1969b.   Charadriiform birds of Cheyenne Bottoms. Part 2. Kansas Orni. Soc.
          Bull. 20(3):17–24.
Pike, Major Z. M.
1810.   An account of an expedition to the sources of the Mississippi and
          through the western parts of Louisiana, to the sources of the Arkansaw
          Kansas, La Platte and Pierre Jaune rivers. C. & A. Conrad & Co.,
          Philadelphia.
Ripley, S. Dillon.
1977.   Rails of the world. David R. Godine, Boston. xx + 406 pp.

Rising, James D.
    1974.   The status and faunal affinities of the summer birds of western Kan-
              sas. Univ. Kansas Sci. Bull. 50(8):347–388.
Rising, James D., and Delbert L. Kilgore, Jr.
    1964.   Notes on birds from southwestern Kansas. Kansas Orni. Soc. Bull.
              15(4):23–25.
Say, Thomas.
    1823.   Account of an expedition from Pittsburg to the Rocky Mountains,
              performed in the years 1819 and '20, by order of the Hon. J. C.
              Calhoun, secretary of war: under the command of Maj. Stephen H.
              Long. 2 vols. H. C. Carey and I. Lea., Philadelphia.
Schorger, Arlie W.
    1955.   The passenger pigeon; its natural history and extinction. Univ. Wis-
              consin Press, Madison. 424 pp.
Schwilling, Marvin D.
    1972.   Arctic loon taken at Wilson Reservoir. Kansas Orni. Soc. Bull.
              23(3):13–14.
    1976.   Wood stork at Marais des Cygnes Waterfowl Management Area, Linn
              County. Kansas Orni. Soc. Bull. 27(1):11.
    1977.   Review of Kansas scoter records. Kansas Orni. Soc. Bull. 28(3):25–27.
Seibel, David.
    1975.   Poor-will nesting in Cowley County, Kansas. Kansas Orni. Soc. Bull.
              26(4):17–19.
    1978.   A directory to the birds of Cowley and Sumner Counties and the Chaplin
              Nature Center. Wichita Audubon Soc. Misc. Publ. 1:1–74.
Self, Huber.
    1978.   Environment and man in Kansas. Regents Press of Kansas, Lawrence.
              288 pp.
Snow, Francis H.
    1872.   A catalogue of the birds of Kansas. Kansas Educ. Jour. 8:376–383.
    1903.   A catalogue of the birds of Kansas. Trans. Kansas Acad. Sci. 18:154–
              176.
Spomer, Ron.
    1981.   The Arctic comes to Kansas. Kansas Wildlife 38(6):26–31.
Sprunt, Alexander, Jr.
    1955.   North American birds of prey. Harper and Bros., New York. 227 pp.
Stephens, Homer A.
    1966.   Observations of eagles in Kansas. Kansas Orni. Soc. Bull. 17(4):23–25.
Stoddard, Herbert.
    1931.   The bob white quail, its habits, preservation, and increase. Scribners,
              New York. 559 pp.
Sutton, George Miksch.
    1967.   Oklahoma Birds. Univ. Oklahoma Press, Norman. xiv + 674 pp.
Terres, John K.
    1980.   The Audubon Society Encyclopaedia of North American birds.
              Knopf, New York. 1109 pp.
Thompson, Kirk.
    1985.   Brown County snows. Kansas Wildlife 42(6):27–30.
Thompson, Max C., Wallace Champeny, and Jay Newton.
    1983.   Records of the Garganey in Kansas. Kansas Orni. Soc. Bull. 34:29–30.

Tordoff, Harrison B.
    1956.   Check-list of the birds of Kansas. Univ. Kansas Publ. Mus. Nat. Hist.
                8:307–359.
Weber, John W.
    1981.   *Larus* gulls of the Pacific Northwest interior with taxonomic comments
                on several forms. Part 1. Continental Birdlife 2(1):1–10.
Wiley, Robert W., and Eric G. Bolen.
    1971.   Eagle-livestock relationships: livestock carcass census and wound
                characteristics. Southwestern Nat. 16:151–169.
Williams, Frances, Ed.
    1985.   Photographs in Southern Great Plains Region section. American Birds
                39:319–320.
Zuvanich, J. R.
    1963.   Forster Terns breeding in Kansas. Kansas Orni. Soc. Bull. 14(1):1–3.

INDEX TO COMMON AND SCIENTIFIC NAMES

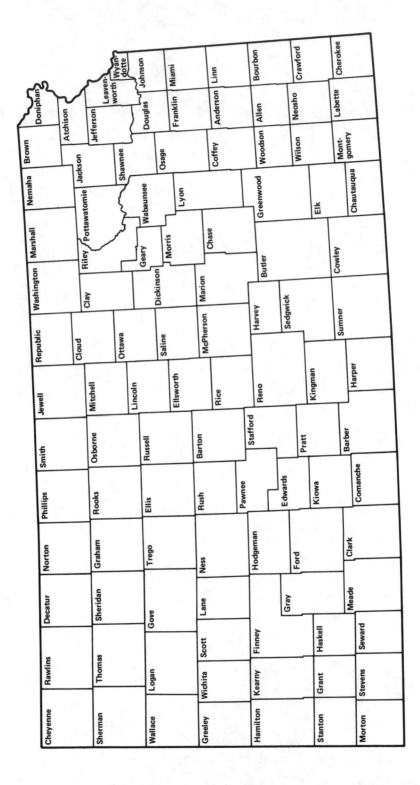